The New Economic Populism

THE NEW ECONOMIC POPULISM

How States Respond to Economic Inequality

William W. Franko
and
Christopher Witko

OXFORD
UNIVERSITY PRESS

OXFORD
UNIVERSITY PRESS

Oxford University Press is a department of the University of Oxford. It furthers
the University's objective of excellence in research, scholarship, and education
by publishing worldwide. Oxford is a registered trade mark of Oxford University
Press in the UK and certain other countries.

Published in the United States of America by Oxford University Press
198 Madison Avenue, New York, NY 10016, United States of America.

Library of Congress Cataloging-in-Publication Data
Names: Franko, William W., author. | Witko, Christopher, author.
Title: The new economic populism : how states respond to economic inequality /
William W. Franko and Christopher Witko.
Description: New York : Oxford University Press, [2018] |
Includes bibliographical references and index.
Identifiers: LCCN 2017013744 (print) | LCCN 2017024847 (ebook) |
ISBN 9780190671020 (Updf) | ISBN 9780190671037 (Epub) |
ISBN 9780190671013 (hardcover : alk. paper)
Subjects: LCSH: Income distribution—United States.
Classification: LCC HC110.I5 (ebook) | LCC HC110.I5 F73 2017 (print) |
DDC 339.2/20973—dc23
LC record available at https://lccn.loc.gov/2017013744

9 8 7 6 5 4 3 2
Printed by Sheridan Books, Inc., United States of America

CONTENTS

FIGURES AND TABLES

FIGURES

TABLES

PREFACE AND ACKNOWLEDGEMENTS

The idea of writing a book on how the U.S. states respond to and shape economic inequality emerged a few years ago after we completed an article on public attitudes toward a proposed income tax on the rich in Washington State. One of the main findings from this work was that people who were more concerned about growing income inequality were much more likely to support the tax increase, and we began to explore whether this was the case for people living in other states and for other policies related to inequality. There has been a lot of research into how politics and policy shape inequality in recent years, but at that time, very little of it had focused on the role of the states. In the years since, fortunately, there has been a growing list of studies that have examined how states respond to inequality and how state policies shape inequality. However, this book length treatment enables us to piece together different empirical studies into a broader understanding of how states are responding to economic inequality, and also show how this fits into broader patterns of American economic policy making. We also hope that some people who do not read academic journals may benefit from reading this book.

The main idea of this book is that the federal government is not doing much to address income inequality, but some state governments are beginning to take sustained efforts to address this problem. Furthermore, we argue, this pattern of federal inaction alongside state action is similar to what we have seen in other periods of rapid economic change in U.S. history, whether it be the period of rapid industrialization in the late 1800s or the Great Depression of the 1930s. The risk of making these types of arguments on a "timely" subject, like inequality, is that the premise of the book could be obliterated by events. For instance, a candidate like Bernie Sanders might have won the Presidential election and focused the efforts of the federal government on inequality. This did not happen, and thus understanding how the states will respond to inequality should be an important topic going forward for observers interested in the dynamics of growing inequality.

Another risk of writing a book on a timely topic is that developments will run counter to your argument. One might say we have an optimistic argument about the ability of American democracy to address the problem of growing income inequality. We believe that attempts by some states to limit and even reduce inequality will spread to other states and even the federal government, which is a view that is based more on our reading of American history than the relatively limited (in a historical sense) empirical data we examine in our statistical analyses. And it must be noted that some recent events could be interpreted as evidence against this argument. Though some states are attempting to limit inequality, other states are taking actions—like limiting the power of unions, enacting regressive tax cuts, etc.—that are likely to make inequality worse.

But from our perspective, this is merely the other side of the same coin. We document that states with a liberal government, with a public aware of inequality, strong labor unions, and an accessible initiative process are more likely to enact policies that are associated with lower inequality. The flip side of this is that states with conservative governments, an unaware public, weak unions and lacking the initiative are not. And it may be that such policies will continue to spread and the future will be bleaker than we envision. However, these policies—like the regressive tax cuts in Kansas that have decimated that state's budget—do not have a good track record of success in raising wages for average Americans, stimulating economic growth or, of course, reducing inequality. Thus, we think that over time the more effective and popular policies—and compared to tax cuts for the wealthy, increases in the minimum wage are much more popular—will win out. Of course, only time will tell, but we believe there is reason for guarded optimism about the future of American inequality.

For some people, the simple fact that we wrote a book about income inequality is probably enough to suggest that we have an aversion to unequal economic outcomes. It is true, and will probably be apparent, that we do not think more inequality is a good thing. This view is at least in part a reflection of the mounting evidence demonstrating that rising inequality leads to many undesirable societal outcomes, like less political participation, more concentrated political power, worse health outcomes, and less economic mobility, just to name a few. This normative belief, however, is basically irrelevant for the analyses we present in the book. Our historical research is based on established events and the empirical chapters are concerned essentially with objective facts—how does public opinion, the initiative, and so forth, shape state policies like taxation, the minimum wage, and the Earned Income Tax Credit. In other words, this study is an academic endeavor and our conclusions are based on systematic, transparent, and evidence-based analyses.

While we recognize that the audience for this book will largely be those in academia, we also hope that some people who do not read academic journals may benefit from our research. To this end, we discuss the results of our analyses in the main text using straightforward summaries along with the aid of visual presentations. The detailed statistical tables that more technically advanced readers will expect are made available in the appendices. Additionally, we hope the topics covered in the book will appeal to instructors, students, and more casual readers who have interests in the political process that go beyond the politics of inequality. This is obviously a book about income disparities and state politics, but it also very much a book about public opinion, public policy, representation, and the historical roots of federalism in the U.S. Finally, we would also like to think the book provides a good example of how to use a variety of methodological approaches to better understand a central research question.

As with any book we have a number of debts to individuals and organizations. First, we are most appreciative of the efficient and excellent work of the staff at Oxford University Press, particularly Angela Chnapko and Alexcee Bechthold. Angela's excellent advice on both substance and style have greatly improve the book. We also thank her for corralling two great anonymous reviewers who pushed us to improve the manuscript substantially. Alexcee's assistance made for an easy process and nice looking final product.

We also must thank a number of scholars who commented on drafts or presentations of the contents of this book. Because parts of chapters 4 and 5 were drawn from previous studies with different coauthors, we thank them for their contributions to these chapters. Specifically, thanks to Nate Kelly for his insights into how government liberalism relates to inequality in Chapter 4, which is based on an article that emerged from a collaboration between Kelly and Witko. He also commented on early drafts of chapter 4.

We owe major gratitude to Caroline Tolbert, who was a coauthor with us on the article that analyzed public support for Proposition 1098. Caroline was also critical in encouraging us to pursue a book project on the role of the states in responding to inequality and read over and commented on drafts of a number of chapters. Without Caroline's encouragement and advice this book would not exist, or at least would have taken much longer to appear.

Others have provided useful comments on presentations of parts of the research. We thank Joe Soss and Sanford Schram, who provided comments on a conference paper version of part of chapter 4. We thank graduate students and faculty members of the Department of Political Science at the University of Iowa for comments on a presentation of the material presented in chapters 3 and 6. Early versions of several chapters were presented at the 2011, 2012, and 2014 Midwest Political Science Association annual meetings, where we received helpful feedback from many gracious participants at each of these conferences. We would especially like to thank Leslie McCall and Chris Ellis for their helpful comments on our work measuring the public's perceptions of inequality. We are also grateful for members of the Class and Inequality sections of the American, Midwest, and Southern political science associations for creating an invaluable academic community that has allowed us to discuss many aspects of this research in a variety of settings.

Witko thanks his colleagues at the University of South Carolina for providing feedback on different ideas and analyses in the book, and in providing guidance about the process of completing a book, especially Dave Darmofal, Susan Miller, Kirk Randazzo and Harvey Starr. More generally, an ongoing collaboration between Witko, Peter Enns, Nate Kelly and Jana Morgan on the politics of inequality has contributed to the understanding of the roots of federal inaction on the matter of inequality discussed in this book.

Franko is grateful for his colleagues in the Department of Political Science at West Virginia University for their support in the final stages of this project. He would also like to acknowledge the important influence of the inequality research from Larry Bartels, Rodney Hero, Theda Skocpol, Benjamin Page, and Lawrence Jacobs. Their seminal work still motivates his research today and without it he likely would never have chosen to study inequality.

Finally, we would like to thank our families. Witko thanks Rebecca, Rachel and Sarah for being understanding while he was banging away on his laptop or away at the office, and for providing fun and adventure when he was not working on this book. Franko's spouse Lindsey has been supportive throughout this process and he recognizes how lucky he is to have her in his life.

The New Economic Populism

CHAPTER 1

Introduction

Donald Trump's 2016 campaign and election surprised nearly everyone. But the fact that a candidate was able to tap into economic discontent to appeal to working-class voters in key battleground states should not be so surprising in an era of stagnant wages for the many with skyrocketing incomes for the few. Though Trump received high levels of support from the white working class, once in office, the newly elected billionaire president appointed a cabinet that has a net worth greater than one-third of American households combined (Calfas 2016). This has raised questions about whether Trump would vigorously pursue the interests of the working class, while highlighting the growing problem of economic inequality in the United States. It is understandable to worry whether such a wealthy cabinet would be "out of touch with ordinary citizens and their needs" (Lee 2016), but income inequality has grown over the last few decades regardless of the wealth, and party affiliation, of those in elected and appointed offices in Washington, DC (Hacker and Pierson 2010). The federal government has been hesitant to address growing income inequality, even while this problem is increasingly salient.

This book examines how, while the federal government in Washington has failed to address inequality and even established policies that have resulted in the expansion of income inequality in recent decades, many state governments have quietly been addressing income inequality, partly in response to a growing public concern over the issue. We argue that this dynamic, where the US government is unable or unwilling to reduce inequality, leaving the states to respond, is consistent with how the country has addressed emerging economic problems in past periods of American history. Policymaking at the national level is in many ways designed to be plodding and onerous, and the states have routinely been the architects of policy solutions to pressing economic challenges from the birth of the Republic, through the Depression, and now in this era of growing inequality. In the pages that follow, we explore why and how certain states have responded to growing income disparity by crafting policies designed to reduce it.

There is growing attention to economic inequality in the United States because in the United States it is extreme. While income and wealth inequalities have grown in many affluent democracies over the last few decades, the United States has the dubious distinction of being the leader in economic inequality among wealthy, industrialized democracies. According to the Organization for Economic Cooperation and Development (OECD) the growth of the top 1% income share in the United States (i.e., the percentage of income that goes to the highest earning 1% of the population) dwarfs that of any other advanced democracy by a large margin. The OECD reports that between 1981 and 2012 the 1% share in the United States grew from 8.2% to 19.3%, while Germany and France experienced top 1% income share increases of 2 percentage points and 0.5 percentage points, respectively (OECD 2014b). The Anglophone countries, such as the United States, the United Kingdom, and Ireland, tend to have higher levels of economic inequality, and the Gini coefficient, another commonly used measure of income inequality, for the United States in recent years has been in line with those of Ireland and Great Britain. Nevertheless, the top 1% income share in the United Kingdom grew from 6.7% to just 12.9% from 1981 to 2012, while in Ireland the change was from 6.7% to only 10.5% (OECD 2014b). Thus, even compared to countries with relatively similar economic and political institutions, a lot more income is collected by the very wealthy in the United States than elsewhere.

One might reasonably say that Americans are just more tolerant of inequality than other countries, but compared to past periods of American history, current levels of economic inequality are very high. As we can see in figure 1.1, in recent years the top 1% income share (excluding capital gains income) is much higher than it has been for several decades, since just prior to the Great Depression. The highest earning 1% of families with incomes above $392,000 in 2013 controlled approximately 20% of pretax income, up from 10.8% in 1982 (Saez 2015). Even careful scholars are referring to the current situation in America as "the new Gilded Age" because of the high levels of inequality and other similarities to the first Gilded Age, including the dominance of the political and policy process by business and the wealthy (Bartels 2008). Systematic data are not available

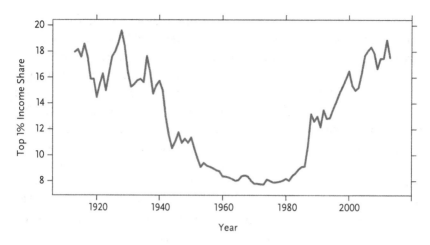

Figure 1.1: US Top 1% Percent Income Share
Source: The World Wealth and Income Database (http://www.wid.world).

prior to the early 1900s, when the consistent collection of the income tax made it possible to gather widespread income data. But historians piecing together a variety of information have argued that income inequality in the contemporary United States is even worse than it was in 1774 (Lindert and Williamson 2012). This is true even if slaves are included in the calculations!

As alarming as these income inequality statistics are, because annual income differences can compound over time, disparities in wealth—income plus stocks and bonds, real estate holdings, and so on—are much greater than those in annual income. The top 1% of the wealthiest Americans hold 41% of all the wealth in the country (Saez and Zucman 2014). Heirs of the Walmart founder, Sam Walton, alone owned more wealth than the bottom 40% of US families in 2012 (Economic Policy Institute 2012). The Forbes 400, the 400 richest Americans, own as much wealth as the bottom 61% of the wealth distribution (Holland 2015). Alarmingly, in his *New York Times* bestseller Thomas Piketty (2014) argued that there is no reason for optimism that the rapid growth of income and wealth inequality will slow any time soon. The fact that Piketty's book, entitled *Capital in the Twenty-First Century*, at over 600 pages and chock full of figures, tables, equations, and references to obscure studies in foreign languages, topped the *New York Times* nonfiction bestseller list ahead of books on the perennially popular subject of Jesus's death (coauthored by Bill O'Reilly of Fox News fame), and *Unbroken*, the inspiring tale of a World War II prisoner of war that ended up being made into a feature film, attests to the growing public concern about and interest in economic inequality in America.

And the public is right to be concerned about growing inequality. Though some inequality is to be expected, and probably necessary in a well-functioning market economy, since the time of Aristotle thinkers have argued that extreme levels of inequality are associated with a host of negative outcomes (Aristotle 1984). This ancient intuition is being confirmed by a growing body of scholarship showing that high levels of inequality are associated with higher rates of sickness and mortality, lessened social mobility, slower economic growth, less investment in public goods like schools and roads, and even violence and civil unrest (Berg, Ostrey, and Zetterlmeyer 2012; Cingano 2014; Kawachi et al. 1997; Wang et al. 1993). Admittedly, whether all of these negative outcomes are actually *caused* by growing inequality remains uncertain, but there is accumulating evidence, even in our own time, that economic inequality is having undesirable consequences.

While some inequality is fine, it is widely agreed that extreme levels of inequality are bad. Of course, we can never be entirely certain ahead of time whether we have reached the point at which inequality will produce dramatic social upheavals and crisis. A not very comforting fact is that throughout history entrenched elites and common citizens alike have often failed to notice the consequences of extreme economic inequality until it is too late. Marie Antoinette, the Romanovs, and others in positions of power have often paid a stiff price throughout history for ignoring a growing gap between the haves and have-nots. One would hope in a modern democracy that events would not head in this direction, and it seems that the United States is far from this type of strife. But perhaps we are experiencing the birth pangs of a more serious crisis to come. The discontent with the economic status quo can be seen in the success of both Bernie Sanders and Donald Trump in the Democratic Party and Republican Party primaries, respectively, and ultimately in Donald Trump's election as president (though racism and sexism appear to have also played an important role). As major protest movements like the Tea Party and Occupy Wall Street emerge, and urban riots, in places like Ferguson and Baltimore, return to America, it is reasonable to ponder, as children might ask on a long car ride, are we there yet?

The riots in Baltimore in 2015, which attracted a great deal of media attention (probably in part due to the highlighting of its urban poverty and violence on HBO's acclaimed series *The Wire*), were directly precipitated by the police killing of Freddy Gray. However, it did not take long for observers, as diverse as President Obama and famed economist Nouriel Roubini, to link the strife in Baltimore to the underlying economic problems faced by the city's residents. Indeed, Baltimore is contemporary America writ small—there are a small number of very wealthy individuals and families alongside stagnant incomes, widespread poverty, and limited opportunities for the many. Among the 50 largest cities in America, Baltimore had the 10th highest income inequality (Associated Press 2014), and a recent study by a group of well-respected economists noted that poor children in Baltimore have among the worst odds of escaping poverty of children in any of the 100 largest counties in the country (Chetty and Hendren 2015). Though some observers blamed the breakdown of the traditional family for the unrest in Baltimore, and that certainly does not help matters, the breakdown of the family is also a consequence of the inability of males with few skills to earn a decent living in the postindustrial economy (Greenstone and Looney 2012). Why get married to someone with a very limited potential to contribute to the economic stability of the family? This inability of individuals with few specialized skills and little education to earn a decent living, combined with the explosion of incomes for a handful of highly compensated professionals and managers, is the raw material of growing income inequality in the United States.

Urban riots sparked by the plight of poor, inner-city residents were also common in the 1960s, a time of comparative equality. But Occupy Wall Street, which started in lower Manhattan, was aimed squarely at growing economic inequality and resonated due to the simple framing of economic conflict as the 99% versus the 1%. Occupy Wall Street protests spread well beyond Manhattan to cities like St. Louis, Madison, and Oakland, and even beyond the United States. These demonstrations were the first mass events to draw attention to growing economic inequality, and they may have been the most widespread protests against economic conditions since the Great Depression, when people took to the streets in many parts of the country to protest joblessness and the lack of any government response to the problems of that era (Piven and Cloward 1979). Though the Occupy movement did not revolutionize the federal government's response to economic inequality, Occupy activists have been successful in campaigns to raise minimum wages in many cities, and they certainly did draw attention to the issue of economic inequality in a way that others had failed to previously (Levitin 2015). In the wake of Occupy Wall Street, even Republican candidates for president must address inequality and explain how their policy proposals will address it.

The growing economic conflict we observe is not solely caused by the anger of the "losers" of the economic status quo, however. After all, despite one of the stingiest welfare states in the affluent world, Tea Partiers and major party politicians have heaped scorn upon the alleged legions of "takers" believed to sit idly and live off the dole. Most infamously, Republican presidential candidate Mitt Romney claimed that 47% of the population does not pay any income taxes at all, and just wants a handout from government. These recent episodes are merely the continuance of a multidecade effort to portray the poor beneficiaries of government welfare programs as lazy and undeserving (Gilens 1999). Thus, while some of the superrich have taken to portraying themselves as undeserving victims of class anger from below (Tom Perkins, a California venture capitalist compared rich folks in the United States to Jews in Nazi Germany), the class conflict that appears to be intensifying in America is certainly a two-way street.

Scholars have argued that growing income inequality and the conflict that it engenders are also a cause of the increasing polarization found in Congress, which prevents much of anything from getting done (McCarty, Poole, and Rosenthal 2006; Garand 2010). This, in turn, perpetuates growing inequality since policies would be needed to reverse the economic status quo and the Congress is increasingly unable to do much of anything (Enns et al. 2014; Hacker and Pierson 2010). In short, the very real economic divisions in the country are already causing substantial political conflict, and with little hope of a short-term solution to fix inequality, it is probable that such conflict will only get worse in the coming years. The government does not only respond to economic inequality, however. Research increasingly shows that government decisions and policies also shape inequality in important ways.

THE FEDERAL GOVERNMENT AND ECONOMIC INEQUALITY

Initially, most research into the causes of growing economic inequality focused naturally enough on economic changes, such as increasing globalization, deindustrialization, the rise of the financial sector, and the lack of a skilled workforce. Hacker and Pierson (2010) convincingly argue that these factors may explain some of the growth of inequality, but ultimately fail to explain a great deal of the variation in income inequality across nations. Put simply, the fact that advanced nations with similar levels of education, exposure to globalization, a well-developed financial sector, and intensive technology use, such as Germany, Canada, and France, have considerably lower levels of inequality shows the limitations of purely economic explanations of rising inequality. There is now a consensus developing among scholars that government activity (and inactivity) has played a major role in expanding economic inequality in the United States in the last few decades (Bartels 2008; Hacker and Pierson 2010; Kelly 2009). Just as the New Deal and Great Society programs probably played a key role in maintaining low levels of inequality over a number of decades from the 1930s through the 1970s, federal government policy has contributed to growing inequality since the late 1970s (Hacker and Pierson 2010).

Compared to citizens in most other affluent nations, Americans are historically more tolerant of socioeconomic inequalities, more likely to view negative economic circumstances as the fault of the individual, less friendly to government intervention in the economy, and thus less likely to look to the government to fix inequality (Inglehart 1997; Kingdon 1999; Lipset 1997). These facts probably help explain why America generally has more inequality than other affluent democracies. Yet most Americans are aware of, and troubled by, the rapidly growing inequality in recent decades, and surveys show that inequality has increased to the point where many Americans would like the government to take steps to reduce it (Bartels 2005; Page, Bartels, and Seawright 2013). Since the end of the Great Depression Americans have generally looked to the federal government to confront major economic challenges facing the nation, and economic inequality is now viewed by the majority as a substantial problem that should be fixed.

However, rather than taking steps to slow the growth of, or reverse, growing economic inequality, the federal government has played a lead role in creating and enacting policies that make inequality worse than it would otherwise be. The growing inequality in America is defined by the divergent economic fortunes of the vast majority of workers and those at the very top of the income distribution. Since the 1970s the incomes of less-skilled workers have not increased at all after adjusting for inflation, but even at the 90th percentile, real income gains have been minimal (Desilver 2014). At the same time that the vast majority of workers have experienced wage stagnation or even decline, the incomes of those at the very top have increased dramatically, as can be seen in figure 1.1. The government can reduce inequality by influencing what firms in the market pay to their employees (with policies such as the minimum wage or laws encouraging collective bargaining) or by redistribution (i.e., taxing the wealthy and spending money on transfers to the less well-off) (Kelly 2009). In both of these policy realms the US government has exacerbated, rather than lessened, inequality in recent years.

Stagnant wages at the bottom of the income distribution and explosive growth at the top have partly different causes, but in each case policies have been enacted that limit wages at the bottom of the income distribution and that cause large increases in income at the top of the income distribution. In some cases, policies that suppress the wages of lower-income wage earners almost automatically increase the earnings of top income earners. And some of the "economic" forces that have caused growing income inequality are themselves influenced by government choices. In the next paragraphs our goal is not to provide a comprehensive understanding of how the federal government may have influenced income inequality, since other scholars have examined this question in great detail (Hacker and Pierson 2010; Kelly 2009). Here we merely wish to highlight how federal policies have led to a decline in wages for those with low incomes and increasing wages for those at the top of the income distribution.

Let's consider one of those major economic changes that has contributed to growing economic inequality, globalization. While we sometimes view globalization and the expansion of economic relationships as an inhuman, unstoppable force, expanding trade relationships with China and other low-wage countries was a political choice over which the government had control. Excellent recent research shows that the expansion of trade with low-wage countries, in particular China, has contributed to declining wages of many workers (Autor, Dorn, and Hanson 2013). Freer trade policies undoubtedly benefit firm managers and shareholders who have access to larger consumer markets and cheaper labor markets, but this does not benefit industrial workers if their jobs are outsourced. In this situation, policymakers chose policies that benefit managers and shareholders at the expense of workers. Indeed, Trump's campaign for president was, in part, fueled by the common belief that these trade deals were good for CEOs but bad for workers. In fact, it is not clear that the federal government made a "bad" choice to expand trade relations with China and other low-wage countries, since these relationships do have many benefits for individuals and firms in the United States and in the low-wage countries. We simply wish to note that economic forces are almost never purely economic, but are influenced by the government, and that in this case the government chose managers, shareholders and middle-class consumers, not employed in the industrial sector, over manufacturing workers, whose unions were resistant to expanding trade with China. Perhaps this was all inevitable, but perhaps the government could have negotiated better deals that would have cost fewer jobs. Certainly this argument is part of the reason President Trump performed well in the Rust Belt in the 2016 election.

The growing weakness of unions, evident in their inability to prevent expanding trade with low-wage countries and shaped by a loss of manufacturing employment, has also reduced the wages of low-skilled workers and increased the wages of highly paid executives. It is generally recognized that collective bargaining leads to higher wages for workers, but collective bargaining through unions also suppresses executive pay. Rosenfeld and Western (2011) argue that unions were critical organizations that kept executive pay more in line with the wages of rank-and-file workers, and that once unions became relatively powerless, executive compensation skyrocketed. While unions have declined in many countries due to structural economic changes, since the election of Ronald Reagan the federal government has taken steps to weaken unions, and consequently unions have declined more in the United States than in many other industrialized nations (Hacker and Pierson 2010).

Even if economic efficiency demanded trade with China and weak unions, the government might have cushioned the blow of industrial job loss and workers' weakened bargaining power. For example, the federal government might have routinely raised the minimum wage to boost earnings in the service sector to make average wages closer to average industrial sector earnings. This would have boosted the earnings of the lowest-income workers and possibly reduced the profits of firms, which might have reduced the compensation of managers and the earnings of shareholders. As we will see later in this book, the federal government has declined to consistently raise the minimum wage in recent decades, even as other forces have put downward pressure on wages to a greater extent than before. Thus, a number of policy actions and inactions simultaneously led to a reduction of the wages of lower-income workers.

Other policies have helped corporations and their managers to earn higher profits and wages, by expanding opportunities for rent-seeking and increasing the ability of firms to take risks, for which the public would ultimately foot the bill. This is perhaps most clearly on display in the financial sector, where deregulatory policies permitted financial institutions to grow larger and to take advantage of unknowledgeable consumers. The wall between commercial and investment banking that was erected during the Great Depression was finally knocked down in the late 1990s at the urging of congressional leaders and members of the Clinton Cabinet, like Robert Rubin, former head of Goldman Sachs (Hacker and Pierson 2010). This allowed financial firms to take on more risk, which placed the entire economy at risk, and necessitated large taxpayer bailouts in the aftermath of the 2008 financial crisis. On a more mundane and routine level, the removal of credit card interest rate caps, the elimination of bankruptcy protection for credit card debt, and the lack of meaningful oversight of financial company activities since the late 1970s allowed financial firms to prey on unknowledgeable consumers. It is no wonder that the average consumer has become much more indebted, while the profits of large financial firms and the compensation of their executives have exploded (Witko 2016), which has been an important driver of economic inequality (Keller and Kelly 2015).

The policy decisions mentioned above affect the income distribution before taxes and expenditures, and are thus "market-conditioning policies" since they affect the "market" income inequality level (Kelly 2009). But the government also influenced the post-tax and transfer income distribution in a similar manner by enacting large tax cuts for the wealthy, especially for those who earn their income through investments. The current top marginal federal income tax rate in the United States is 39.6%, down from 70% in the late 1970s and early 1980s (Tax Foundation 2015). Capital gains tax rates, or taxes on investment income, have also been reduced from nearly 40% to under 20% since the late 1970s (Tax Policy Center 2015). These tax policy changes have kept more money in the pockets of the wealthy than they otherwise might have had, while depriving the federal government of revenue that could be used on a variety of programs to benefit the general public.

These changes did not take place simply because they were someone's Platonic ideal of good public policy (though for some, they certainly were). The inequality-enhancing aspect of these policies was a feature, not a bug. In their excellent book on how the federal government contributed to growing inequality in the last few decades, Hacker and Pierson (2010) note that the wealthy beneficiaries of growing inequality are very skilled at using their money to lobby for policies that benefit the wealthy, and block those that would harm them. Tax cuts for the wealthy, deregulation of the financial sector, and attacks on unions were all driven by the political acumen of organized wealth. The fact that it is extremely difficult to get much of anything done in Washington, DC, these days discourages changes that would reduce the incomes or wealth of the very rich (Enns et al. 2014), even as the public becomes more concerned about inequality. And the increased resources of the wealthy in our era of high inequality may enhance their ability to change unfavorable policies and solidify favorable policies.

Though the resurgence of the Republican Party since 1980 has likely helped the wealthy, Hacker and Pierson (2010) point out that the resources of the rich have proven irresistible to many Democrats, in some ways pushing that party to the right. This was most notable in the person of Bill Clinton, and Hillary Clinton appears to have lost the 2016 presidential election, in part, because of the weak support from white, working-class voters. But the affinity for business and the wealthy can also be seen in many lesser-known Democratic members of Congress, appointed officials, and party strategists. Thus, it cannot come as a surprise that that the US Congress is generally not responsive to the preferences of average Americans (Bartels 2008; Gilens 2012) or that well-funded interest groups have great influence over national policy outcomes (Gilens and Page 2014).

Overall, the federal government has not only failed to respond to inequality, but has in many ways made it worse.

THE NEW ECONOMIC POPULISM IN THE STATES

The end result is that while the public has looked to Washington for answers to economic problems since the end of the Great Depression, the federal government has demonstrated little interest in, or capacity for, reducing inequality. Though Donald Trump ran as an atypical, populist Republican, it appears that his economic agenda is being driven by more traditional Republican sentiments. Among the first priorities for the Trump administration is privatizing social insurance programs like Medicare and cutting taxes for the wealthy. Thus, people concerned about inequality will not find much in the way of comfort in Washington, DC. While it would be nice for the federal government to take steps to address inequality because of the greater capacity and resources at its disposal, rather than waiting for this to happen, the states are beginning to meaningfully address growing economic inequality through a variety of means, depending on specific state economic, political, and institutional conditions. We call this trend "the new economic populism," and it provides the book's title.

We will show in this book that in response to a growing awareness of increasing income inequality, and federal inaction in the face of this trend, many states are taking steps to combat inequality, from increasing minimum wages, to raising taxes on the wealthy and expanding tax credits for low-income workers. This is not happening evenly across all states, but when and where inequality is growing more rapidly, and the public is aware of and concerned about this issue, and where policymaking institutions are favorable to changes that benefit the lower and middle classes, states are beginning to tackle economic inequality. These state actions are "populist," because as the federal government proves less responsive to public preferences and needs, states are increasingly an important locus of majoritarian policymaking aimed at reducing the income gap. The policies that we look at in this book in detail—the minimum wage, tax credits for the poor, and tax increases on the wealthy—are generally quite popular with the average citizen and are likely to reduce income inequality, unlike mere populist rhetoric. This trend is "new" because since the Great Depression, Americans have become accustomed to the federal government playing an equalizing role in the economy, while states have more often crafted inegalitarian policies, such as regressive taxes or racially discriminatory laws. Furthermore, this response to growing economic inequality has begun to gain momentum in the last 10 or 15 years. Thus, what we call the new economic populism represents a significant departure from the governmental division of labor that prevailed for several decades.

It may seem strange to argue that there is a movement of states actively fighting inequality when, as a result of the elections of November 2016, a quite conservative Republican Party is in control of more state governments than at any time since the late 1920s. And indeed, not all states are embracing egalitarian economic policies. Many states will continue or renew efforts to pursue policies that scholars think will make inequality worse—like enacting so-called right-to-work laws that weaken unions and the bargaining power of workers. But on the same day that Republicans achieved stunning electoral success in 2016, voters in several states enacted minimum wage increases or rejected minimum wage decreases via the popular initiative, even in such conservative states as South Dakota. Voters in California, where more than 10% of Americans live, extended a large tax increase on the wealthy. In the past, state policies that address major economic problems have spread to other states, localities, and the federal government, so state activity holds the promise of addressing contemporary economic inequalities throughout most of the country, despite the sometimes isolated nature of the states' responses.

A key argument that we make in this book, and which provides the backdrop for our examination of state responses to income inequality, is that the current federal inaction and the states' responses are consistent with the governmental division of labor in other periods of rapid economic change in American history. In chapter 2 we argue that the states have long addressed emerging economic problems that the federal government was either unwilling or unable to address. This has been the case since almost the founding of the nation. The period of the 1930s through the 1960s, when the federal government aggressively took the lead in addressing economic problems, is the exception rather than the rule. Indeed, what many view as the triumph of federal government activism, the New Deal, followed a long period of foot dragging in Washington and was largely an amalgamation of policies crafted in the states in the preceding years. Though the federal government is in many ways best equipped to address growing inequality, its unwillingness to do so is not surprising when we consider this broader historical backdrop.

We explain in chapter 2 that the federal government was designed by Madison and his colleagues not to do much, and it often achieves stunning success in this regard. Because of the institutional design of the US government, with its many veto points, it is very easy for the "winners" of changing economic circumstances to gain control of at least one veto point and prevent changes to the economic status quo from which they benefit. In contrast, the variation in economic conditions, in the concerns and preferences of the publics, which groups hold power in government, and the variation in political institutions found among the states means that new approaches to economic problems are more likely to be developed and implemented by the states than by the federal government. All of these points are laid out in chapter 2, and in the remainder of the book we apply this framework to contemporary inequality and consider in more detail how the public's views of inequality, who holds power in government institutions, and the availability of the initiative as a policymaking tool shape states' responses to economic inequality.

In chapter 3 we present the variation that exists in income inequality across the states, and variation in public concern about income inequality, as measured by opinion polls. Though politicians may decide to tackle income inequality even in the absence of public concern about it, government responses are more likely when and where there is a growing awareness of, and concern about, inequality, as the analyses in this book confirm. To examine this connection, we develop novel and robust population estimates of public opinion awareness of income inequality in the states from 1987 to 2010 using multilevel regression, imputation, and poststratification weights using national survey data. These state public opinion estimates of concern about inequality are the first of their kind. Using these estimates, we see in chapter 3 that the growth in public concern about inequality responds in part to objective increases in inequality, but also that state political conditions, particularly mass partisanship, shape perceptions of inequality. In the next chapters, we explore the ways in which a growing public awareness of inequality acts as an antecedent or predecessor to the new economic populism, since it shapes the ideology of public officials and the types of policies that are pursued by government.

Though it appears based on recent research that Republicans and many Democrats in Washington, DC, are unresponsive to the poor and middle class, some governments in the states are taking action to reduce income inequality. Comparative research, and research in the United States, shows that left-leaning politicians are most concerned about inequality and most likely to try to reduce it (Kelly and Witko 2012). In chapter 4, we argue that in states where there is a greater awareness of inequality, the public will have a greater desire to elect politicians who will advance the economic interests of the lower and middle classes, and that strategic politicians will take advantage of the lack of federal action to try to reduce inequality. Our analyses using the measures of public awareness developed in chapter 3 as explanatory variables show that as public awareness of inequality grows, government officials indeed move to the left. These shifts have been, in turn, associated with lower income inequality between 1987 and 2010.

In the next few chapters we explore some of the mechanisms that state governments have used to respond to inequality. We explore both redistributive tax policies (the earned income tax credit and taxes on the wealthy) and market-conditioning policies (the minimum wage). We also explore how aspects of state policymaking institutions that we do not find in Washington, DC, particularly the initiative, may push policy in a more egalitarian direction. The initiative can allow citizens to produce more egalitarian policies even in the absence of left-leaning parties in control of government, because the initiative process circumvents elected policymakers. In fact, the ballot initiative was instituted during the Progressive Era precisely in response to the perception that wealthy economic interests had excessive influence over elected officials (Magleby 1984; Bowler, Donovan, and Tolbert 1998; Smith and Tolbert 2004).

Most of our analyses rely on aggregate data, but in chapter 5 we examine how public perceptions of inequality influence the formation of tax policy preferences at the microlevel, by taking advantage of Washington State's highly redistributive Initiative 1098. This proposal, dubbed the millionaire's tax, allowed citizens to vote directly to increase taxes on the wealthy, in the context of a policy debate that very much focused on the growth of income inequality. This episode provides us a rare opportunity to understand how inequality shapes individual voter attitudes toward redistribution and increasing taxes on the wealthy in the context of specific policy debates in which discussion of inequality features prominently, a rare circumstance in recent decades since inequality has generally not been salient with the public, and few tax increases on the wealthy have been proposed. Drawing on a survey of Washington State's registered voters, and unique questions designed by the authors, we find that voters who were more concerned about income inequality were more supportive of this tax increase on the wealthy. Though this initiative did not pass, even initiatives that do not pass can move policy in the direction their proponents favor (Gerber 1999). In fact, a very similar measure, Proposition 30, was enacted in California in 2012 and then extended for 12 years in 2016. We also find that awareness of inequality is associated with top income tax rates across states during the period of our analysis. The research in this chapter suggests that raising taxes on the wealthy is likely to appeal to more voters as income inequality becomes more salient.

Whereas in chapter 5 we looked at policy aimed at redistributing money from the rich to the poor, in the following two chapters we examine how attitudes toward inequality and other factors shape policies intended to boost the pre- and post-tax incomes of the poor. In chapter 6 we examine how the state minimum wage has responded to a growing awareness of inequality and other state political factors. The minimum wage was initially pursued by the states a number of years before the federal government adopted a minimum wage in the 1930s. However, the minimum wage law is still jointly controlled by the states and the federal government, allowing us to directly examine how federal inaction in raising the minimum wage spurs state minimum wage increases. We find that federal inaction, a public awareness of growing inequality, and state government liberalism are significant predictors of increases in state minimum wages. We find also that the minimum wage is more likely to be increased in states with the initiative, even in states that are relatively conservative.

In chapter 7 we examine how state adoptions of the earned income tax credit, an alternative means of boosting the incomes of the working poor by adjusting their incomes with the tax code, were influenced by the growing awareness of inequality and other state-specific factors. Unlike the minimum wage, the earned income tax credit was originally enacted by the federal government in the 1970s, and since it is essentially a tax cut, it has been acceptable to conservatives until very recently, when conservatives have criticized the fact that many citizens do not pay any income taxes (e.g., Mitt Romney's 47% of people don't pay taxes). As some Republicans have begun to question this policy at the federal level, we see that it has been expanded substantially at the state level as the public has become more concerned about income inequality. And we show that unlike minimum wage increases, both liberal and conservative governments adopted EITC laws at similar rates. In addition, states where individuals have become more aware of inequality and where labor unions are strong are also more likely to adopt the EITC. In chapter 7, we also investigate the extent to which the EITC and the minimum wage can be viewed as contradictory or complementary approaches to raising wages for low-income workers.

In chapter 8 we conclude by recapping our arguments and empirical results, and discussing the possibilities for the "new economic populism" to promote egalitarian economic outcomes in the face of continuing gridlock and the dominance over Washington, DC's policymaking institutions by business, the wealthy, and a conservative Republican Party. Contemporary observers concerned about inequality are discouraged when they place their gaze on Washington, DC, and this discouragement is understandable.

But many states are actually addressing inequality now, and these policies are working. Admittedly, many states continue to embrace the policies that have contributed to growing inequality, such as tax cuts for the wealthy and weakening labor unions. But as the public grows more concerned about inequality, policies that address these income disparities will become more popular, and policies that exacerbate inequality will become less so. Over time, if history is a guide, more egalitarian policies will spread across the states, and ultimately to the federal government. Thus, the new economic populism has the potential to transform American public policy and economics.

A brief note about methodology is warranted here. In most of our chapters we present the results of statistical analyses of our hypotheses and arguments. Statistical analysis is indispensable when analyzing a large number of data points, which is certainly what we have when we examine the 50 US states over more than two decades. Social scientists are familiar with the use of statistical analysis, but we hope that nonacademics will also find this book interesting and useful. Therefore, the reader should keep in mind that all statistical models are abstractions of reality. They necessarily limit themselves to a relatively small number of salient factors that can be measured and modeled to explain outcomes of interest. We are not implying that other factors are irrelevant, and we must remain aware that policy change is a messy and idiosyncratic business. For instance, no two campaigns to raise the minimum wage are exactly alike. We address some of this complexity in the various chapters that focus on specific policies, before turning to the statistical analyses. Nevertheless, we lose some of the drama of political struggle as it actually occurs. On the other hand, we hope the reader will agree that there is value in using statistical analysis of the commonalities among different episodes of policy change across the different states to understand how these seemingly isolated events form something more than isolated incidents. Though all policy debates are somewhat different, it is clear that many states are responding in similar ways to growing inequality, and we are able to understand why this is the case with our approach. We are also able to place this current spasm of policymaking in a broader theoretical and historical perspective with our abstract approach.

Presenting the results of statistical analyses to lay audiences is also tricky, since most people are not familiar with statistical methods, outputs, and tables. Thus, whenever possible, we use maps and figures to visualize the empirical results and make the findings fairly easy to understand. While we use sophisticated statistical analyses to estimate the models and develop new statewide estimates of public opinion about the problem of income inequality, using a fairly complex procedure, the results are presented in an easy-to-comprehend visual format that requires no prior knowledge of statistics; statistical details are relegated to appendixes for our fellow scholars. We hope that this will allow lay readers to proceed past unwanted details and gain a great deal from the book, while scholars can probe the research design and statistical and measurement approaches used throughout this book.

CHAPTER 2

Economic Inequality, Federalism, and the New Economic Populism

History does not repeat itself, but it rhymes.

Attributed to Mark Twain

A newly elected Democratic president was tackling an economic crisis fueled by bank failures and resulting in high unemployment. According to critics from the left, the government was not addressing these problems aggressively or rapidly enough. The dissatisfaction with the economic conditions in the country led to large protests in a number of major American cities. From the right, the president was deemed a socialist, and his agenda was vigorously opposed by many organized business interests and the wealthy. These critics feared that the American way of life and system of government was imperiled by the expanding scope of government intervention into the economy. State government officials across the political spectrum were critical of both federal government action *and* inaction. This scenario will be familiar to anyone who achieved adulthood before the financial crisis of 2008 and the early months of the first Obama administration. But it would also be familiar to their grandparents or great grandparents, as the scenario equally well describes the first years of Franklin Delano Roosevelt's first term in office.

The conventional history is that FDR's New Deal was critical to mitigating the economic trauma of the Great Depression (though revisionist historians on the right certainly dispute this) and ultimately it may very well have been. Before these federal programs were enacted, however, some states were more aggressively tackling the joblessness and poverty associated with this crisis, and more generally the problems associated with modern, industrial capitalism for years and even decades. In fact, the New Deal was pursued only after years of extensive human suffering and federal foot-dragging, and was ultimately largely "borrowed" from earlier state policy innovations (Downey 2010). Despite the experience of the period from the 1930s through the 1960s, when the federal government led the way in tackling emerging economic problems, we see this pattern throughout American history—the federal government has often hesitated to respond to emerging economic problems, and the states have played a lead role in crafting policy responses during times of economic change and tumult. Our main focus in this book is to understand, in our own time, how the states are challenging current federal inaction to tackle economic inequality by engaging in what we call the "new economic populism." In this chapter, however, we take a step back and place the new economic populism into a broader historical and theoretical perspective on the division of labor in economic policymaking in American federalism.

We begin by discussing how and why the federal government often fails to address emerging economic threats, and how historically states have seized this opportunity or been forced to act to address economic problems because of this federal inaction. We then turn to a discussion of how the same constitutional design that makes it difficult for the federal government to act encourages states to address new economic problems. Next, we explain that not all states are equally likely to address growing economic problems, but point out that the severity of an economic problem and the resulting public preferences for government to address that problem, the types of ideologies and interests represented in the policymaking institutions of government, and the presence of particular political institutions, notably the initiative, all influence the likelihood that a state will address a growing economic problem.

In the last part of the chapter we turn our attention to the contemporary period and growing economic inequality. We discuss how, consistent with past eras, the federal government has largely failed to address this issue and, in fact, made inequality worse. We then turn to a discussion of how a number of states have begun to pursue a new economic populism to address growing economic disparities, and why particular states are more likely to address the problem of growing inequality, laying the groundwork for the remainder of the book.

Though Americans are ideologically committed to limited government, in all countries the government, or what scholars often call "the state," plays a major role in the economy (North 1981; Polanyi 1944). A capitalist economy is impossible without the state, or at least one has never yet existed without a relatively strong state. There are several reasons why this is the case. First, the rule of law through courts is critical to establishing the enforcement of contracts, without which modern commerce is impossible. In addition, even libertarians typically agree that the government is necessary, or at least very useful, in addressing market failures, such as negative externalities, imperfect information, or inadequate public goods. Even the most libertarian-minded among us typically believe that the government should levy taxes in order to provide for a military to supply the public defense, for example, and think that it is reasonable for the government to establish currencies and define and enforce weights and measures. Because the government *will* tax and spend, and engage in some economic regulation, even from the most extreme laissez-faire perspective, the state will play some role in how society adapts to economic change. But, of course, many observers agree that beyond addressing basic market failures and enforcing contracts, the government can play a positive role in the economy, with policy designed to both encourage positive economic change and protect citizens against looming economic threats, roles that governments have played for centuries (Polanyi 1944).

It is a truism that Americans typically prefer a smaller and more limited government than those in most other affluent democracies. But, paradoxically, this "protective" function of government—to help citizens confront the challenges associated with major economic changes—may actually be especially important in America, because the American economy is historically noted for its innovation and dynamism. America has been on the cutting edge of economic change for a very long time, and remains so today. This innovation has created great wealth and high standards of living, but rapid economic change also creates tremendous economic trauma for those business owners that are put out of business by new forms of economic competition or business organization, and for the workers who are downsized or outsourced, or whose skills no longer fit what is needed by the economy and who consequently see the value of their labor rapidly decline. Economic change creates winners and losers, and the losers are seldom happy with these changes, as they see their incomes and standards of living deteriorate (Witko 2016). But even for those that fare well, in terms of income and standard of living, during economic transitions, the social changes that accompany major economic changes, like the shift from the farm to the factory, or women entering the workforce en masse, can still be jarring.

Because of American political culture and ideology, which favor limited government, throughout American history the proper role of government in protecting citizens against the rough edges of modern capitalism has been vigorously debated. But the federal government, which is limited in many ways by the Constitution, shares economic policymaking authority with the state governments, adding another layer of complexity to this discussion that takes place in all countries. Of the policies that are explicitly designed to primarily influence the performance of the economy, or provide for the economic welfare of the population, the states have a constitutionally circumscribed role in only monetary and currency policy and trade policy, though even for the latter, most states do still have foreign trade offices and seek to expand exports to US trade partners. Setting these few policies aside, along with the federal government, the states are directly involved in designing fiscal, regulatory, and social policies, all of which affect economic outcomes.

Though the US Congress has the constitutional authority to regulate interstate commerce, states also engage in a variety of important regulatory activity (Teske 2004), and in some cases carry most of the burden of regulating very large industries that have important economic implications, such as the insurance industry (Meier 1988). The states are also now the main driver in crafting so-called developmental policies that are designed to stimulate economic growth and employment (Peterson 1995). More education spending, for example, is done by the states than the federal government, and the states are the leaders in funding the nation's transportation infrastructure (Witko and Newmark 2010). States have typically followed the lead of the federal government in redistributive policy (Peterson 1995) because, scholars have argued, they wish to limit redistribution in their jurisdictions to avoid being a "welfare magnet" (Bailey and Rom 2004). Nevertheless, states have considerable discretion over health and welfare eligibility requirements and benefit levels (Fellowes and Rowe 2004), and, as we will discuss below, the states initially crafted many of the welfare and social insurance programs that are the basis of the federal welfare state. Finally, states can also influence economic outcomes through the use of fiscal policy, that is, taxing and spending (Prillaman and Meier 2014; Hatch and Rigby 2014; Witko and Newmark 2010; Kelly and Witko 2014).

Given this variety of economic policy tools at their disposal, it is not surprising that states have been found to influence a number of different economic outcomes, including economic growth (Hendrick and Garand 1991; Jones 1990; Prillaman and Meier 2014), job growth and employment (Hansen 1999; Kelly and Witko 2014; Jones 1990), and even income inequality (Barrilleaux and Davis 2003; Freund and Morris 2005; Hatch and Rigby 2015; Kelly and Witko 2012; Langer 2001). However, because they share power with the federal government and face both internal and external policymaking constraints, the ability of states to shape economic outcomes is greater under some circumstances than others (Kelly and Witko 2012; 2014). When the federal government fails to act to address a problem, this creates a space in which states can take the lead (Kelly and Witko 2012). This does not mean that all states will choose to take the lead. We often speak of the "states" doing things, but of course what we mean is that individual policymakers in state institutions choose to act. Thus, whether action takes place depends on the calculations of individual policymakers within the states. But often politicians in some states decide that it is in their interest to act to address a problem, even while federal politicians have decided not to, or been unable to.

Many people now take it for granted that the federal government should be the leader in confronting major economic problems because of its greater expertise and resources. But this is largely a conceit of the New Deal and Great Society eras. Throughout much of American history, though the possibility of action was hotly debated in Washington, DC, in critical moments the national government did *not* aggressively intervene in the market to protect citizens against or otherwise manage emerging economic threats. More often the federal government has eventually taken action, but only *after* a number of states have developed and tested policy solutions to emerging economic problems and threats.

The Pre–Civil War Era

The beliefs about what is appropriate and necessary for government to do have changed substantially along with changing economic conditions throughout the entire world over the last 250 years. Yet even as these views have evolved, debates about the proper scope of federal activity (given the expectations of government action at a particular time) in America extend back to the earliest days of the Republic. As a newly independent nation, the United States was suddenly thrust into economic competition with countries like France and the United Kingdom, which did not believe in limited government and laissez-faire capitalism. A lack of state intervention in the economy was a major problem for those wishing to have the United States compete on the global economic stage, since all major economic powers at the time had interventionist production and trade policies. Noting that rapid population growth and an abundance of natural resources could make America an economic power, Alexander Hamilton argued that the government should subsidize manufacturing, enact protective tariffs, and support the development of infrastructure to allow manufacturing to thrive (Hamilton 1791). Alas, with the exception of the tariff, Hamilton's ideas were rejected by the Congress (Katz and Lee 2011). In the event, the United States did become a major manufacturing power, but perhaps several decades later than would have been the case if Hamilton's plan were followed.

Even for Jeffersonian opponents of Hamilton's vision for an economic superpower that could rival the great countries of Europe, it was quickly clear that a simple economy of yeoman farmers still required a system of transportation infrastructure to link internal markets in what was even then geographically a large country, and which grew dramatically after the Louisiana Purchase. This led some politicians to again argue that the federal government should play a lead role in what were then called "internal improvements," but what we would call infrastructure development today (Goodrich 1948). Formidable proponents, like Henry Clay, argued that the federal government should take the lead in funding and building infrastructure in his "American System," and the federal government did sometimes invest in private companies building roads and canals (Goodrich 1948). Ultimately, however, a robust federal role in funding infrastructure was rejected in the 1830s, when legislation to fund a national highway system failed in Congress, and President Andrew Jackson vetoed a bill that would have permitted the federal government to buy stock in a private company building the Maysville Road in Kentucky (Baker 2002). Thus, the federal government played a minimal role in planning or funding such engineering feats of the early 1800s as the Erie Canal. In contrast, state governments typically played a lead role in spurring such developments by creating public authorities and chartering corporations, which allowed private individuals to join together to raise the vast sums of capital needed to create large infrastructure projects. These debates about the federal government's role in funding infrastructure persist until today, of course, and the view that the federal government should not play a major role in funding infrastructure has its champions even in recent Congresses. Nevertheless, over time the federal role in this area has expanded considerably despite multidecade opposition to taking a lead role in infrastructure.

Of course the most divisive issue in the early years of the Republic was slavery. Through a modern lens we tend to view slavery in almost purely moral terms, and justifiably so, but it was ultimately an economic system, in which a minority were mercilessly exploited in order for others to profit economically from their labor (Williams 1944). We correctly view the federal government as the entity that once and for all eliminated slavery and the de jure legal cast system surrounding it, through the Civil War and subsequent constitutional amendments and statutes. But despite heated debates as early as the Constitutional Convention, the federal government was not very active in abolishing slavery in the first several decades of the Republic. Indeed, slavery was built into the Constitution, and federal institutions and laws played a key role in prolonging slavery and extending its geographical reach, with actions such as the Missouri Compromise and the *Dred Scott* decision, despite the fact that even at the time of the writing of the Constitution there was substantial opposition to slavery. In fact, by the time the Constitution was written a number of northern states had already outlawed slavery (Kaminski 1995). So even on this matter where the power of the federal government was decisive in ultimately eliminating slavery in the southern states, the federal government still *followed* several of the states in abolishing slavery, and by several decades at that.

Prior to the Civil War, the potential role of the federal government in the economy was circumscribed by the limited scope and reach of markets as they then existed. Yet, since the founding of the Republic, there have been strong and famously eloquent proponents of an expanded role for the federal government in the economy in the name of addressing economic problems faced by both capitalists and average citizens. Prior to the Civil War, federal policymakers often rejected this expanded role. As industrialization took place after the Civil War, proponents of a more activist federal government again pressed for federal action to address the problems that this economic change was creating, and again, the federal government initially rejected playing a lead role in helping citizens confront this major economic shift.

Government Responses to Industrialization

In the decades after the Civil War the nation was transformed from a largely rural society, where most people worked in agriculture in the wilderness or small towns, to one in which the population was more often working in industry, crowded together in cities as a result of the coming of industrial capitalism. In 1860, nearly 80% of the population lived in areas that the Census Bureau defined as rural, but by 1920 less than half of the population lived in such places.[1] This change dramatically transformed the economy and virtually every other aspect of society. The appalling working and living conditions endured by many in the rapidly growing cities were vividly documented in the photographs of Jacob Riis, and captured in print by muckrakers such as Upton Sinclair in his famous book *The Jungle*.

Industrialization had critical economic implications for everyone. For nimble firms and entrepreneurs, the larger scale of economic enterprises and expanding national and international markets created the potential for much greater profits and wealth. But there were downsides for many in society. Farmers suffered because they were reliant on huge firms in often noncompetitive environments for insuring and transporting their products, which created new opportunities for exploitation. Small businesses were threatened, and often put out of business or swallowed up, by the giant new corporations. For workers, industrialization created many new jobs, but the new production processes also created dangerous and unhealthy working environments, and the competition for jobs among low-skilled laborers in some industries and areas gave employers the upper hand in negotiating contracts with workers, leading to low wages, long working hours, and unsafe working conditions. Industrialization was simultaneously an economic miracle *and* disaster.

Not surprisingly, given how widespread the effects of industrialization were, the public began to demand solutions to these downsides of industrial production. In the late 1800s and early 1900s the Populist and Progressive movements forged programs to address the economic and social problems associated with industrialization and the development of a modern national economy. These activists advocated for regulation of natural monopolies like railroads and utilities, and for government authority to break up trusts. Social legislation, such as child labor laws and maximum-hour laws, aimed at ameliorating the worst abuses of the industrial labor market, were also advanced. At the federal level, these plans found a vigorous champion in the person of William Jennings Bryan (Kazin 2006). Aside from his infamous work as an antievolution attorney in the "Scopes Monkey Trial," William Jennings Bryan is probably best known for being the only person to be nominated as a presidential candidate by a major party three separate times. Thus, his brand of populism had substantial appeal.

Alas, not quite enough appeal, as Bryan lost all three times to his Republican opponent. These repeated defeats have multiple causes, but certainly the opposition of the "robber barons" and industrialists played an important role in his electoral tribulations. Senator Mark Hanna, the campaign manager and fundraiser for President McKinley, who defeated Bryan in his first attempt at the presidency in 1896, raised what were then staggering sums from corporations and businessmen, in exchange for the promise of a laissez-faire and limited government approach to the economy, even as the Republican Party wanted to expand the activity of the federal government in other realms, such as by the establishment of overseas colonies (Williams 2010). Powerful members of Congress, such as Senator Nelson Aldrich of Connecticut, had close business and personal relationships with titans of industry such as John D. Rockefeller—Rockefeller's son would become Aldrich's son-in-law (Smith 2014). Thus, even if Bryan had been elected president it is doubtful that his agenda would have met with much success in the Congress given the forces arrayed against him. The Populist and Progressive agendas did not entirely fail at the federal level, but even when laws such as the Sherman Antitrust Act were passed by Congress (in 1890), they were often weakly enforced by presidents and presidential appointees who were beholden to big money.

It was therefore largely left to the state governments to develop and implement policies to combat the problems of modern industrial capitalism in the late 1800s and early 1900s. The minimum wage and eight-hour workday, child labor laws, "mother's" pensions, and worker's compensation insurance all began at the state level (Amenta et al. 1987; Allswang 2000; Hofstader 1955). Cognizant of the fact that the new extraordinary wealth of industrial firms could be used to control the political system, the Progressives and Populists also successfully enacted institutional reforms like direct primaries, the Australian ballot, women's suffrage, the "merit" system to staff government bureaucracies, campaign finance regulations, and direct democracy (the initiative, referendum, and recall). These institutional changes were designed to weaken party machines, limit the ability of private interests to influence the political process, expand citizen control over policymaking, and, in the case of the initiative, allow citizens to circumvent elected officials and the wealthy interests that controlled them in the policy process (McGerr 2005). It was only much later that the federal government adopted most of these policy and institutional changes, which initially spread among the states. For instance, it was approximately three decades between the passage of the first state minimum wage law and the adoption of a national minimum wage law in the Fair Labor Standards Act, passed as part of the New Deal (Grossman 1978).

Not only did the federal government fail to address the problems of industrialization, but federal institutions even attempted to prevent the states from doing so. Most notoriously, the Supreme Court interpreted the Constitution and federal statutes to limit the power of the state governments to regulate business and increase government taxation and spending. One of the more infamous examples was found in the *Lochner* case, in which the Court determined that laws limiting hours (and implicitly regulating other working conditions) violated the right of individuals to enter into contracts, which was interpreted as a guarantee of the due process clause of the 14th Amendment (Frankfurter 1916). Indeed, the Supreme Court has often been an institution preventing subnational governments that would like to address emerging economic problems from doing so. For instance, in an earlier era the *Dred Scott* case helped ensure the spread and persistence of slavery, and it also prevented a robust federal response to the Depression, as we discuss next.

The Great Depression and Great Society

FDR's New Deal may or may not have saved America from the Great Depression depending on one's perspective, but for our purposes it is important to remember that even as the problems of a modern, industrial economy were laid bare after the stock market crash and resulting depression, the federal government dithered for years. In the initial phases of the Great Depression, President Herbert Hoover, who presided over the stock market crash of 1929, preferred charity rather than federal government action, and later viewed the New Deal as a major infringement on liberty (Schlesinger 2003). But even after FDR's election, it was more than five years before some New Deal programs were implemented, due partly to Supreme Court recalcitrance (Carson and Kleinerman 2002). Nevertheless, in the years preceding the Court's acceptance of the New Deal, and the expansion of federal policy activity to address the Depression, the state "laboratories of democracy" pursued a variety of policies intended to ameliorate the problems of unprecedented unemployment and poverty.

Indeed, parts of the New Deal program were taken directly from Populist and Progressive policies that had been enacted in the states years or even decades before. FDR's secretary of labor, Frances Perkins, was an architect of many of these programs while she served governors, Al Smith and FDR himself, in New York (Downey 2010). Other cornerstones of the New Deal, for example, the minimum wage, a federal system of unemployment insurance, and pensions for the elderly, disabled, and widowed (part of the Social Security Act) had been enacted in states over the preceding few decades. Massachusetts and Wisconsin, for example, crafted unemployment insurance laws years before FDR's election, and a dozen states had old-age pension laws that would serve as the model for Social Security by 1932 (Amenta and Carruthers 1988). As the Great Depression caused widespread misery, state politicians and policymakers proposed even more dramatic action, which directly affected the crafting of the New Deal. For instance, Upton Sinclair's campaign for governor of California and his EPIC (End Poverty in California) plan attracted the attention and admiration of federal New Dealers like Harry Hopkins, and provided further impetus to programs like Social Security, pushing the New Deal to be more expansive (Singleton 2000). In short, virtually all aspects of the New Deal had already been tried or were then being proposed in the states when the federal New Deal was being crafted. Before the New Deal "saved" America from the Depression, the states had for decades been engaging in policy experimentation to address the economic problems of industrial capitalism, which manifested themselves in extreme form during the Depression.

Following on the heels of the Great Depression, World War II led to an expanded role for government in almost every aspect of the economy— from working with employers and employees on collective bargaining agreements and labor peace, to dictating which products would be manufactured by the War Production Board (O'Brian and Fleischman 1944). Though such actions would never have been tolerated in peacetime, with victories over the Great Depression and the Axis there was an apparent willingness to see the federal government use its power and authority to improve the economic lives of Americans. In the wake of World War II the federal government took the lead in addressing socioeconomic problems of the postwar era. The GI Bill, the interstate highway system, and ultimately the Great Society and the War on Poverty were programs designed to help Americans thrive economically and to protect citizens from the worst aspects of modern capitalism.

In contrast with earlier periods, these postwar programs did not have much precedent at the state level and were largely the creation of federal politicians, bureaucrats, advocates, and academic experts (Zelizer 2015). This expansion of the federal government into the economy seemed natural—in a complex world with numerous economic (and military) threats to citizens, the federal government has more resources, expertise, and policy tools with which to confront economic challenges. In addition, after the victories over the Depression and the Axis, people had confidence in the federal government. Furthermore, for many decades certain state governments had demonstrated consistently that they would not ensure equal economic rights for all citizens. Some of the Great Society and War on Poverty programs were specifically designed to circumvent recalcitrant state governments that would not support the goals of eliminating poverty and enhancing opportunity for all citizens, since they were dominated by segregationists and thus would not give minorities a fair shot at government benefits (Zelizer 2015).

Thus, from the late 1930s through the mid-1960s the federal government took the lead in addressing economic problems faced by the nation. We do not mean to imply that the states did nothing to address economic problems and challenges from the New Deal to the Great Society. Many state policymakers used the willingness of the federal government to take a larger role in the economy to push their own goals, while other states did not. For instance, de facto partnerships between the federal and some state governments, fueled by federally funded research grants and returning veterans with GI Bill money, spurred the expansion of high-quality higher education systems in many states. The era from the 1930s to the 1960s may have been the heyday of what is sometimes called cooperative federalism—the federal and state governments acting in tandem, with the federal government using its superior resources to push states to address economic problems like poverty and unemployment.

Nor are we saying that federal government action was inconsequential before the New Deal. Even before the New Deal and Great Society eras, federal government action, however late it may have been, was important, because not all state governments were inclined to act on major economic problems. This is most obvious in the case of slavery, where slaveholders in the South were made to abandon the practice under force of arms, but even Populist and Progressive reforms were not adopted in all states (Aldrich 2015). So federal government action was essential to putting these laws into place for the entire country. The same is true of the New Deal. And even during periods of general federal recalcitrance, the federal government did take some steps to address emerging economic problems (e.g., the Sherman Antitrust Act and the Tillman Act, which regulated campaign finance in 1904). Our point is simply that the federal government is seldom the first to tackle an emerging economic problem, and by the time it does address an economic problem, the states have usually already been addressing it for some time and have provided examples of policy that can be used by the federal government. Thus, the period of the late 1930s through the late 1960s was something of an anomaly in American history up to that time. Furthermore, this federal activism was to prove short-lived.

Backlash: The 1970s to the Present

Hacker and Pierson (2010) argue that the policies of the 1930s through the 1960s were very successful at creating a society of rising wages and standards of living and broadly shared prosperity. Indeed, economic inequality was relatively low and remained low during this period. Of course, there were those who did not see benefit in this economic status quo and did not agree with this new role for the federal government, even at the height of federal triumphalism in the 1960s. For instance, Republican presidential candidate Barry Goldwater did not support the federal Civil Rights Act, which was clearly a large expansion of government into commerce, because he thought it was an overreach by the federal government and violated states' rights. At the time, these voices were a distinct minority within the halls of government, in the media and in universities, but as the Great Society and War on Poverty advanced, the federal policy activism in confronting economic threats provoked a backlash from numerous conservative politicians and thought leaders (Quadagno 1994).

President Nixon is generally seen as one of the first political beneficiaries of this backlash (Perlstein 2009), but subsequent presidents and congressional majorities have come to power to some degree on the prolonged displeasure with the liberal programs and federal activism of the 1960s. While not shy about using the power of the federal government to achieve his political aims, in the early 1970s President Nixon initiated some early steps to limit the expansion of federal power and devolve some power back to the states. The move to return power to the states and limit the activity of the federal government accelerated throughout the 1980s and 1990s. In 1986 President Ronald Reagan joked that the scariest words in the English language were "I'm from the government and I'm here to help." This was barely more than 20 years after LBJ's Great Society and War on Poverty were launched. A leading spokesperson of the resurgent right, Grover Norquist, famously quipped that he wanted to shrink the size of government so it could be drowned in a bathtub.

Reagan's election, along with a Republican Senate in 1980, represented a sea change in Washington, DC. While the government expanded in the realm of defense, the growth of social programs and regulation were slowed and taxes were reduced. After the Republican Party gained control of the Congress for the first time in decades, following the 1994 election, further steps to limit the activism of the federal government were initiated. The new Republican congressional majority that took power in 1995 had a number of economic policy proposals in its "Contract with America," intended to limit the size and economic intervention of the federal government by limiting regulation, avoiding unfunded mandates for state governments, and cutting taxes (Rae 1998). The 104th Congress engaged in a new kind of activism, one that was largely aimed at dismantling Progressive Era, New Deal, Great Society, and War on Poverty programs (Hacker and Pierson 2010).

In some ways the three-decade attack on these programs has been a remarkable failure. During the Reagan administration a Democratic House prevented major changes to these programs, and President Clinton prevented many of the policy changes that the 104th Congress would have preferred. More generally, even in the absence of Democratic "veto players," programs like Medicare and Social Security remain very popular, and it does not look like they are going anywhere in the near future. After all, even under unified Republican government during George W. Bush's term in office these programs were not seriously threatened despite the president's desire to fundamentally reshape them by, for example, privatizing Social Security. Yet the conservative attacks on the New Deal and Great Society programs have been very successful in other ways. In the realm of finance, there has been an almost a complete dismantling of New Deal era regulation (Hacker and Pierson 2010; Keller and Kelly 2015; Witko 2016), with arguably disastrous consequences for the United States and global economy. Similarly, organized labor has been attacked and weakened by conservative presidents and their appointees (Tope and Jacobs 2009). And major tax cuts for wealthy investors, high-income earners, and rich heirs have been a major theme of the last three decades of American politics. Not all of these reversals were the product of Republicans who had long been suspicious of federal policy activism—the Clinton administration and many key Democrats in Congress were critical to the process of financial deregulation, and it was Bill Clinton who signed a bill to "end welfare as we know it" (Hacker and Pierson 2010).

More often, however, rather than changing older policies, the federal government has simply failed to address emerging economic problems and changing economic circumstances. Hacker and Pierson (2010) call this failure of the government to change existing policies to confront new economic realities "policy drift." Perhaps nowhere are the effects of federal inaction clearer than on the issue of the minimum wage, since if it is not raised, its value deteriorates through inflation. The federal government routinely increased the federal minimum wage from the 1930s through the 1970s to counter the effects of inflation, but since Reagan's election this has happened far less frequently. In the 30 years from 1950 to 1980 the federal government increased the minimum wage 18 times, while in the 31 years from 1980 to 2011 the minimum wage increased only 9 times (US Department of Labor 2015). As defined benefit pensions have disappeared in the last generation, the federal government has done little to address this problem (Hacker 2004). The steady work, annual wage increases, and good retirement benefits that were the hallmark of the post-World War II economy have disappeared, and been replaced by low-wage service sector jobs and growing economic insecurity (Rehm, Hacker, and Schlesinger 2012). It is remarkable how little policy has changed to address these new economic realities. Thus, though few major economic and social policies of the New Deal and Great Society were completely dismantled, there were few policies designed to address new or worsening economic problems, including inequality, as we discuss below. Undoubtedly, this partly reflects the success of the attacks on the government as incompetent and incapable of skillfully addressing economic problems, which has been a constant them in American political discourse over the last several decades.

There are exceptions to this pattern of inaction, of course. The Affordable Care Act is a major policy innovation designed to address the problems faced by American workers—as steady work becomes less common, this creates a major problem, since in the US health insurance is tied to employment for people under 65. The Affordable Care Act should help to address this problem. But it is notable that even here, the states are given a major role in establishing what this policy will eventually look like, with key authority over whether to establish an insurance exchange or expand Medicaid. The refusal of certain states to expand Medicaid has meant that hundreds of thousands of individuals who could be covered by this health insurance program are not. The law was nearly undone but for the decision of the Supreme Court to uphold the legality of federal insurance exchanges in the *Burwell* case. In addition, as the price of passage, the Obama administration had to make major concessions to big business. For insurance companies, the Obama administration did not push the so-called public option, which would have allowed people under 65 to choose government health insurance. And of course Republicans in Washington, DC, are promising to repeal this law with a repeal law already passing through the House of Representatives as of this writing.

The 2008 financial crisis and resulting recession, the most severe economic problems the country has faced since the Great Depression, was of such a magnitude that the federal government was forced to do something. In fact, it did quite a lot in the immediate aftermath of the crisis. There were bailouts of large banks and automakers, a stimulus designed to create jobs, and new banking regulation enacting. Naturally, many critics on the right objected to these policies as government overreach and thought that the government should be doing very little other than letting the pain play out. Critics on the left, such as economist and *New York Times* columnist Paul Krugman, argued that these policies did not go nearly far enough.

But it is undeniable that after the initial burst of major legislative activity, the federal government has done relatively little to address the lingering problems of the recession and financial crisis, contributing to high levels of unemployment that persisted much longer than in the typical post–World War II recession. In fact, gridlock in Congress has prevented the government from doing much of anything at all. Even performing basic tasks of government—like passing a budget or increasing the debt capacity of the federal government—are nearly out of reach. This means that addressing the longer-term problem of growing economic inequality is highly unlikely. Though this federal inactivity is frustrating to liberals, who see economic history through the lens of the New Deal and Great Society eras, federal inaction in the face of economic threats and challenges has been the norm, not the exception, throughout American history. Next we discuss why this is so often the case and why, therefore, the states often take the lead in addressing economic.

WHY THE FEDS FAIL AND THE STATES TAKE THE LEAD

There are political cultural, institutional, and practical political reasons why the federal government has historically *not* taken the lead in addressing economic problems, which has left a vacuum for the states to fill. Early in the Republic there was a strong cultural or philosophical bias against an "energetic" federal government, which was in part a response to the government overreach of the colonial era. When the Constitutional Convention was called, there was widespread dissatisfaction with the Articles of Confederation, which governed the 13 states at the time. Many of the provisions of the Articles of Confederation—such as a lack of centralized taxing authority, inability to create money, and a weak executive—prevented a true national government from emerging. There was considerable agreement that the Articles needed to be revised, but substantial disagreement over how "energetic" the new government should be, and how many powers it should have compared to the states, with many critics preferring to keep significant governing authority at the state level (Storing 1981). The result of the constitutional debate was a federal government with fairly limited formal powers, particularly in the realm of domestic affairs. This hesitancy to expansively use the power of the federal government could be seen in debates over internal improvements in the very early years of the Republic. Though most people are comfortable with a larger, more powerful government these days, this strain of suspicion about the power of the federal government is still fairly widespread, as we can see in contemporary policy debates.

On top of any philosophical or cultural preferences for limited federal government, the embodiment of these ideas in the Constitution limits the power and ability of the federal government to act in very tangible ways, and poses few such limits on the states. The federal government is given exclusive power in just a few areas (foreign trade, coining money, etc.), and these are mostly in foreign policy and defense. In domestic economic policy, the supremacy clause indicates that federal law is the supreme law of the land when the federal government is acting within its legal authority. But if the federal government does little, for practical purposes this is not a constraint on the states at all. And the 10th Amendment reserved powers clause states that powers not explicitly given to the federal government in the Constitution are reserved for the states or the people. This means that the states in some sense have more legal authority with which to act to address problems, since as far as the US Constitution is concerned, they can address any substantive policy matter that is not exclusively granted to the federal government.

In contrast, there are numerous limits on the federal government's ability to act in the Constitution. Congressional action is limited to the 17 enumerated powers, while the powers of the executive and the Supreme Court are even fewer. It is true that the interstate commerce clause and necessary and proper clause allowed for a future expansion of federal government activities beyond those specifically listed, but until the 1930s these clauses were typically interpreted narrowly by policymakers and the courts. As a result, for the first several decades of American history the federal government did relatively little in terms of economic policymaking. Under these circumstances it was natural for citizens to look to state governments for redress of economic grievances. As the esteemed scholar of American democracy Theodore Lowi put it, "nineteenth century social movements focused on the state capitals, not the national capital, whenever demands or frustrations focused on public objects" (1984).

Second, separation of powers and checks and balances mean that even when the federal government is acting in a legitimate sphere of authority, and some federal officials would like to confront economic problems, as a practical matter, it is very difficult to enact new policy. The framers of the new Constitution did prefer a "republican government," that is, a government that is ultimately accountable to the "public" via elections. However, they were also worried that "measures are too often decided, not according to the rules of justice and the rights of the minor party, but by the superior force of an interested and overbearing majority" (Madison 1789). So they sought to limit the ability of the majority to enact its preferences. It should be pointed out that, of course, a true majority faction would be impossible in Madison's day since the majority of adult inhabitants of the United States lacked meaningful political rights. And, in his concern about minority rights, Madison certainly was not referring to racial or ethnic groups, but instead was concerned about the rights of economic minorities, since, as he notes in Federalist 10, "The most common and durable source of factions has been the various and unequal distribution of property." Thus, when a major economic change emerges that threatens the majority, Madison's scheme was *designed* to make it difficult for this majority to prevail in the federal policy process.

In some ways the Constitution has become more responsive to the public by amendments such as the direct election of senators, and the expansion of the franchise. However, at the same time that these developments have taken place, other remarkably antidemocratic practices have emerged within US policymaking institutions, especially the US Senate. A single member of the US Senate can prevent action on important matters like legislation and judicial and executive branch appointments. A determined minority can pretty much stall anything they want. Practices that enable this—such as the filibuster, or the ability of senators to place "holds" on nominees—are not found in the Constitution, and can thus be changed more easily, but further magnify the Madisonian ideal of stifling majorities.

The flip side of majorities being easily stifled is that because of the numerous veto points designed into federal policy institutions it is comparatively easy for a powerful minority to prevent policy change. Madison was concerned that an oppressive majority could take over the federal government, and the Constitution was designed to prevent this. But he and other framers were less worried about the possibility that a minority could take over government and prevent positive changes. But the ability of a minority to prevent the enactment of new policies is arguably every bit as much a threat as a powerful majority. And during periods of major economic change, because of the structure of federal policymaking institutions, and an abundance of economic resources, the minority of winners of economic change have the means to control these veto points, bringing us to the practical political reason why the federal government often fails to act to confront economic challenges.

Periods of economic change like war, the Industrial Revolution, or the "financialization" of the economy today produce tremendous wealth (Witko 2016). But major economic changes also create major economic dislocations and traumas, and it is natural for citizens that are economically threatened to look to the state to ameliorate these threats (Polanyi 1944). The "winners" of the economic status quo will have the incentive and means to block policies that change the status quo that enriches them. These wealthy individuals and interests often invest their significant sums of money into politics to do precisely this. During the Progressive Era this often involved outright bribery. After, laws were enacted, and norms changed, which led to the decline of such overt corruption, but business and the wealthy still invest heavily in lobbying and funding election campaigns (Witko 2013), which can gain them the allegiance of members of Congress and presidents (Hacker and Pierson 2010). Even unelected bureaucrats or judges often identify with the winners of economic change, or are subject to indirect pressures from them, as we can see from the history of Supreme Court rulings striking down Progressive reforms and New Deal programs. Because of the presence of numerous veto points in the federal government, it is comparatively easy for powerful interests to prevent policy action in the federal government, even if favored by a majority, as we discuss below in the context of income inequality.

Ultimately, despite the veto points and powerful interests, politicians are responsible to the public via elections. This means that determined public opinion can, at times, overcome these impediments to action in the federal government. However, due to the large size and diversity of the United States, a majority of elected officials are unlikely to get intense demands from the public to act to address particular economic problems since those problems are not felt equally across the United States at any one time. In an economic disaster the magnitude of the Great Depression, unified public opinion may want the government to do something. But in more normal circumstances of slowly evolving economic change, this intensity of opinion throughout the country is unlikely. For instance, while the decline of manufacturing was a major problem in the Rust Belt, where there were calls for protectionist measures and a national industrial policy, the Sun Belt was thriving economically (Graham 1994). This means that the average voter may not be very concerned about substantial economic disruptions. Even when a huge swath of the country is experiencing economic hardship, if the remainder is not, the federal government is less likely to act.

FEDERALISM AND GOVERNMENT RESPONSES TO INEQUALITY

The historical pattern of federal inaction and state policy activity in the face of changing economic conditions is very much on display in the current context of growing economic inequality. While income inequality has been growing for a few decades, the issue burst into the public consciousness during the Occupy Wall Street protests, beginning in Manhattan and spreading to various cities in 2010. Though some attempted portray these protestors as a disgruntled (and disheveled) minority, opinion polls show broad concern about growing inequality. For instance, a 2014 Pew Survey found that 65% of Americans believe the gap between the rich and everyone else has increased over the last decade, and this view is shared by majorities across nearly all groups in the public, including 68% of Democrats and 61% of Republicans (Pew 2014).

Polls also show a growing willingness to have the government use its authority to reduce inequality. Broadly speaking, government may take two approaches to pursuing inequality. First, government can engage in redistribution by taxing the wealthy and spending the revenue on programs for the poor and middle class. Second, government can enact policies that raise the pretax wages of workers. These have been called redistribution and market-conditioning policies, respectively (Kelly 2009). We have seen increasing support for both redistribution and market-conditioning policies in recent years. The same Pew survey mentioned above found that "raising taxes on the wealthy and corporations to expand programs for the poor" is favored by 54% of Americans. In early 2015, when asked whether the government should use heavy taxes on the rich to "redistribute wealth" 52% of Americans agreed, the largest percentage since the question was first asked in 1939 (Newport 2015). This is quite remarkable considering the use of the loaded term "redistribute."

Conservatives tend to be less supportive of explicit redistribution, which limits the attractiveness of such policies to many, but other market-conditioning egalitarian policies that do not involve redistribution and new taxing and spending, such as the minimum wage, have high levels of public support, even among conservatives. In 2014, 70% of Americans expressed support for raising the minimum wage from $7.25 to $10 per hour (CBS / New York Times 2015). Despite these opinions, there have not been large increases in taxes on the wealthy in recent years, nor has the federal government frequently raised the minimum wage very often.

One possibility is that inequality is neglected because it grows slowly and is not salient with the public, and this may explain federal inaction. But other issues with similar characteristics—most notably the deficit—attract tremendous attention from policymakers and have led to important changes in government policy (such as sequestration, or future spending caps legislated into the budget process that result in automatic budget cuts). So the issue characteristics of inequality alone cannot explain why it is not addressed. Nor can public acceptance of inequality. We have seen that despite relatively antistatist views in the United States, a majority of Americans are concerned about growing economic inequality and want the government to do something about it.

This nonresponse to inequality and the exacerbation of inequality seem puzzling in a system that is supposed to be responsive to the average voter, at a time when economic inequality is becoming more of a public concern. But against the broader historical backdrop discussed previously, the failure of the government to act to slow inequality, and even to exacerbate it by helping the winners of economic inequality see desired policies enacted or to veto undesired policy changes, is not so surprising. The usual factors that have prevented the government from addressing major economic problems in the past—the structure of policymaking institutions and the power of the beneficiaries of economic change—can explain why demands to address inequality are unmet now in Washington, DC.

According to political science research, during this period of growing inequality, the political power of the wealthy has increased, and responsiveness to the average member of the public has declined. While the US federal government seems to have been broadly responsive in the post–World War II era, according to some analysis (Erikson, MacKuen, and Stimson 1999), there is mounting evidence that the federal government is not very responsive to the poor and middle class any longer. For instance, Larry Bartels (2005; 2008) demonstrates that the US Senate is primarily responsive to the preferences of the wealthy. Republicans in the US Senate respond only to the preferences of the rich, and Democrats respond to the wealthy and, sometimes, the middle class. The poor go mostly unheard by both parties. Bartels also chronicles how federal government fiscal policies have favored the interests of the affluent, from the Bush tax cuts of 2001 and 2003 that dramatically reduced top marginal rates, to the failure to raise the federal minimum wage, to the repeal of the estate tax.

Similarly, Martin Gilens (2012) and Gilens and Page (2014) show in their important work that the preferences and organizations of the wealthy often influence policy outcomes, while middle-class preferences and those of the poor seldom have such an effect. While these groups may get what they want when they agree with the wealthy (Enns 2015), on issues pitting the poor against the wealthy, the poor are almost certain to lose. These preference gaps matter a great deal since, compared to the very wealthy, the poor and middle class are more likely to think that government should actively reduce inequality, and more supportive of policies like redistribution or the strengthening of unions to achieve this goal (Page, Bartels, and Seawright 2013).

Perhaps it is not surprising that politicians are not very responsive to the poor because they are less likely to vote (Brady, Verba, and Schlozman 1995; Franko, Kelly, and Witko 2016). But Bartels's research shows that gaps in voter turnout cannot fully explain the lack of responsiveness to lower-income Americans (Bartels 2006). No doubt, this reflects, in part, that in America's system of pluralist democracy, interest groups are also an important means of representation and the rich are increasingly injecting their resources into politics. As income inequality has grown, so too has the dominance of lobbying and contributing to campaigns by business and the wealthy (Drutman 2015; Hacker and Pierson 2010; Witko 2013). Adding to the growing power of business and the wealthy, politicians are increasingly likely to have personal wealth and come from the business world themselves in recent years (Carnes 2012; Witko and Friedman 2008).

Taken together, these findings have caused some observers to ask whether the United States is becoming an oligarchy (Winters and Page 2009). Oligarchy or not, it is clear that policy that is enacted more often reflects the preferences—and interests—of business and the wealthy, and that policies opposed by these interests are less likely to be enacted in Washington, DC. Even policies with widespread economic benefits for many in the public, like the Affordable Care Act, must accommodate the preferences of powerful business interests. For example, the legislation ensured that the government could not offer cheap health insurance options to consumers to compete with options offered by the private insurance industry. While not as beneficial as it might have been, the ACA was still a step in the right direction. In contrast, there is mounting evidence that other policies pursued by the federal government in recent decades like regressive tax cuts for the wealthy, financial deregulation, a weakening of protections to organize unions, and failing to raise the minimum wage have contributed to growing inequality (Enns et al. 2014; Hacker and Pierson 2010; Keller and Kelly 2015; Kelly and Witko 2012; Smeeding 2005; Western and Rosenfeld 2011).

Against this backdrop of inaction and harmful action, why has the public not risen up to assert itself? It is hard for the majority to counter the power of business and the wealthy because of the large number of veto points in the US political system, which are controlled by the wealthy and business interests (Bonica et al. 2013; Enns et al. 2014). Stepan and Linz (2011) found that countries with more veto points in their policy process have higher levels of inequality, and the United States has more than almost any other country (it is tied with Brazil). A single chamber of the Congress, the president, or even a single senator can prevent the enactment of policy favored by millions of Americans. This dynamic has prevented egalitarian economic policies preferred by the vast majority of Americans—like an increase in the minimum wage—from being enacted.

Adding to the problems of majorities, the growing partisan polarization in America exacerbates the American constitutional design to make it even harder to get things done. Schattschneider (1960) thought that programmatic, ideological parties could ensure that the public would have a voice in government by limiting the power of wealthy special interests by giving the mass public clear choices in terms of two strong parties. This may be true in elections, since it does seem that growing inequality has contributed to the relatively distinct party platforms in recent decades (McCarty, Poole, and Rothenberg 2006). Yet, within the Congress, polarized parties seem to make it harder to get much of any policy enacted, which leads to growing inequality as the economic status quo creates increasing inequality, which would need to be addressed by public policy (Enns et al. 2014; Hacker and Pierson 2010). Unfortunately, given this combination of forces there does not seem to be any clear end in sight to this inequality-producing and reinforcing status quo in Washington, DC.

The States and the New Economic Populism

This federal government inaction in the face of rising inequality has spurred a number of states to enact policies that have the effect of slowing the growth of, and reducing inequality, a trend that we call the "new economic populism." Though the Constitution predisposes the federal government to inaction, the Constitution allows for the states to take broad policy initiative, and the variation in state economic, political, and institutional conditions will often lead to responses to emerging economic problems in at least some states, that we do not see in the federal government. Furthermore, federal inaction creates a policy vacuum that can be filled by the states during times of economic hardship. Federalism creates possibilities for entrepreneurial policymakers in the states to address problems even as the federal government neglects to do so.

Scholarly conceptions of the nature of American federalism have informed, and evolved in response to, the shifting divisions of powers and activities of state and federal governments over time. Prior to the Progressive Era or even the Great Depression, scholars and the enforcers of the vertical division of power in American government, the courts, often adopted an implicit or explicit framework of dual federalism. This is the idea that the federal government is sovereign in certain areas (like monetary or currency matters and trade) but that the states are sovereign in other matters (like education or enforcing community morals) (Boyd 1997). As long as the economy was fairly local and the scope of government involvement in it limited, this arrangement held and worked more or less well. But this system clearly began to break down in the latter part of the 1800s, as the increasingly complex economy demanded broader government involvement and economic problems crossed state boundaries.

As the regulation of businesses and economic activity took shape, and the welfare state developed throughout the early 1900s and through the New Deal and Great Society eras, it was very clear that the creation of federal and state programs, and shared responsibilities for both levels of government in federal programs, had created a very different type of federalism than existed previously. The federalism that emerged in this period is often referred to as "cooperative federalism," because the states and the federal government share responsibility to address shared goals (Boyd 1997). The Affordable Care Act might reasonably be viewed as an example of cooperative federalism. In what counts as poetic language for a social scientist, Morton Grodzins (1960) called dual federalism "layer cake" federalism, because there were clear divisions of authority between the levels of government and this new type of cooperative federalism "marble cake" federalism, because there were not clear layers of responsibility for different problems or policy realms, but instead the division of power between states and the feds was messier.

As noted above, since the late 1960s and certainly since the early 1980s the federal government has often neglected to play a leading role in addressing new economic problems, and sought to shift more responsibility to the states, which is sometimes called the "new federalism" (Boyd 1997). The federal government taking a less aggressive role in confronting many problems has led to what Derthick (2010) calls "compensatory" federalism, where the states have the authority and ability to step in to address problems that the federal government is failing to tackle. She examines this in the context of the failure to regulate greenhouse gas emissions, but the idea is very applicable to the context of economic inequality. The failure of the federal government creates a situation where states have an enhanced ability to influence the income distribution should they choose to do so (Kelly and Witko 2012). Freeman and Rogers (2007) discuss the possibility of a "progressive federalism," which would allow the states to better confront economic and other problems. And they recommend federal policy actions, like equalization payments to poor states to ensure that they have fiscal capacity similar to wealthier states, to help states confront problems. But even in the absence of institutional and policy changes that would help the states be more aggressive in tackling problems, which are very unlikely to be pursued at the moment given the conservative outlook of many policymakers and general gridlock in DC, we show in this book that many states are already responding to growing economic inequality as the federal government fails to.

The new economic populism then, is a type of state action enabled by federalism that begins with the acknowledgment that at the moment the federal government is unable to do much of anything, let alone tackle a multidecade problem like economic inequality. Though state governments are subject to many of the same problems as the federal government, because of a similar institutional structures and political dynamics, for status quo economic interests to prevent *any* state action they would need to control veto points in all state governments. While Madison argued that a faction within a state would be unlikely to combine with other state factions to control the federal government in Federalist 10, it is equally unlikely that a single faction that is powerful in the federal government would be able to simultaneously control all or most state governments, for a number of reasons.

First, because of the variation in state economies and societies, some states will experience economic hardships much more rapidly and intensely than other states. More severe economic problems attract the public's attention, which can in turn make it more likely for the government to address economic problems. For instance, the rapid disappearance of manufacturing jobs or "deindustrialization" in the 1970s and 1980s was an acute problem where there were more workers reliant on manufacturing for employment in the "the Rust Belt." And while the federal government never created a comprehensive industrial policy to address the decline of manufacturing jobs, a number of Rust Belt states went very far in this direction (Gray and Lowery 1990). Similarly, inequality varies across the states. There is a major debate about the relationship between inequality and redistribution in the political economy literature generated by the classic article by Meltzer and Richard (1981), and one reason we think that inequality may not automatically lead to more redistribution by government is that not all publics will have the same awareness of and concern about even similar levels of inequality. Of course, some individuals are more concerned about inequality and where these individuals—namely liberal, Democrats—are more numerous there should be a greater awareness of inequality, even controlling for objective levels of inequality. The states allow us to examine this possibility because of the variation in inequality and mass partisanship.

Second, the strength of competing economic interests in interest group and party systems varies across states. It is likely that the "winners" of contemporary economic change will prefer the economic status quo and use their resources to maintain it. In this era of growing economic inequality we have seen that the wealthy and business have become more organized at the state level (Hertel-Fernandez, Skocpol, and Lynch 2016). Groups like the American Legislative Exchange Council (ALEC), and Americans for Prosperity, funded by corporations and wealthy individuals and families, such as the Koch brothers, have been successful in pushing policies in a more inegalitarian direction in some states, much as we have seen in Washington, DC, but have been less influential in other states (Hertel-Fernandez et al. 2016). Yet in many states countervailing groups that oppose business and the wealthy in the policy process, especially unions, remain very strong compared to in the nation as a whole (Radcliff and Saiz 1998; Witko and Newmark 2005).

Furthermore, big business and the wealthy have more opposition in the party system in some states compared to Washington, DC. It is possible that state policymakers will take action to address emerging economic problems, even where the public is not *yet* concerned about an issue because they are personally alarmed by it or see some future political advantage in pursuing it. As with the mass public, politicians affiliated with left-leaning parties are much more willing to intervene in the economy against the wishes of business and the wealthy for both ideological and constituency reasons, and are probably more sensitive to inequality. Though conservative Republicans have seen more electoral success in federal elections and many states in recent decades, other states have stayed similar or even gone further to the left in terms of the ideology of their elected officials. In these states, business and the wealthy will have a more limited ability to shape policy outcomes, and policies will be more egalitarian. Indeed, we think it is probable that as inequality increases and the public becomes more aware of it, this may spur increasing liberalism in the government of some states, where liberal politicians can take advantage of the vacuum created by federal inaction to push policies in more egalitarian directions that are in line with their personal beliefs and electoral interests. The opposite can be said of conservative politicians, of course. Thus, the new economic populism may mean more divergent policies and ultimately economic outcomes.

Finally, some state institutional environments have fewer veto points than others, and there are institutions that allow the public to largely circumvent elected officials and interest groups altogether. Fewer states allow the filibuster, historically many state governors have had more limited veto authority, and state judges are often directly elected by the people, meaning that they are less likely to thwart the will of strong majorities. Most importantly, direct democracy allows policy entrepreneurs to completely circumvent most institutional veto points and allow the public to directly make policy via the initiative with a simple up-or-down vote (which is still subject to judicial review). Indeed, it was conditions very much like those now seen in America that gave rise to direct democracy, which refers to the initiative, the referendum, and the recall.[2]

Citizens in 19 states voted to add one or more of these populist mechanisms to their state constitutions during the early 1900s, and a handful of states adopted some of these institutions in later decades (Cronin 1999). The theory behind the initiative is simple. If you give the public the ability to directly craft legislation and thus bypass interest groups, parties, and politicians, policy will be more reflective of the public's preferences. Though agreement is by no means universal, many studies show that policy is more in line with public preferences in initiative states (Matsusaka 1995; Bowler and Donovan; 1998; Arceneaux 2002; Burden 2005).

One concern is that, just as republican institutions like elections were subverted by organized wealth during the Gilded Age, the initiative has become the tool of wealthy special interests. Even in the Progressive Era, when the initiative was just first being used, opponents and proponents of ballot measures raised large sums of money to persuade voters (Allswang 2000). Of course these expenditures have skyrocketed in recent years, as we discuss in the context of Proposition 1098. The large-scale spending associated with many ballot campaigns has led critics to view the initiative as just another tool of wealthy special interests. However, Gerber (1999) demonstrates that citizen groups are the largest beneficiaries of direct democracy and that wealthy economic interests are able to use their resources to stop policy, but not generally to advance policy that contrasts with the preferences of the public. And Gerber (1999; 1996) also argues that even if an initiative fails, it can push policy enacted by the legislature in a given state closer to public preferences, because the initiative focuses policymaking on certain issues, and state legislatures and governors will often enact more mild versions of initiatives in order to forestall more extreme policy emerging from the direct democracy process.

Since its adoption in the early 1900s, the initiative has been an important tool allowing states to more rapidly adjust to the shifting public preferences that accompany new economic realities. As state governments were not responsive to public preferences for programs helping them deal with industrialization, the initiative was used to force policymaking in these areas. From 1904 through the beginning of the Great Depression, the initiative was a tool that was used to adjust policy to these new realities. The initiative was used to pursue income, land, and property taxes, to establish maximum weekly working hours and minimum wages, and prohibit child labor, often decades before the federal government enacted such laws. In many cases these initiatives actually failed, but they did popularize policies like the progressive income tax. And in some cases, these policies were successful, as when the initiative was used to limit child labor in Arkansas in 1914, predating similar federal legislation by several years.[3]

Federal inaction was most notable during the early part of the Great Depression, and during this period many states considered ballot initiatives designed to address the problems of modern industrial capitalism put so vividly on display by the Depression. In California, the 1938 "Ham and Eggs" Proposition 25 included the repeal of the sales tax and the creation of gross (progressive) income tax (Allswang 2000). The text of the measure stated that "anyone qualified to vote in California and aged fifty or older without a job would receive $30 of 'warrants' every week. Each $1 warrant would require a two-cent tax paid weekly to keep the note valid until redeemed. The warrants would be legal tender for payment of state taxes." (Ballotpedia 2016). The name "Ham and Eggs" came from the opportunity to trade a breakfast of oatmeal for ham and eggs. Despite the failure of two Ham and Eggs ballot measures, the campaigns publicized the problems of poverty and inequality, and the ideas underlying these policies would later influence the design of federal social security (Mitchell 1992). Others have suggested that failing ballot propositions can shift policy more in line with public preferences within a state (Gerber 1999), but we see here that even failing ballot propositions can spread beyond a single state to other states and even up to the federal government. After both state and federal governments had responded to the new requirements of industrialization with the crafting of a welfare state funded by progressive taxation, the initiative became a rarely used policy tool from the 1940s through the 1960s (Cronin 1999), but we have seen the re-emergence of the initiative in recent decades as the problems of deindustrialization appeared, and as inequality grows dramatically.

Thus, while it is always difficult for the federal government to respond to economic problems, and some states may opt not to, it is usually possible and, from the standpoint of voters or politicians, desirable for at least some states to do so. And, because successful, popular policies are often emulated by other states, and even the federal government, the fact that some states are likely to act creates the possibility for an eventual large scale or system-wide response to economic inequality, even if it begins in somewhat isolated fashion.

Overall then, we expect that in the states, where there is more variation in levels of inequality, the characteristics of state populations, the power of different actors and presence of different institutions, there is likely to be more responsiveness to opinion, and more of an opportunity for opinion to shape government and public policies, in at least some states. Our basic conceptual model can be seen in figure 2.1. Specifically, we expect that objective inequality will shape public perceptions of inequality, but that these perceptions will also be filtered through the characteristics of

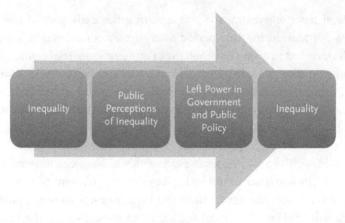

Figure 2.1: Conceptual Model of the New Economic Populism

state populations, in particular mass partisanship. Regardless of its precise cause, a growing public awareness of inequality will push government to the left, since left governments are associated with more egalitarian outcomes, as we explain more in chapter 4. In turn, left government power will push policy in a more egalitarian direction. But even in conservative states where liberal governments have little chance of being elected, public perceptions of inequality may result in some more egalitarian policies being enacted, especially where citizens have the ability to make policy directly via the initiative. Then, these governments and policies will themselves shape inequality, returning to the beginning of the cycle. None of these variables are determinative. For instance, liberal states will not always pursue egalitarian policies with equal fervor, and conservative states will sometimes pursue egalitarian policies. But on average where the population is more aware of growing inequality, where the government is liberal, and so forth, we will see more policies enacted to reduce inequality.

Of course, reality is far messier than this highly abstract conceptual model. It involves struggle between those pursuing egalitarian policies and outcomes and those wishing to preserve the status quo or even pursue policies that would exacerbate inequality. Periods of rapid advance may be followed by stunning defeats and setbacks. Nevertheless, this conceptual model can help us to make sense of a broad array of disparate events and facts, and as we will show in later chapters, it works to describe reality fairly well. Specifically, we demonstrate that in the states a greater public concern about inequality is associated with more left-leaning governments, more support for egalitarian policies at the individual level, and a greater likelihood that egalitarian policies are enacted by state governments.

It may seem strange to argue that federalism allows for egalitarian policy responses to inequality, since this is the exact opposite of how federalism is often viewed, particularly by left-leaning observers and by scholars (Wildavsky 1985). There is no doubt that federalism and the policymaking authority reserved to the states has sometimes permitted egregious inequalities to form and persist, with slavery and Jim Crow in the South being notorious examples (Aldrich 2015; Gonzalez and King 2004; Wildavsky 1985; Key 1949). On the other hand, when the federal government ignores an economic problem, the autonomous policy space created by federalism provides room for the states to use their authority to challenge the status quo, *if their governments or citizens are so motivated and the circumstances permit the formulation of such policies*. For instance, as discussed above, many states outlawed slavery well before the Civil War, and, in another example, several states granted women the right to vote before passage of the 19th Amendment to the US Constitution guaranteed the right to vote for (white) women in all states. Thus, when the federal government is inactive or even hostile to equality, federalism and state policy autonomy are important in reducing inequities, and we think that state policy action is currently important in tackling inequality.

To create more egalitarian outcomes, policies must either reduce the incomes of the wealthy or boost the incomes of the poor and middle class. During the "Great Compression," or the reduction in inequality from the 1930s through the 1960s the federal government used each of these approaches to reduce inequality. The federal government, which was usually controlled by a Democratic Congress and president, used a combination of high taxes on the wealthy and expanding social welfare programs to redistribute income, while policies like the regulation of industry, investment in infrastructure and education, the encouragement of labor unions and collective bargaining, and minimum wages boosted the wages of workers even before redistribution took place (Hacker and Pierson 2010). These policies, which are typically considered liberal or left-leaning, may have unintended negative consequences, but their effect on the income distribution is fairly clear based on both American experience and comparisons among countries (Bartels 2008; Bradley et al. 2003; Kelly 2009). Because of this knowledge from academic studies and historical experience, reducing inequality is, relatively speaking, a conceptually simple task, since we already know which policies reliably reduce economic inequality. For instance, we know with quite a bit of certainty that more progressive taxation and a higher minimum wage will lead to more equal outcomes. In his bestseller, Thomas Piketty (2014) recommended a "wealth tax" as a way to prevent growing inequality.

Such policies are unlikely to be enacted by the federal government at this time. From this standpoint, one important role of the states in combating inequality is demonstrating the strategy and tactics to get policies enacted that have not been tried in decades (like large tax increases on the wealthy), to show that they are politically acceptable or even popular, and to reaffirm that they work. For instance, the states are revealing which arguments in favor of higher taxes on the wealthy and which types of tax increases can gain majority support, what types of minimum wage laws will face the least political resistance from business and have the broadest support, and other similar questions. These state experiments provide valuable data for politicians and policymakers that can be used in future attempts to reduce inequality by other states or by Washington, DC. Of course not every policy that might reduce inequality has been discovered, and the states have a role to play in identifying new policy innovations that might also lead to lower inequality. And some of the policies that we suspect may reduce inequality will fail to do so or have other undesirable consequences, which make them suspect. But state action will provide us with these examples and lessons.

Admittedly, to this point not all states have actively attempted to fight growing inequality. This reflects variation in the institutions, presence, and power of different groups, the strength of the Left in government, and public opinion, as described above. In perhaps the most notable example, led by newly elected Republican governor and former US senator Sam Brownback, the state of Kansas has placed restrictions on aid to the poor and enacted regressive tax cuts that have reduced the tax bills of the wealthy, while drastically reducing the revenue available for government programs, including education. These policies have been an objective disaster for Kansas. Not only have they failed to spur the rapid economic growth proponents envisioned, they have led to unprecedented budget cuts leading to, among other negative consequences, the early closure of schools for lack of money (Jones 2015). While Brownback was elected to a second term in 2014, in 2016 several of his legislative allies were defeated in Republican primaries by more centrist Republicans (Lowery 2016). Such visible failures discourage other politicians from supporting such policies.

Nevertheless, even if a more moderate legislature reverses course, it is unlikely that Kansas will suddenly embrace a highly egalitarian economic agenda. For the citizens of such states, federal action is ultimately necessary to address growing inequality. In addition, the federal government has more power and resources with which to affect inequality, should it attempt to do so. But as long as some states enact successful policies that do address inequality, these efforts will likely diffuse, since states mimic other states' successful innovations (Boehmke and Witmer 2004; Shipan and Volden 2008). This means that there is potential for many states to address economic inequality, even in the absence of federal action. And, as in the past, state attempts to address economic problems are likely to spread to the federal government if they work and prove popular, and in the meantime states are having a real effect on the income distributions within their borders. Thus, the new economic populism emerging in some states is already making a difference there, but holds the promise of transforming politics, policy, and inequality in the coming decades.

Therefore, action in just a handful of states can have important consequences for systematic responses to growing inequality. Human action cannot be easily predicted, of course, but certain conditions make it more likely for states to tackle growing inequality. Some mix of the right economic conditions (increasing inequality), a serious public concern about inequality, reasonably powerful unions, left-leaning governments, and majoritarian policymaking institutions like the initiative will increase the chances that states will seek to slow and reverse growing inequality. There is a lot of variation in these factors across the states, and in the subsequent chapters we explain how the variation in these factors has shaped state responses to growing income inequality thus far.

We examine both market-conditioning policies intended to boost the wages of the poor (the minimum wage) and redistributive policies that affect the incomes of the wealthy (progressive tax increases) and the poor (the earned income tax credit). Before turning to these examinations of specific policies in chapters 5, 6, and 7, however, we begin by taking a broad view of inequality and government responses to inequality in the next two chapters. In chapter 3 we consider how variation in objective inequality contributes to variation in the public awareness of growing inequality in the 50 states. In chapter 4 we examine the relationship between a growing awareness of inequality, how left-leaning the government is, and income inequality in the states.

CHAPTER 3

Growing Inequality and Public Awareness of Inequality in the States

The former president of the United States, Barack Obama, declared that income inequality is "the defining challenge of our time," and in his 2015 State of the Union address asked, "Will we accept an economy where only a few of us do spectacularly well"? Thus, it appears the issue of inequality has gone mainstream. The current prominence of discourse related to income differences emerged in the wake of the recent financial crisis and was propelled by the ensuing protests across the country—related to the Occupy Wall Street movement—that looked to place a spotlight on the perceived unfairness of the US economy. But just how aware of growing inequality are Americans? And how does this vary across the states in response to different levels of inequality and political characteristics of the states?

These questions are important for our understanding of state responses to rising inequality, or what we refer to as the new economic populism. It is possible that the government may respond to growing inequality even if the public is unaware of or unconcerned about it, because policymakers do pursue their autonomous issue preferences at times. Yet in a democracy public concern about an issue is expected to make a government response more likely. If the public responds to objective changes in inequality, and the government responds to these changes in public opinion, then state governments may have something like a thermostatic response to growing inequality. The public's distaste for and concern about inequality, as measured in national polls, has already been discussed, but the federal government has been largely unresponsive to these growing concerns for the reasons we discussed in chapter 2.

In this chapter we begin by examining whether variation in public awareness of inequality is responsive to actual objective changes in inequality, which is the first stage of the conceptual model. Though inequality has increased in virtually all states, an awareness of inequality has not increased in many states. Some of this variation reflects very different trends in inequality in the 50 states. Some states have witnessed a much more rapid growth in inequality, some have seen income differences expand at a more subtle rate, and others have endured inconsistent trends where inequality has grown, leveled out, and even decreased at different points in time. We do find that the public is more aware of growing inequality where the scope of the problem is objectively greater. But, to foreshadow the results of our statistical analysis, not all of the variation in awareness of inequality is explained by different rates of growing inequality. We also find that political factors, in particular, the partisanship of state residents, shapes awareness of inequality. Part of being a Democrat in the modern United States is to have a greater sensitivity to inequality of outcomes, so heavily Democratic states have higher aggregate levels of awareness of inequality. The importance of mass partisanship or ideology to the process of gaining an awareness of inequality can explain why even some state publics with similar levels or patterns of growth in inequality may have different responses to it. Furthermore, the longer-term secular trend toward Republican Party identification in many states can also help explain why growing inequality has not translated into as great a concern about growing inequality as one might expect.

In this chapter we first describe the recent trends in state inequality over the past several decades and show that income inequality has evolved differently across the states. Then we discuss what we know about the public's knowledge of inequality from existing research and explain why we expect to find a connection between rising inequality and public awareness of inequality. Finally, we introduce our unique state-level measure of perceptions of economic inequality, which is used to demonstrate that people are responsive to the unique changes in inequality that occur in the states, but also that perceptions of inequality systematically vary depending on the political and social context.

THE EVOLUTION OF INCOME INEQUALITY IN THE AMERICAN STATES

Since the late 1970s and early 1980s income inequality has increased dramatically in America. Figure 3.1 shows the Gini coefficient (a common way

Figure 3.1: National Household Income Inequality (Gini Coefficient), 1970–2012
Source: Frank (2009).

to measure inequality) of national household income inequality. This figure represents income from a variety of sources, but does not include government cash grants or programs (Temporary Assistance to Needy Families cash payments, food stamps, etc.), and is thus "preredistribution" income inequality. The Gini coefficient provides information about the concentration of income, in this case across households. A perfectly equal income distribution where households all have the same income would have a Gini coefficient of 0, and if all income were concentrated in one household, the Gini coefficient would be 1, so higher values indicate more inequality. Changes in the Gini coefficient over time do not, in themselves, tell us whose income is changing. An increase in the Gini coefficient could mean that the wealthy are earning the same amount while low-income households are earning less. Or it could be the case that most households have growing incomes, but that the wealthy households' incomes are growing more rapidly.

We know from research in the United States that the increasing income inequality is driven by stagnant wages for most earners, along with rapidly growing incomes for the top earners (Piketty, and Saez 2003. These two drivers of inequality are demonstrated in figure 3.2, which plots the share of total income going to the top 1% of earners along with the total share going to the bottom 20%. This figure provides a good indicator of how the overall distribution of income has evolved over time in the United States, with the portion of total national income going to the very wealthy rising at an astonishing pace, while those at the bottom of the income distribution have experienced a steady decline in their share of total income in recent years. It is clear that the growth in top incomes closely resembles the trend of the US Gini coefficient presented in figure 3.1, suggesting that a sizable portion of the overall expansion of inequality is attributable to the substantial rise in top incomes.

We take it for granted at this point that income inequality has increased dramatically in America in the last few decades. And inequality has increased in most states, but there nevertheless remains tremendous variation in levels of, and trends in, inequality across states. Some states have levels of

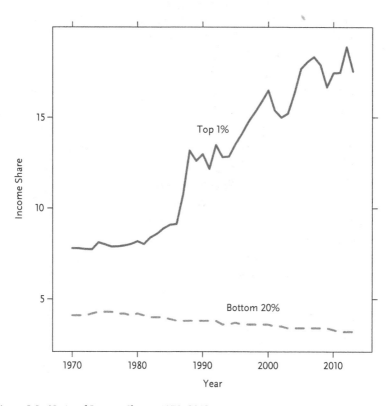

Figure 3.2: National Income Shares, 1970–2012
Source: World Wealth and Income Database (http://www.wid.world) and US Census Bureau.

inequality that are similar to the historically low levels of income inequality that existed nationally in the late 1960s, while other states have levels higher than the current national average, and which are actually similar to developing nations. Similarly, some states have seen large increases in the last few decades, while others have seen essentially flat income inequality.

Figure 3.3 shows 2012 household-level income inequality in the US states. The 0 point on the figure represents the national state average Gini coefficient (.464), and the bars represent deviations from the mean state average. We can see that there is substantial variation in income inequality across the states. Alaska, Hawaii, Maine, Iowa, and West Virginia are the five states with the lowest income inequality. In contrast, Connecticut, Florida, Nevada, New York, and Wyoming are the five states with the highest levels of income inequality according to their Gini coefficients in 2012.

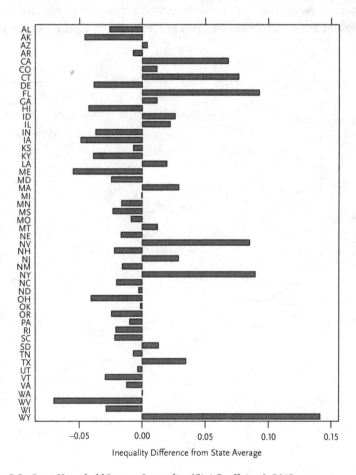

Figure 3.3: State Household Income Inequality (Gini Coefficient), 2012

To put these Gini coefficients in perspective, Alaska and West Virginia have income inequality levels that are about the same as national income inequality in the 1970s. In contrast, New York and Connecticut have income inequality levels similar to Zimbabwe in the mid-2000s, when the last data are available for that country, and just a bit lower than Brazil. The latter country is notorious for its historical income inequality, but is now making a concerted effort to reduce the gap between the rich and poor (Central Intelligence Agency 2012; Solt 2008, 2009; Stepan and Linz 2011).

Not only is there significant variation in current levels of inequality across the states, the states have also experienced very different growth trajectories of inequality. Over the last few decades not a single state has experienced a meaningful decrease in inequality, but a few states have had only modest increases or essentially held steady. In other states, the growth in income inequality has been dramatic. But even among these states with rapidly growing inequality, the exact timing of major increases in income inequality varies considerably. In order to demonstrate the variation in these trends, figure 3.4 shows the Gini coefficient of preredistribution household income inequality in four states that experienced moderate or large increases in inequality from 1970 to 2012.

These four states are not intended to be representative, but were instead chosen to show the extent of variation in the growth of inequality across states (interested readers can find similar plots for all states by geographic region in figures B.1, B.2, B.3, and B.4 in appendix B). Iowa and Nevada, for instance, have similar levels of inequality in the early 1970s, but the growth of the Gini coefficient in each state is quite distinct. The rise of inequality in Iowa is relatively consistent and moderate overall, while Nevada experiences a number of fluctuations throughout the time period, with large jumps in inequality in the 1980s and most recently after the 2008 recession. The expansion of income inequality in New York is also mostly consistent, but, unlike Iowa, the overall extent of growth is substantial. Similar to New York, Texas also experienced a large increase in the Gini coefficient during the first two decades of this time span, but the growth in inequality appears to level off after 1990.

A broader, historical view of trends in state inequality is presented in figure 3.5. The five US maps in this figure represent the state Gini coefficients at the beginning of each decade from 1970 to 2010. Lighter-shaded states are those with lower levels of income inequality, while the darker states indicate higher levels of inequality. Consistent with our discussion of the income gap to this point, we can see that most states had relatively small income differences in 1970 compared to 2010. Even in this era of relative equality, however, variation is still apparent among the states.

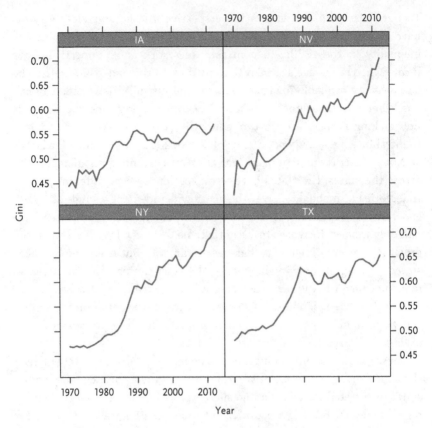

Figure 3.4: Income Inequality Trends across Four States (Gini Coefficient), 1970–2012
Source: Frank (2009).

Interestingly, a number of small Plains states, like Nebraska and North Dakota—states that are more recently characterized as having average or below-average levels of inequality—were some of the most unequal states during this time. As the decades progress, states like California, Wyoming, New York, and Florida begin to stand out as the income gap in these states rapidly increases. Other states have a noticeably consistent color across each map (e.g., Oregon, Ohio, and South Carolina), suggesting the growth of inequality over time has been much more gradual in these states.

Why is there such variation in the level and trajectory of income inequality across states? At first glance, it does not seem that politics could play a major role since the most unequal states in 2010 are both very liberal (New York and Connecticut) and very conservative (Texas and Louisiana). And the same is true of the states with the least inequality in the income distribution. The three states with the lowest inequality have reputations as being politically conservative, while the next two states, which have very

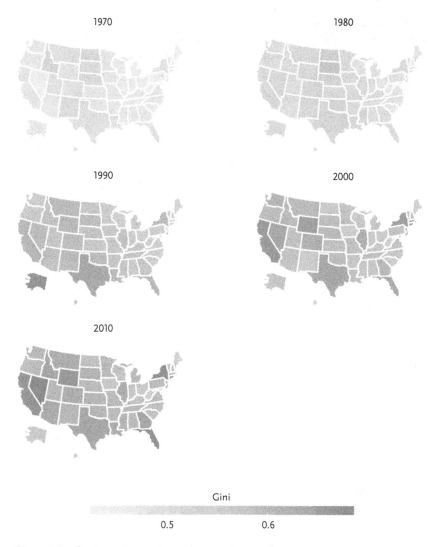

Figure 3.5: Changes in Income Inequality over Time in the 50 States, 1970–2010

similar levels of inequality (Vermont and Hawaii), are among the most liberal. This simply shows that economic and demographic differences across the states, and not politics and public policy alone, are critical to understanding levels of income inequality. For example, states with large numbers of immigrants from Latin America and other developing countries, who tend to be less educated than native-born Americans or immigrants from more developed countries, and therefore have substantially lower incomes, will have greater income disparities (Davies and Wooton 1992; Xu, Garand, and Zhu 2016).

Similarly, economic activity explains some of the variation in inequality across states. States with a greater presence of service sector industries that are reliant on unskilled labor (e.g., tourism industry employees in Florida) or low-skilled industries like agriculture will have higher income inequality. The same is true of states with large concentrations of unusually high-income occupations (e.g., financial industry employees in New York and hedge fund managers in Connecticut). California, which has a high level of inequality, has a large agricultural sector and a lot of higher earners in the entertainment and technology industries.

It is evident that income inequality in the states has developed in distinct ways over time. We will return to the question of why the income gap has followed contrasting trajectories across the states in later chapters, and specifically the role that politics and policy plays in shaping the income distribution. But first we ask whether the state publics are aware of these changes in economic inequality. While the data clearly indicate that income differences have generally expanded over time, it is unclear if the public is cognizant of this growing inequality. In other words, we ask if people in states with rapid income growth are more aware of this growth during times when it is growing rapidly, or have these trends gone largely unnoticed? As suggested above, we believe that the public's understanding of growing inequality has important policy implications, since a citizenry that has little awareness of the changes in economic inequality will be unlikely to demand a policy response to these economic changes.

WHAT WE KNOW ABOUT HOW THE PUBLIC UNDERSTANDS INEQUALITY

Scholars have been interested in public attitudes about inequality for some time. A number of early studies that are relevant to our work here focused on the broad concepts of fairness and equality to make sense of how individuals view unequal social, political, and economic outcomes. This research finds that core values, such as individualism and equal opportunity, play a large role in shaping beliefs about why inequality exists and whether unequal outcomes should be tolerated (Feldman 1988; Kluegel and Smith 1986; McClosky and Zaller 1984). The combination of the findings from this foundational work and the increased prevalence of opinion polling has led to several important studies assessing the public's understanding of income inequality more specifically, and whether these attitudes affect policy preferences that are related to the distribution of income (Bartels 2005; 2008; Hayes

2013; Lupia et al. 2007; McCall 2013; McCall and Kenworthy 2009; Page and Jacobs 2009).

One general conclusion resulting from these studies is that many Americans believe a combination of equal opportunity and hard work is the best path to financial success. For instance, more than three-fourths of the public agrees that it is possible for someone who is poor to become rich through hard work (Page and Jacobs 2009). In other words, at least in the abstract, many people still have faith in the American dream. However, somewhat contradictory to the notion that one's economic status is the result of a fair and meritocratic system, a large portion of the public also appears to be concerned about growing inequality (McCall and Kenworthy 2009; Page and Jacobs 2009). If hard work solely determined one's position, then any inequalities are justified. Despite this, in recent years a strong majority of the public consistently agrees that "differences in income in America are too large" (McCall and Kenworthy 2009). This suggests that people not only consider equality of opportunity when thinking about inequality, but also care about unequal outcome.

With evidence supporting the claim that the public is aware of, and does care about, growing economic inequality in hand, scholars have asked whether this concern shapes policy attitudes. Unlike the literature discussed above that explores the relationship between the income distribution and levels of government redistribution, this work focuses on how individuals view inequality and if their beliefs about economic disparities influence opinions on public policy. In general, these studies suggest that those who are more concerned about income differences, and place more emphasis on egalitarian principles, are also more likely to support egalitarian policies like taxing the rich and providing assistance to the poor (Bartels 2008; Franko, Tolbert, and Witko 2013; Hayes 2013; McCall 2013; McCall and Kenworthy 2009).

Less agreement exists, however, on the causal nature of this inequality-policy relationship and the degree to which concern about inequality factors into policy decisions in practice. For instance, although the public exhibits a growing disapproval of inequality, a majority of Americans supported the 2001 Bush tax cuts, which were anything but egalitarian. These tax cuts heavily favored the wealthy, and it is likely that this policy has contributed to the continued expansion of income inequality (Bartels 2005; 2008). Further casting doubt on the idea that views of inequality affect the public's policy preferences is the finding that support for redistributive policies has changed very little over the past two-plus decades, which is surprising since income inequality and public concern about inequality have grown considerably (McCall 2013; McCall and Kenworthy

2009). If individuals link their concern for inequality to preferences on specific policies, a public aware of and concerned about economic inequality would be expected to increase its support for redistribution, but we have not seen this.

The uncertainty surrounding the connection between inequality and preferences for egalitarian policy brings us back to the basic question of how aware the public is of income inequality in the first place. The above discussion suggests most Americans have at least a basic understanding of economic inequality. Though people tend to underestimate the extent of wage disparities, the average person knows that the CEO of a large corporation makes much more money than an unskilled factory worker (McCall 2013; Page and Jacobs 2009). And when asking if the income difference between the rich and the poor has increased, decreased, or stayed the same in recent years, three-fourths of the public correctly says it has increased (Bartels 2008).

When more closely evaluating the public's response to questions about the growth of inequality over time, however, the results are less encouraging. Referring to the survey question inquiring about income differences over the last 20 years, Bartels suggests that even though most people say these differences have grown, this appears "to reflect cynical folk wisdom more than close attention to actual economic trends" (2008, 129). Similarly, when examining aggregate responses to a Harris Poll question asking individuals whether it is true that "the rich get richer and the poor get poorer," a question consistently asked since the 1960s, the public's perceptions of economic inequality are seemingly unresponsive to the remarkable expansion of inequality beginning in the 1980s (Bartels 2008).

These findings cast doubt on how much the public really knows about, and responds to, income inequality. Evidence of whether a connection exists between growing inequality and citizen perceptions of inequality is mixed and far from conclusive. As discussed above, making sense of how citizens perceive inequality is essential since it has implications for the extent of the public's concern about inequality, and ultimately how inequality is addressed through public policy—if the issue is addressed at all. Some of the uncertainty surrounding the nature of the relationship between economic outcomes and citizen perceptions may be resolved by taking a different approach to how we examine the public's understanding of economic inequality. National-level surveys do not account for the tremendous variation in trajectories of inequality across the states, or for the ways that varying political conditions may filter economic information.

In our assessment of how the public views income inequality we focus on two factors related to opinion formation that have largely been overlooked by existing research. The first, which is consistent with the central argument of the book, is that we consider the economic and political aspects of state environments that might influence how people understand income differences. As we have discussed in detail above, inequality has developed in distinct ways across the states, and it is likely that these contextual differences shape the public's attitudes about the distribution of income. Second, if we want to know whether the public is aware of recent *changes* in the income gap—that is, if we want to learn about reactions to growing economic inequality—we need to examine changes in perceptions of inequality over time. Very few studies have assessed whether local economic context is related to evaluations of inequality[1] or if views on inequality follow trends in actual changes in income differences,[2] and no research to our knowledge has studied the public's awareness of inequality when taking into account both state context and trends in economic inequality across the states over time, as we do here. Below we introduce a new measure of the public's aggregate awareness of income differences for every state, which allows us to examine whether this collective opinion is shaped by objective trends in state economic inequality.

Two important questions related to the effect of state changes in inequality on attitudes about income differences are whether it is reasonable to expect individuals (1) to be knowledgeable enough to understand and develop opinions about income inequality and (2) to be aware of and responsive to their local economic environment. Although the prospect of uncovering an informed public that understands and cares about economic inequality seems unlikely in the context of evidence suggesting that most Americans are not very knowledgeable about income disparities (e.g., Bartels 2005), a number of notable studies argue that public opinion is quite stable and meaningful when observed in the aggregate (Erikson, Mackuen, and Stimson 2002; Page and Shapiro 1992). This research suggests that even if many individuals do respond to questions about political and economic conditions in ways that are not consistent with objective reality and even illogical, many people also have rational responses to changing political or economic circumstances. When taken collectively, we can make sense of public opinion because those who act randomly will essentially cancel out. For most issues, this leads to a public opinion that is stable over time, with changes generally occurring slowly in response to actual changes in the political or economic environment. This implies that those who systematically change their attitudes in response to actual information will be the main cause of shifts in aggregate public opinion. Since aggregation is the key to understanding public opinion from the macro perspective, emphasis is typically placed on viewing the structured movements of opinion over time.

It is particularly relevant for the study of income inequality that objective economic conditions appear related to political and policy positions, at least some of the time. Perhaps the most prevalent line of research linking economic conditions to political behavior is the economic voting literature (Kinder and Kiewiet 1981; Lewis-Beck 1988; Lewis-Beck and Stegmaier 2007). The basic premise of economic voting is that voters expect government officials to be competent managers of the economy. When economic conditions are promising, the public rewards the governing party by keeping it in office, and when the economy is poor, voters punish the current office-holders by electing the opposing party. Not only does an abundance of evidence support the economic voting thesis, but election forecasters regularly produce accurate predictions of election outcomes using economic growth as the fundamental factor in their models (Abramowitz 1988; Bartels and Zaller 2001; Gelman and King 1993; Lewis-Beck and Rice 1992). This means that, in some ways, the public is using economic information in its voting decisions. In addition to elections, the economy also affects other aspects of political behavior, for example, presidential approval and partisanship, and aggregate perceptions of economic conditions tend to reflect objective measures of economic growth (De Boef and Kellstedt 2004; Erikson, Mackuen, and Stimson 2002; Hopkins 2012).

So even though most Americans are not experts on the economy, collective opinion seemingly follows general economic trends. Most people do not actively seek out detailed information about the economy, but they are regularly exposed to signals related to current economic conditions. Media coverage of topics like unemployment, inflation, and the stock market filters down to the public directly when individuals follow the news and indirectly through people's everyday interactions with others, who may be unemployed or are able to retire early because of a good stock market (Erikson, Mackuen, and Stimson 2002).

Similarly, exposure to certain types of economic information can also serve as signals of inequality. Although the media does not tend to explicitly cover the issue of income differences very much, it does cover inequality in other ways by emphasizing comparisons among groups or by focusing on inequality-related themes (McCall 2013). For instance, newspaper articles on the topics of social class and job insecurity tend to use phrases related to executive salaries, the rich, and job prospects or incomes of the poor

(McCall 2013). In addition, people's own experiences—seeing their own or a family member's wages stagnate, while seeing more high-end cars in the parking lot at the mall—may clue them in to growing inequality. This suggests the possibility that the public might use information about various aspects of economic outcomes when thinking about income inequality, even if people are unfamiliar with specific inequality statistics per se, which most Americans surely are. Some individuals will place more importance on some aspects of the economy than others, and not everyone will have the same factors in mind when developing perceptions of inequality. Some may focus more on media reports about CEO pay or the fabulous incomes of hedge fund managers, while others are more concerned about unemployment and poverty at the bottom end of the income scale. Overall, though, aggregate perceptions of inequality will reflect an assessment of different aspects of salient economic outcomes for different people, and some people will misperceive reality, but on average opinion should be responsive to growing economic inequality.

Furthermore, a long line of literature suggests that citizens are well aware of their state environments. Differences in the political, economic, and social contexts of the American states have substantial consequences for political outcomes (Erikson, Wright, and McIver 1993), which have important implications for state economies. And many people appear to be aware of these state differences. Evidence suggests state-level economic factors influence voting behavior (Books and Prysby 1999; Ebeid and Rodden 2006; Reeves and Gimpel 2012) and that opinion is generally responsive to local economic conditions (Newman et al. 2013). These distinctions in state context may have a significant influence on public beliefs about inequality, yet most research of this kind has focused on national opinion.

There are some impediments for the public when responding to economic inequality, however. One impediment to public awareness of inequality is that unlike other economic outcomes, such as economic growth, unemployment, or the health of the stock market, there are no widely agreed-upon and well-known indicators used to report inequality. The Gini coefficient, which we discussed at the beginning of this chapter, is a relatively obscure and complex statistic. Income percentage shares are more intuitive, but have not been widely reported in the media until fairly recently. Thus, there may not be as tight a link between inequality and perception of inequality as we would find with unemployment, for example. But overall public awareness of inequality should grow when inequality expands.

Another reason that awareness of inequality may not be strongly linked with objective inequality is that awareness of inequality is not a purely economic phenomenon. Instead, some individuals are predisposed to be more sensitive to inequality of outcomes than others. A particularly interesting finding from Bartels's (2008) work is that party identification can be an important intervening influence between the public's views on inequality and other attitudes related to policy and redistribution. This is largely because partisanship reflects core ideological beliefs that are closely related to ideas like egalitarianism and individualism. While all Americans value equality, the type of equality valued differs. Because of their ideology and underlying values, Democrats are likely to be more sensitive to inequality of outcomes than Republicans, who tend to focus more on legal impediments to equality of opportunity (Verba 1987). Whether partisanship causally makes people more or less sensitive to inequality of outcome, or people self-select into parties that fit their preexisting views, is unimportant for our purposes. Either way, in states with more individuals that identify as Democrats there should be a greater awareness of inequality.

GROWING INCOME DIFFERENCES AND PUBLIC AWARENESS OF INEQUALITY

To gain insight into the public's understanding of economic inequality, a measure of inequality awareness over time for each state is needed. To obtain such a measure we first need a survey question that is asked regularly over time, and that captures the extent to which individuals comprehend growing economic inequality. Second, the question used should be included in a survey designed in such a way that it allows for estimates of opinion at the state level. Although few surveys have consistently asked questions about income inequality over the years, one question in particular has been asked by several polling organizations dating back to the 1980s. The relatively straightforward question (briefly mentioned above) asks if people believe "the rich are getting richer and the poor are getting poorer." Not only has the question been asked regularly over time, but it also uses a simple comparison—between those who are rich and those who are poor—to tap into perceptions of income differences. Altogether, the question was asked on 34 national surveys during the 1987–2012 period, with an average of more than 1,500 respondents per survey and a combined total of over 53,000 individuals polled.

While it is important that we have a regularly asked survey question spanning over 25 years that taps into the public's perceptions of inequality, it is equally important to have measures at the state level. One hurdle that we face with the survey questions we have identified is that all of the polls were designed to collect national samples of the US adult population, which is common for most surveys addressing issues related to American politics. This is problematic when attempting to make inferences about state residents, however, since most national polls do not have enough geographic coverage to reliably estimate opinion by simply averaging responses from each state. We avoid this issue by using a recently developed opinion estimation technique—referred to as multilevel regression and poststratification, or MRP—that allows researchers to accurately measure public attitudes at the state level using typical national samples. We detail the specifics of this strategy in the appendix (also see Franko 2017), but to summarize, perceptions of inequality are first modeled for all respondents in each survey using a few important demographic characteristics, and including estimates of differences in opinions by state. We then combine these individual estimates with actual state demographics from the US census to adjust the estimates for any differences between the individuals surveyed in each state, and the true state population.

A first look at the public's awareness of economic inequality is presented in figure 3.6, which shows over-time trends in awareness across the states. What is initially striking is that while inequality has grown in most states, awareness of inequality has often not. In most states it ends up about where it began. It is true that most states demonstrate large spikes in increasing awareness in the early part of the series, when inequality was objectively growing very rapidly (in figures 3.2 and 3.3 we can see that the most rapid growth in income inequality occurred in the late 1980s), but we see declines in the awareness of inequality in many states in the later part of the series, when inequality was still growing, albeit typically less rapidly. Nevertheless, there are differences in the timing of growing and decreasing awareness across the states. The sharp downward trend in perceptions exhibited by Georgia and Texas are certainly different from the less pronounced trends seen in Maryland, Michigan, and Rhode Island. Even in states with a general decrease in awareness of inequality, we see some periods of rapid growth in awareness of inequality. Are these shifting levels of awareness in inequality associated with the actual annual variation in the growth of inequality in the states?

To determine whether the public responds to growing inequality with an increasing awareness of inequality, it is important to examine how *changes* in awareness of inequality correspond to *changes* in the growth of inequality, since slow increases in inequality would not be expected to produce growing awareness as much as large increases. Figure 3.7 demonstrates annual changes in perceived inequality along with annual changes in the top 10% share of total income, one way to measure income inequality, for

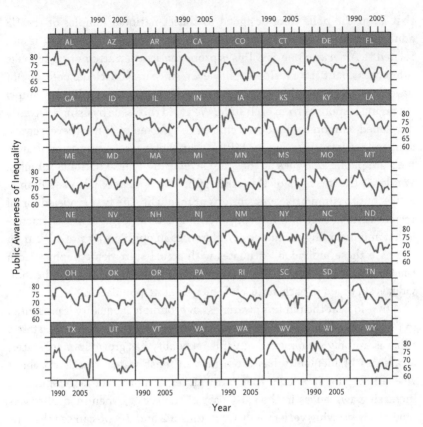

Figure 3.6: Trends in Public Awareness of Economic Inequality, 1987–2012

several states. The plot illustrates an association between changes in state top incomes and perceived inequality. The frequent shifts in public awareness of inequality that could easily be dismissed as arbitrary opinion change appear to be, to a certain extent, a result of similar changes in the share of top incomes. Thus, what we find when examining how objective measures of inequality affect the public's collective awareness of inequality is a classic time-series example of a relationship that exists between two variables that is masked by variable trending. When differencing both measures, we are able to observe how each variable deviates from those trends, allowing us to get a better sense of how they are related to one another.[3]

In any case, it should be noted that the correlation between the top 10% income share and awareness of inequality across all states is relatively modest, at .21. This suggests that while objective changes in inequality may inform changes in the awareness of inequality, it is far from a one-to-one relationship, and that other factors aside from objective economic conditions affect the perception of inequality. That is, different publics react

The New Economic Populism

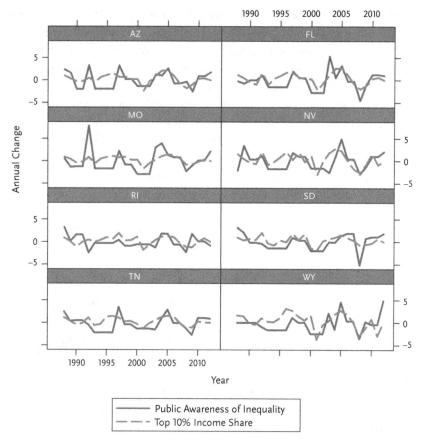

Figure 3.7: Changes in Awareness of Economic Inequality and Top 10% Income Share in Eight States, 1987–2012

differently to growing economic inequality owing to either their own characteristics or the characteristics of their states.

Thus, here we consider whether, once we account for other factors that are likely to shape awareness of inequality, there is a significant relationship between objective inequality and awareness of inequality. In addition to examining the relationship between the top 10% income share measure introduced in figure 3.7 and awareness of inequality, we also investigate the top 1% income share measure and the Gini coefficient.[4] A full list of the variables and data sources used in the analysis can be found in appendix table A.2.

As noted, inequality can be difficult to directly observe, so we begin by considering how other more easily observable economic outcomes related to, but distinct from, economic inequality may shape perceptions of inequality. It may be that rather than being concerned about inequality per se, the public associates inequality with poor conditions for lower-income earners or becomes more aware of inequality as poverty grows. And while inequality is hard to observe, high levels of poverty are relatively easy to observe since poverty is easily understood, routinely reported in the media, and experienced on a personal level (unlike inequality, which is only an aggregate social phenomenon and is not directly felt by any one person). Therefore, the poverty rate is used as an indicator of how well lower-income groups are faring economically. Similar to the way individuals might perceive a connection between top incomes and economic inequality, information related to poverty may also provide signals about income differences.[5] Per capita income (in thousands of dollars) is included as a way to account for the general economic health of a state from the perspective of typical wage earners. When the state as a whole is doing well financially, people may view this as a sign that everyone is prospering and that inequality is not growing or is even in decline. As noted, partisanship probably shapes people's sensitivity to inequality, and thus the difference between the percentage of each state's Democratic and Republican identifiers is also considered to examine whether partisanship plays a role in perceptions of inequality. Finally, we control for union density (the percentage of non-agricultural workers belonging to unions) since belonging to a union is likely to lead to the greater exposure to information related to the growth of inequality, since labor unions and organizations are essentially the only organizations to consistently highlight the inequality-producing aspects of policies that have been pursued over the last few decades.[6]

We present the central findings from our analysis in figure 3.8.[7] The top panel of the plot shows the effects of top 10% income share, the poverty rate, and partisanship on changes in aggregate public awareness of inequality. The bottom panel is nearly identical, with the only difference being that the top 10% income share measure is replaced with the top 1% income share. All of the estimated effects presented for both models in figure 3.8 are statistically different from zero. Discussed in more detail below, the effects for the model using the Gini coefficient are not included in the plot since the estimates suggest the effect of this particular measure of inequality does not have a statistically significant influence on awareness of inequality. To allow us to make reasonable comparisons across the three variables, each bar demonstrates the total effect of each state factor (i.e., top income share, poverty, and partisanship) on inequality awareness when increasing each variable by one standard deviation.[8]

Our results suggest, first, that the public is aware of changes in state income inequality. Specifically, yearly increases in both the top 10% and 1% state income shares lead to statistically significant increases in perceived

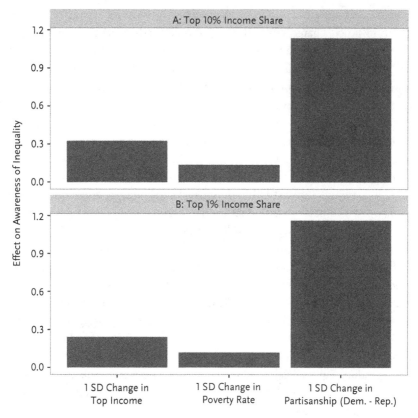

Figure 3.8: The Effects of State Income Inequality, Poverty, and Partisanship on Public Awareness of Inequality, 1987–2012
Note: Estimates are based on the model results presented in appendix table B.1.

inequality among state residents. We do not find a similar relationship between the state perceptions of inequality and changes in the Gini coefficient, however, which is why we only present the effects for the top income share measures. In some ways, this is not surprising. As discussed above, the public's ability to follow trends in economic inequality is dependent on the availability of information that might provide signals related to differences in income for various groups in society. The Gini coefficient is a fairly complex indicator of inequality, as it uses information about the income of each percentile. If the public sees the Gini coefficient reported in the news media, it is unlikely to understand what it is, and it is also not something that is in any sense directly observable. In contrast, stories about the growing incomes of high earners, from athletes to CEOs, are a staple of news media coverage of the economy and are relatively easy to understand. In addition, the growing incomes of the wealthy are in some ways observable even by the poor and middle class if they see the wealthy driving nicer cars, living in fancier gated communities, and so forth. When average people compare the incomes and lifestyles of the very wealthy to their own, it is easy to see that inequality is growing, even if the average person lacks statistical information. And the top income share measures are probably also more intuitive for the typical American.

But, of course, as we could guess based on the bivariate correlation, objective inequality is not the only thing that shapes awareness of inequality. In addition to top incomes, increases in the state poverty rate lead to a larger percentage of the public agreeing that the gap between rich and poor is growing. The status of the most disadvantaged groups in a state also appears to have an influence on how the public understands inequality, suggesting that people are at least indirectly attuned to the least well-off in their state when thinking about growing income differences.

Finally, the political makeup of a state also affects how the public views inequality. Indeed, this variable actually has the largest effect on the awareness of inequality. As previous research has found, partisanship can have an important influence on attitudes about economic inequality (Bartels 2008; Franko, Tolbert, and Witko 2013). The results are clear and as expected: increases in Democratic identifiers (relative to Republicans) in a state produce a greater perception of growing inequality, while the opposite effect exists when Republican identification increases. If we substitute variables measuring the percentage of the public that identifies as liberal and conservative, we find similar results. This finding suggests that one major reason we have seen relatively constant awareness of inequality in many states even while objective inequality is increasing, is that since the mid-1980s a number of states have shifted from a large number of Democratic Party identifiers and liberals to a large number of Republican identifiers and conservatives. The percentage of Democratic identifiers dropped by nearly seven points on average across the states between 1987 and 2010.[9] Republicans and conservatives are simply less likely to acknowledge that the rich are getting richer and the poor are getting poorer, so the large, secular shift away from the Democratic Party (driven by many long-term factors like the shift of the South toward the Republican Party) in some ways masks a growing public awareness of inequality over time.

CONCLUSION

The recent expansion of economic inequality in the United States has not only raised moral concerns about fairness but has also been linked to a number of tangible societal consequences. Income inequality may lead to decreases in economic productivity, stability, and growth (Stiglitz 2012), more political power for the wealthy (Solt 2011; Solt, Habel, and Grant 2011), increases in party polarization (McCarty, Poole, and Rosenthal 2006), less political participation (Solt 2008), and deficient health outcomes (Wilkinson and Pickett 2011). The public is likely to play a role, perhaps even a significant one, in how income disparities and the problems resulting from them are addressed. A public that is unaware of or ambivalent about the state of American inequality, however, is unlikely to emphasize income differences as an important political issue and insist on solutions that are intended to alleviate inequality.

This suggests that understanding how the public perceives inequality is an important first step in determining how the issue is addressed in the future. While most research has studied views of inequality from a national perspective, we also know that state context can shape economic and political attitudes. This study takes advantage of the differences in inequality growth in the states to examine whether the public is aware of changing income differences. Using a unique measure of state-level awareness of inequality, the results presented here show that the public is cognizant of changes in economic inequality. Over-time changes in state top income shares and state poverty rates are two key economic indicators that significantly shape perceived inequality. However, there is not a simple one-to-one relationship between changes in inequality and perceived inequality, since other factors shape perceptions of inequality. In particular, the state political context also appears to influence how the public views inequality, with states with more Democratic identifiers perceiving more inequality, and the opposite being the case for states with more Republican identifiers.

Providing evidence of an American public that is aware of changing economic inequality is essential for the general study of attitudes about income differences. While awareness of inequality certainly does not equate to concern for inequality, a public that is responsive to wealth disparities has a greater potential to be involved in political discussions about inequality than a public that is unaware of these economic changes. We find that, indeed, growing inequality is associated with awareness of inequality, but there is also a large element of the awareness of inequality that is determined by individuals' partisanship/party membership and ideological leanings. The long-term shift away from Democratic identification in the states has reduced awareness of inequality, somewhat offsetting the effect of growing levels of inequality.

We also see annual variation that is not explained by long-term trends. Some of this is simply statistical noise, and some of this short-term variation reflects short-term variation in inequality. Yet some of it also reflects that the salience of economic factors in general, and inequality specifically, varies over time. Thus, while objective inequality is significantly associated with awareness of inequality, we do not see a monotonically growing concern about inequality to accompany the monotonically growing inequality in many states. This has important implications for policy, since if awareness of inequality influences policy, then it is not necessarily the case that state policy would monotonically become more liberal over time in response to high inequality.

If it is awareness of inequality, rather than simply objective levels of income inequality, that makes egalitarian policy more likely, this can help to explain why research often fails to find a simple relationship between increasing inequality and more redistribution by the government (Meltzer and Richard 1981; Moene and Wallerstein 2001). In the following chapters, therefore, we investigate the relationship between an awareness of inequality and egalitarian policies. In the next chapter we consider how this awareness of inequality may be translated into differences in the ideological composition of government, and ultimately differences in the income distribution.

CHAPTER 4

Awareness of Inequality and Government Liberalism

What are the implications of growing public awareness of inequality for politics and policy in the US states? Does a growing public awareness of inequality translate into action that reduces inequality? In chapter 3 we showed that inequality has grown considerably in most states, yet there is substantial variation in the trajectory of growing inequality and in the overall level of inequality in recent years. We also demonstrated in chapter 3 that where inequality has grown more rapidly, the public perceives a growing income gap between rich and poor. That is, when inequality is growing rapidly, the public recognizes this trend. Yet other aspects of a state's political and economic context also shape awareness of inequality. The remainder of the book is devoted to understanding how a growing public awareness of inequality translates into policies that have the potential to slow the growth of, and perhaps even reduce, inequality, and how the presence of other political and institutional factors may lead to policies likely to reduce inequality.

The question of whether a growing public awareness of inequality can translate into actions that slow the growth of inequality or reduce it altogether is critically important. Textbook theories of democracy would lead us to believe that when the voting public is concerned about a problem, it is more likely that the government will address the problem. If this is the case, and a growing awareness of inequality leads to policies that reduce inequality, then because public awareness of inequality does respond to actual levels of inequality to some degree, democracy provides a "thermostatic" means of limiting the growth of inequality along the lines envisioned by Meltzer and Richard (1981). If, by contrast, awareness of inequality does not lead to corrective action, then democracy is unable to prevent high levels of inequality from persisting. Note that even within this framework, if the public does not care about inequality even if it is very high, it is less likely that democratic governments will address it. Of course, governments sometimes address problems that the public is not concerned very much about, and this may sometimes be the case with inequality. But most theories of democracy and the public policy process expect that the likelihood of government action to address a problem will increase if the public is concerned about that problem.

There are a number of policies that a growing concern about inequality might influence in the states, and we explore several of these policy mechanisms in the remaining chapters. The particular political and policy response to inequality will vary depending on the structure of policymaking institutions, more general public policy attitudes, and the power of different actors in the state government. In this chapter, we consider whether a growing concern about inequality is associated with governments that are more likely to reduce inequality. These governments, based on the comparative and American politics literatures, are those that are more left wing or liberal (in the American sense). Because scholars of comparative and American politics argue that left-leaning governments produce a more equal income distribution, it would make sense that citizens concerned about growing inequality would actively choose such governments and try to shift the preferences of office holders in a more liberal direction once they are elected. Furthermore, even if the electorate is completely passive, in the presence of a growing concern about inequality, entrepreneurial politicians can be expected to shift to the left to avoid serious electoral challenges, gain re-election, or build public support for a run for higher office.

In the data analysis section of this chapter we show that, since the mid-1980s, when and where the public is more aware of growing inequality, the government in the state is more liberal, even after we control for historical government liberalism and the more general liberalism of public opinion in a state. In turn, we show that more liberal state governments are also associated with lower levels of inequality during the period 1987–2010. State government liberalism appears to have little relationship with the share of income going to very top wage earners, but when we examine a broader range of higher earners and the state Gini coefficient of income, we see that government liberalism is associated with a more equal income distribution during the period that we examine.

PUBLIC OPINION TOWARD INEQUALITY AND
GOVERNMENT RESPONSES

As already noted in chapter 2, if we focus only on Washington, DC, we should doubt that growing inequality and a growing awareness of inequality will lead to changes in government and public policy that are likely to slow or reverse these trends. Bonica et al. (2013) present a number of reasons why, looking at the national government, democracy has not "cured" growing income inequality. One reason may be that, though the national public does seem more aware of growing inequality over time (Kelly and Enns 2010), the public has not consistently demanded governments or policies that would be likely to reduce inequality. Indeed, the public has sometimes embraced national-level policies that are likely to make inequality considerably worse (Bartels 2005). On the other hand, the public also demonstrates high levels of support for policies that would probably reduce inequality, such as tax increases on the very wealthy and increases in the minimum wage (Page, Bartels, and Seawright 2013), which have not been enacted frequently by the Congress.

Why have such popular proposals not been advanced by the federal government? One possible answer is that there is a growing upper-class bias in the interest group system (Hacker and Pierson 2010), and business interests and the very wealthy often oppose policies that would reduce inequality. And, as unions have declined, members of both parties have become more reliant on the resources of the upper classes to be elected to office and pursue policy changes (Hacker and Pierson 2010; Witko 2013). For instance, it was Bill Clinton's administration that in many respects completed Reagan's deregulatory agenda in the financial sector. Given the upper-class bias in the interest system, it can hardly be surprising that research shows a general lack of responsiveness to the preferences of the mass public alongside heightened responsiveness to the preferences of the wealthy at the constituency level (Bartels 2008; Gilens 2012).

In addition, the gridlock in national policymaking institutions, especially the US Senate, prevents any change to the policy status quo (Enns et al. 2014). As policies that reduce taxes on the wealthy, weaken unions, and otherwise exacerbate inequality now represent the status quo, this policy gridlock reinforces growing income inequality. This means that even when the public chooses to elect seemingly liberal politicians to office in Washington, DC, these individuals are often incapable of enacting new policies that benefit the lower and middle classes and reduce income inequality. Even President Obama's prized Affordable Care Act, which undoubtedly benefits many lower- and middle-income Americans, could only be enacted after making concessions to business that will cost taxpayers hundreds of billions of dollars in the coming decades. In Washington, politics and policy are not fixing inequality.

A key argument in this book, however, is that variation in the states allows a greater possibility for political and policy responses to growing economic inequality in some states. First, the dysfunction and gridlock that characterize Washington, DC, are not present in most states because they have laws or constitutional requirements mandating the passage of essential legislation like budgets. In addition, the states often lack a number of the gridlock-inducing institutions found in Washington, DC. The US Senate is probably the lead institution for promoting gridlock (Enns et al. 2014) because of the filibuster and other practices. Many states do not have the minoritarian institutions of filibusters and holds, which allow a single member of the Senate to prevent legislative action, and in only a few states are filibusters or the threat of filibusters routinely used to prevent legislative action (Grossman 2015).

In addition to these institutional differences in the states, there is substantial variation in the extent to which state interest group systems are dominated by business and the wealthy, versus systems open to a larger number and kind of organized interests that represent lower- and middle-income voters and interests. Whereas unions are quite weak in national government because of low overall union density in the United States (only about 10% of private sectors workers are in unions), in some states more than 20% of the workforce is represented in collective bargaining by unions, and unions remain powerful in politics in those states.

In addition, while the national electorate has grown more conservative and Republican over the last few decades (Kelly and Enns 2010), there is substantial variation in state public opinion liberalism. Opinion in most states has become more conservative, but it should be obvious to even casual observers that the public in states like New York and Vermont is more liberal than in states like Alabama or Utah, and this variation in borne out in studies of state public opinion (Enns and Koch 2013). Even if they become aware of growing inequality, we showed in the last chapter that citizens in very conservative states are unlikely to embrace liberal government—though even in conservative states there is widespread support for some liberal policies, such as the minimum wage, which we examine in chapter 6. In other states, however, a more moderate or even liberal tradition allows for the state governments to become more left-leaning. Furthermore, politicians acting strategically to win future elections or election to higher office one day may find it in their interest to move to the left to address growing inequality in liberal states. State governments have a number of policy tools that they may use to shape the income distribution, and it is left-leaning governments that are most likely to use these tools. Thus, as inequality grows and the public awareness of it follows, one possible consequence is growing government liberalism.

STATE GOVERNMENT POLICY TOOLS TO INFLUENCE
THE INCOME DISTRIBUTION

It is natural to think of the federal government when we think of public efforts to reduce inequality since it has typically played this role over the last several decades. Furthermore, discussions of government reductions in inequality often revolve around explicit redistribution of income via taxation and transfers, and the federal government takes the lead here (Peterson 1995). In addition, the federal government has more resources and policymaking authority with which to influence the income distribution than state governments have. The most recent financial crisis that began in 2008 showed the benefits of an active federal government and the constraints faced by the states. While the states were forced to slash spending on a variety of programs, resulting in contractionary fiscal policy, the federal government was able to engage in at least some deficit spending and stimulate economic growth and job creation. Even so, many critics of the federal government argued that it was not doing enough. And what if the federal government fails to address a problem altogether or makes it worse, as with inequality? A key argument in this book is that state governments have substantial resources and policy authority to create more equitable economic outcomes should they choose to do so.

Existing research shows that states policies influence such economic outcomes as economic growth, employment, and inequality (Kelly and Witko 2012; 2014; Jones 1990; Prillaman and Meier 2014). One reason that people tend to underestimate the possibility that the states can influence income inequality is that they focus on redistribution. And, as noted, the federal government has taken the lead in income redistribution since the New Deal era (Peterson 1995). Though many states had some modest redistributive programs prior to the 1930s, as we have discussed, it is New Deal programs like Social Security and Aid to Families with Dependent Children (now Temporary Assistance to Needy Families, or TANF) and Great Society programs like Medicare and Medicaid (along with other smaller programs like Women, Infants, and Children, or WIC) that "do" most of the redistribution in America. What is usually referred to as "welfare", that is, cash payments to the poorest people in America, is the federally designed

Temporary Assistance to Needy Families (TANF), the successor to Aid to Families with Dependent Children (AFDC), which was created as part of the New Deal. The federal government also has a host of smaller programs that provide in-kind benefits to the poor in the areas of food and nutrition (Supplemental Nutrition Assistance Program, or SNAP, and WIC), rent and energy subsidies, and so forth. And Medicaid is a large and increasingly costly program that provides health insurance for the very poor, which is an important cash-like benefit given the ever-growing cost of health insurance. These programs are redistributive in that they are funded by general tax revenue from a progressive federal tax structure (albeit one that has become less progressive in recent decades).

Furthermore, it is often argued that there are strong incentives for states to *allow* the federal government to take the lead in income redistribution (Peterson 1995). This reflects that states must compete for wealthy residents and business investment, and high taxes to fund generous welfare programs are generally thought to repel these entities but attract poor people, creating a further burden on state taxpayers. It is believed that because states want to avoid becoming a "welfare magnet" (Bailey and Rom 2004; Fellowes and Rowe 2004), they will be unlikely to engage in very much explicit income redistribution via progressive taxation and transfers beyond what the federal government requires. State tax systems are relatively flat, and independent state "welfare" programs are relatively modest.

Yet it would be wrong to say that the states do nothing in terms of income redistribution via transfers or progressive social insurance programs. Though all state income tax systems are relatively "flat" compared to the federal government income tax system, some states have more progressive tax structures than others (Prillaman and Meier 2014). For instance, California, which probably has the most progressive income tax systems of any state, has brackets ranging from 1% on income under around $8,000 to 13.3% on income above $1,000,000. Other states like New York, New Jersey, and Oregon also have fairly progressive income tax systems with top rates of around 9%. In contrast, some states lack an income tax altogether and fund much of government operations with the sales tax, which is a highly regressive approach. Thus, while state tax systems are much flatter than the federal system, there is quite a bit of variation, and some states do take more from wealthier taxpayers to fund government operations.

In addition, though states have few large, independent welfare programs, many American welfare state programs are "federalized," meaning that the state governments play an explicit role in funding the programs and determining eligibility and benefit levels. Indeed, this state policy authority over welfare programs was expanded when AFDC was replaced with TANF in 1995 (Bailey and Rom 2004; Plotnick and Winters 1985; Soss et al. 2001). For instance, states have the ability to fund cash assistance to TANF recipients beyond the federal limit of 60 months with their own funds, and a handful of states have opted to do so. States also have the option of increasing cash benefit levels or keeping them indexed to inflation. A large number of states have opted to allow cash benefits to be paid to recipients even if they begin to earn substantial income, so-called earnings-disregard provisions. Of course, many other states have chosen to restrict TANF expenditures to the fullest extent possible under federal law (Gais and Weaver 2002).

In a very recent prominent example, under the Affordable Care Act states have the discretion to expand their Medicaid programs to cover more beneficiaries, with the federal government covering most of the bill, but with states having to pay a portion of the cost. Prior to the passage of the Affordable Care Act, states were given a great deal of discretion in funding and benefit decisions for the State Children's Health Insurance Program (S-CHIP). Thus, while states have always had some degree of discretion over certain federally initiated redistributive policies, recent welfare state policy changes enacted by the federal government have expanded the role of state governments in such policies. And, despite the incentive to avoid becoming a welfare magnet, as we noted above in the context of TANF some states have chosen to expand benefit levels and eligibility requirements further than is mandated by federal law (Bailey and Rom 2004; Fellowes and Rowe 2004). Furthermore, at the "street level," bureaucrats can use their discretion to expand or contract the scope of programs, and these decisions have meaningful effects on overall benefits distributed (Schneider and Jacoby 1996; Soss et al. 2001).

In addition to these federal programs, some states have created their own relatively modest transfer and social insurance programs. For instance, in recent years a handful of states, California, New Jersey, Rhode Island, and Washington, have adopted paid family leave policies, and because total possible benefits are capped, this program is of greater benefit (as a percentage of total income) for low- and middle-income workers than the wealthy. In short, through a variety of programs state policy action may influence the income distribution via taxes and transfers, even though the federal government plays the lead role in redistributive policy.

In addition to potentially influencing inequality via explicit income redistribution, states can also shape the income distribution by enacting market-conditioning policies, which affect wages before taxing and spending take place. Again, certain market-conditioning policies are the purview of the federal government. Monetary policy is the most obvious example, in which states have essentially no direct role (though even here they have an indirect role in that people residing in states are appointed to the Federal Open Market Committee, and they consider the economic condition of their state when making decisions). The federal government also plays the major role in crafting trade policy, though states often have foreign trade offices and do engage in negotiations about specific trade arrangements with foreign companies and governments.

Some market-conditioning policies, like the minimum wage, are jointly influenced by both the federal and the state governments (Kelly and Witko 2012), as we will discuss in some detail in chapter 6. But there are an almost infinite number of potential regulatory, labor market, tax, and other policies that can condition market outcomes and are within the purview of the states. For example, governments can make it easier to form unions, enabling workers to capture more corporate profits, reducing inequality. Many state governments have made it easier for public sector workers to form unions in recent years, for example. They can also mandate better wages and benefits for companies that wish to bid on public contracts. Additionally, governments can also use fiscal policy to invest in public goods, like universities or transportation infrastructure, that enable some groups to gain skills or directly create economic growth and spur employment (Kelly and Witko 2014; Witko and Newmark 2010). There is evidence that federal policies affect national income inequality via both redistribution and market-conditioning policies (Enns et al. 2014; Hacker and Pierson 2010; Kelly 2005; 2009). And some state-level research shows that taxing, spending, minimum wage, and other policies also shape the income distribution at the state level (Barrilleaux and Davis 2003; Freund and Morris 2005; Hatch and Rigby 2014; Kelly and Witko 2014; Langer 2001).

Since 1980, and especially since 1995, the Republican Party has more often controlled the institutions of the federal government. This conservative governing party has been less committed to ensuring equitable economic outcomes than the Democratic Party that preceded it. While Hacker and Pierson (2010) rightly point out that inequality has grown even with Democratic presidents, there is little doubt that the Congress has shifted dramatically to the right since the GOP takeover in 1995. This means that the federal government has been less active in fighting inequality, and Republican control of the federal government is generally associated with higher levels of inequality (Kelly 2009). The federal inaction on inequality creates a policy vacuum that the states can fill. Thus, in recent years states have both the means and the opportunity to shape the income distribution, *if they choose to do so.*

The presence of these tools to influence the income distribution raises the question of why certain governments take action to reduce inequality, while others do not. It seems almost trivial to point out that the ideology and constituency preferences of governments are a critical determinant of the policies that they pursue in office, but this simple idea is important for understanding how governments respond to economic inequality. Just as liberal Democrats in the mass public are more concerned about inequality, the literature in political science makes it clear that more left-leaning or liberal governments (in the American sense; we use the terms interchangeably here) are more likely to choose to use their policymaking authority and resources to produce a more equal income distribution.

Comparative politics scholars working within the tradition of power resources theory (PRT) assume that lower-class groups have different policy and distributional preferences than managers and investors, with the former supporting policies that lead to a more equitable income distribution and the latter a more unequal distribution (Korpi 1978; Huber and Stephens 2001). PRT scholars think that unions and left parties are the two main organizations that help the lower and working classes achieve more equitable economic outcomes in the market and policy process, respectively. And comparative research shows that left-wing national governments are indeed associated with more egalitarian policies and economic outcomes (Bradley et al. 2003; Huber et al. 2006; Moller et al. 2003.

Left-leaning governments are expected to provide more egalitarian policies and outcomes because lower-income voters are an important core constituency for these parties and these parties are often based on an ideology (Marxism) that views advancing the political and economic interests of the working class as its core responsibility and historical purpose. Policies that influence the income distribution often have fairly obvious distributional consequences, but they involve trade-offs between different economic goals, or among different economic actors. For instance, in one of the more famous examples, an easy-money policy may stimulate growth and employment that is good for the working class, but it might also lead to higher than expected inflation, which is bad for creditors, who tend to be wealthier individuals and institutions (Hibbs 1977). Similarly, increasing the minimum wage will increase the incomes of lower-paid workers, but it will reduce the income of managers and owners somewhat. Raising taxes on the wealthy to fund expanded education programs takes money away from certain (wealthy) taxpayers to fund benefits that accrue to the many. Left-leaning parties find these types of trade-offs that improve the income of the middle and lower classes, but potentially harm the incomes of the upper classes, acceptable because they rely on lower-income voters for support, and they are often ideologically committed to more equitable economic outcomes. The opposite is true of conservative parties with more affluent constituents.

It is important to note that the effects of public policies are often uncertain and contested. However, even conservatives do not typically dispute the first-order, short-term equalizing effect of left-wing or liberal economic policies. If the top marginal tax rates increase, in the short term it *will* lead to less money in the pockets of the wealthy. This is why high taxes on the wealthy are sometimes decried as "punishing success." Opponents of high taxes also argue that they will slow future rates of economic growth, by reducing the incentive of entrepreneurs to take risks and create new economic activity and jobs. And these criticisms may very well be true, at least under certain circumstances. But for our purposes, whether left-leaning or conservative policies are better or worse in any absolute or objective sense is irrelevant; we are simply interested in noting that left-leaning/ liberal policies are generally agreed by political actors and scholars to produce a more equal income distribution in the short term, whatever other problems they may create in the short or long term.

One problem with applying PRT to the American context is that a true left-wing party, that is, a communist, socialist, or labor party, has never held national or statewide elective office. Indeed, the absence of such left-wing parties in America has puzzled generations of scholars. Compared to most other affluent democracies, class conflict in the US party system is largely muted, and since there are not any popular true left-wing parties the social-class makeup of the parties is relatively heterogeneous. Nevertheless, historically some left-wing parties did demonstrate regional strength. The fairly left-wing Populist Party was strong in parts of the South and Midwest, and socialist parties did control government in some cities, like Milwaukee. When the Democratic Party moved to the left and adopted a somewhat left-wing set of redistributive and labor regulation policies during the New Deal era, these left-wing parties were essentially absorbed into the Democratic Party (Hirano and Snyder 2007). Thus, at the national level, since at least the 1930s and probably as far back as the 1890s, the Democratic Party has been economically to the left of the Republican Party.

If the experience of other countries is reproduced in America, we should observe that lower-income voters have greater allegiance to the Democratic Party, while wealthier voters are more likely to identify as Republicans. And when the Democratic Party controls government, policies and the income distribution should be more egalitarian. Contemporary surveys do indicate that the poor and middle class have different distributional and policy preferences than the affluent and very wealthy (Kelly and Enns 2010; Page, Bartels, and Seawright 2013). In addition, though there is variation across regions, poorer voters on balance demonstrate a preference for more liberal politicians and parties in America (Gelman et al. 2008; Kelly and Witko 2012). Furthermore, a growing literature in American politics indicates that Democratic control of the national government is associated with more egalitarian policies and lower levels of economic inequality, at least until around the 1980s (Bartels 2008; Hibbs 1977; Kelly 2009; Kelly and Witko 2012; Witko 2016).

It is obvious that most of the major expansions in the welfare state occurred under Democratic governments and that the Republicans are historically associated with policies like tax cuts for the wealthy. Bartels (2008) finds that lower-income groups experience more rapid economic growth under Democratic presidents. In a narrative analysis, Hacker and Pierson (2010) argue that the rise of the Republican Party in the early 1980s coincided with a number of policy changes that have increased economic inequality. And Kelly (2005; 2009) finds that Democratic control of the institutions of the federal government is associated with more equal economic outcomes. Witko (2016) finds that, until around the 1990s, the Democratic Party was less likely to deregulate the financial sector, and Keller and Kelly (2016) find that this regulation translated into lower levels of inequality under Democrats. None of these major policy changes were necessarily driven by a concern about economic inequality per se. For instance, the welfare reforms of the 1930s and 1960s were intended to address poverty. But when poverty is addressed by increasing the income of the poor, this will naturally reduce inequality.

As with national-level studies, state-level studies typically show that left-leaning state governments are associated with economic outcomes more beneficial to the poor and working class (Kelly and Witko 2012; 2014). It seems logical then, that when the public is concerned about inequality, it would be more likely to choose politicians that are liberal, or urge their elected officials to take more liberal policy stands. Though citizens are unaware of the academic research, the idea that liberal politicians and policies promote equality (even if wrongheadedly to their critics) is widespread. The public usually does not typically express a great deal of concern about the income distribution in surveys compared to other pressing problems (like national security or unemployment), but an increasingly unequal income distribution is intertwined with things that the public cares a great deal about—slowing wage growth, inequalities in the education system, a lack of good jobs for the low-skilled, and so forth. Thus, if at least some members of the public choose candidates on the basis of their approaches to these problems (for instance, by their support for a higher minimum wage or for more school funding), or push their existing elected officials to support more left-leaning policies as a result of these problems, then at the margin, and controlling for other factors, when there is a growing concern about inequality, we should also see increasing government liberalism.

The above admittedly makes some heroic assumptions about the public, that it is somewhat knowledgeable and somewhat engaged—propositions that receive some support in the literature (Erikson, Mackuen, and Stimson 2002). However, even if income inequality is never a major political issue at the top of the government's agenda or policy debates, and the public seldom thinks about it or factors inequality or closely related problems into its voting choices or choices of when to pressure representatives to pursue a policy, a growing public concern about inequality can translate into more liberal government by a process of "rational anticipation." This phrase, used by Stimson, MacKuen, and Erikson (1995), describes a situation in which politicians anticipate the developing preferences of the electorate in order to avoid potential trouble in future elections, or to entrepreneurially build support among the electorate for their political career and policies that they may prefer for a variety of reasons.

As a concern about inequality grows, individuals whose career and livelihood depend on staying on the pulse of the public should provide more of what the public wants even before it is explicitly demanded. If the public begins to become more concerned about economic inequality, politicians may begin to pursue more liberal policy to build support for future elections or higher office. Initially, this may just mean acknowledging that a problem exists, as even Republican presidential candidates are beginning to do with income inequality. But as a problem intensifies, the public may demand and politicians may provide policies actually intended to lower inequality, and politicians may fear resisting such policies. For instance, for a politician that does not have an extremely conservative constituency, resisting minimum wage increases is certain to be very unpopular, and it is something that an opponent could exploit in a future election. And politicians might be able to exploit a growing awareness of inequality to pursue their own, independently developed, liberal predispositions since a hallmark of liberal ideology is the preference for more state intervention in the economy to produce more equal outcomes (Soss et al. 2001). At this point, there is very limited research on how a growing concern about inequality may translate into government ideology, but this is precisely what we examine in the analysis below.

Nationally, it is fairly clear that a growing concern with inequality has not uniformly translated into more liberal governments. While there is some evidence that congressional Democrats have moved to the left, this is not true of presidents, let alone Republican politicians, who have moved to the right (Poole and Rosenthal 1998). And since 1980 Republicans have more often controlled the White House and the chambers of Congress than they did in the period from the 1930s through the 1970s. However, as we note in chapter 2, the differential concern about inequality across the country means that this may not be as likely to be a major issue in national campaigns or while governing Washington, DC, as it will be in states where inequality has increased the most. Furthermore, the power of business and the wealthy in the interest and party systems in DC means that both parties are more reliant on these actors for resources than ever before (Witko 2013), making them less likely to tackle inequality. In contrast, states vary in the extent to which their interest systems are dominated by business and the wealthy, and more importantly, in the extent to which their citizens are concerned about inequality. We expect that a growing concern about inequality, therefore, will be associated with more liberal state governments after we control for past government liberalism and government public opinion liberalism in the US states.

EXAMINING THE RELATIONSHIP BETWEEN PUBLIC AWARENESS OF INEQUALITY AND GOVERNMENT LIBERALISM

To examine the effect of public awareness of growing inequality on state government liberalism we use the measure of awareness introduced and presented in chapter 3 as the key explanatory variable. The measure of state government liberalism that we use, discussed more below, is available through 2010. Thus, our analyses cover the time period of 1987–2010 in this chapter. We discuss how we measure government liberalism, and discuss the other factors that we control for in our analysis of the relationship between awareness and government liberalism below.[1]

Measuring State Governments' "Leftism"

Cross-national studies measure the power of the Left in government using measures like the percentage of time that left-wing parties controlled a majority or a governing coalition in the national government. While the United States lacks a true left-wing (i.e., socialist or labor) party, in the national government the Democratic Party has been to the left of the Republican Party at least since the 1930s. Measuring government left-ism or government liberalism at the state level is not so straightforward, however, because there is substantial variation in the degree to which the Democratic Party is truly a liberal party or even to the left of the Republican Party at certain times in certain states. Most obviously, in the South the Democratic Party has historically been quite conservative in many states and there was very little Republican strength, while in other regions the Democratic Party was well to the left of the Republican Party and there was often robust party competition. In the time period we ana-lyze in this chapter (1987–2010), the Democratic Party is to the left of the Republican Party in every state, but the Democratic Party in states like New York or California is still much more liberal than the Democratic Party in states like Mississippi or Alabama, certainly in the late 1980s and probably even today. Thus, for our purposes it is useful to consider how concerns about inequality are associated with shifts in government ideology and then how this government ideology is associated with the income distribution.

Therefore, to measure how liberal a state government is we use Berry et al.'s (2010) measure of state government ideology. This measure com-bines information about partisan control of government and the "leftness" of both parties in a way that is comparable across states. This is done by applying an ideological score to each state party based on the ideology of their copartisans in the state's national congressional delegation.[2] Using common ideological scores derived from national politics makes it pos-sible to compare the liberalism of state parties using a common metric that approximates the national partisan divide. These state party ideology scores are then weighted by partisan control of the institutions of state government (each legislative chamber at .25 and the governor .50) to pro-duce the final measure of state government ideology. Thus, in states where a more liberal party controls more of the institutions of government, the overall state ideology score will be higher.

Other Factors Influencing State Governments' Liberalism

Of course, an awareness of inequality is not the only variable that influ-ences state government liberalism. Most obviously, the liberalism of gov-ernments does not just dramatically change from year to year, so past government liberalism is a constraint on current government liberalism. Even if current politicians adjust in response to growing concerns about income inequality, conservative or moderate politicians are not going to become left-wingers. Furthermore, as we discussed above, how liberal or conservative the citizens are in a particular state, which obviously varies tremendously across states, can be expected to influence how liberal the government is since liberal citizens will elect more liberal politicians (Erikson, Wright, and McIver 1993), and government officials should anticipate liberal opinion in anticipation of future elections (Erikson, MacKuen, and Stimson 2002). Liberal public opinion exerts a direct effect on the liberalism of government via elections, and also creates space for enterprising politicians to move to the left if that is where their preferences lie. To measure the liberalism of public opinion, we use a measure of state policy "mood" created by Enns and Koch (2013). This measure of public opinion is modeled on Stimson's well-regarded and oft-used national-level measure of public opinion liberalism mood. It measures how liberal the public is in different states by using a large number of questions about a variety of public opinions obtained from thousands of surveys across the states over a number of decades. Specifically, Enns and Koch (2012) use the MRP approach that was used to create the awareness of inequality measures, and discussed in chapter 2, to generate state-level estimates of opinion using survey data.

There are also a number of demographic controls included that may be associated with government liberalism: per capita income, the percentage of the population above 60 (which may affect the demand for liberalism), and the percentage of the population that is white (which can lead to more conservatism). National-level factors may also influence the ideology of state governments. For example, since the 1970s the country has generally become more conservative (Stimson 1999) and this certainly influences the ideology of elected officials. Similarly, national economic trends, foreign policy crises and so forth may all influence the ideology of state government officials. Rather than trying to control for each of these factors in the analysis with a large number of variables, we simply control for year "random effects" so that these year effects that influence all states equally at a given time do not confound our inferences about the state-level variables that we are most interested in.[3] Since we are not concerned with the substantive effects of these random year effects, we do not discuss them in the results section below.

To examine the effect of these variables on state government liberalism we perform linear regression analysis. We discuss details of the approach we used as well as present complete statistical tables in the appendices. In the main part of the chapter we simply present figures summarizing the effect of an awareness of inequality on government liberalism after controlling for the other factors. For comparison purposes, we also show how past government liberalism is associated with current government liberalism.

HOW CONCERNS ABOUT INEQUALITY ARE ASSOCIATED WITH GOVERNMENT LIBERALISM

After conducting the analysis, unsurprisingly we find that past values of state government liberalism are significantly associated with current values of state government liberalism. So too are public opinion liberalism and the percentage of the population that is white (a greater white percentage is associated with more conservative government). But we also find that a larger concern about growing economic inequality is also associated with higher levels of future state government liberalism. In figure 4.1 we present the total expected long-term effect of a one standard deviation increase in public awareness of inequality and a comparable change in

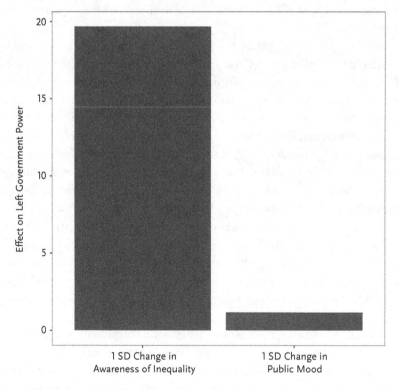

Figure 4.1: The Long-Run Effect of Awareness of Inequality on Government Liberalism
Note: Estimates are based on the model results presented in appendix table B.3.

public mood (i.e., a one standard deviation increase) on state government liberalism.[4] The total increase in state government liberalism of a plus one standard deviation change in awareness of inequality is just under 20 units in increased government liberalism. By comparison, the total effect of a plus one standard deviation change in public mood leads to an increase of just over one unit in government liberalism. The short-term (i.e., next year) effects of such a change are not included in this figure, and the short-term effect of mood is about 60% larger than that of inequality awareness (2.6 units vs. 1.6), however.

To further put these results into context, the expected difference produced in state government liberalism by a standard deviation increase in awareness about inequality is about the same size as the difference in government liberalism between Louisiana and Connecticut in the year 2010 (which was 19.1 points). This is obviously considerable. It should be noted that our modeling approach likely understates the true long-term effect size of public mood because public mood does not change rapidly and it also shapes past levels of government liberalism, which we control for in the model. That is, some of the effect size of public mood is incorporated in the coefficient for past government liberalism, which has a large effect on current government liberalism. Nevertheless, the fact that we observe that an awareness of inequality is a significant determinant of government liberalism, even after we control for past government liberalism and public mood, is an important finding, and indicates that as an awareness of inequality increases the government becomes substantially more liberal in a given state.

How does this abstract finding look in actual practice? Let's consider two states with high levels of inequality that were highlighted in the previous chapter, Massachusetts and Texas.

Both states have seen relatively large increases in inequality, and are among the most unequal states. The responses of the public and government have been quite different, however. In Massachusetts awareness of inequality has fluctuated but stayed relatively constant over time. In contrast, in Texas, awareness of inequality has declined. And, not surprisingly then, while Massachusetts entered some relatively conservative (for Massachusetts) periods of government, with the elections of Republican governors William Weld and Mitt Romney, Texas has seen a steady march to the right during the time period of this study. As one observer said of Texas policymakers in the *Dallas Morning News* "elected leaders aren't about to raise the minimum wage; they brag about the lack of union power; and they're proud of being a low-tax, low-service, low-regulation state" (Schnurman 2014). Texas has pioneered such laws as drug testing welfare recipients.

In contrast, when he was elected as the first openly gay president of the Massachusetts Senate, Democrat Stanley Rosenberg promised to wage a war on inequality and (Miller 2015), and even Republican Charlie Baker has felt pressure to embrace some left policies like minimum wage increases and equal-pay laws (Billis 2016), which are rejected by conservative Republicans in other states and in Washington, DC. This does not mean that inequality in Massachusetts will necessarily be lower than what it would otherwise be in Massachusetts, but the fact that policymakers are trying to reduce inequality is probably a step in the right direction to actually doing so. Next, we turn to this question of how government liberalism translates back into actual levels of economic inequality.

GOVERNMENT LIBERALISM AND INEQUALITY

Prior research examining different time periods has examined whether government liberalism in the states is associated with inequality. For instance, Kelly and Witko (2012) find that state government liberalism is significantly associated with reduced inequality in the period after the Republican takeover of Congress in 1994, but not during the roughly 20-year period before this time. Thus, it is not clear whether the relationship will hold during this different time period since the effect of state government liberalism on inequality does appear to shift somewhat over time (Kelly and Witko 2012), reflecting that different levels of federal activity probably create different opportunities for state politicians to influence the income distribution.

The measures of inequality that we examine as outcomes in this analysis were presented in chapter 3. We examine the relationship between government liberalism and state-level Gini coefficients, the top 10% income share and the top 1% income share. Given that these data were generated by Mark W. Frank using income tax returns, it is important to note that these measures of income inequality are pretax, pretransfer. The federal government does the most to use taxes and transfers to redistribute income, and previous research has found that while the state governments do reduce income inequality by taxes and transfers, most of the cross-state variation in levels of income inequality is explained by variation in market inequality (Kelly and Witko 2012). Therefore, it is sensible to use pretax, pretransfer measures of inequality to assess how state government liberalism and other factors influence state income inequality. This will also provide conservative estimates of the ability of the states to influence the income distribution, since it does not include any redistribution that may take place via taxes and transfers.

Other Factors Influencing State-Level Inequality

Other factors also influence economic inequality at the state level. Labor unions are also thought to be an important organization influencing the income distribution, and as we will see in subsequent chapters, they importantly shape egalitarian policies. Given the fact that we return to them again in subsequent chapters, it is worth discussing how unions might influence the income distribution in more detail. Previous studies find fairly consistent support for the conclusion that high levels of union membership are associated with lower levels of inequality (Bradley et al. 2003; Huber et al. 2006; Moller et al. 2003). Scholars working from a PRT perspective tend to view labor unions as primarily advancing the interests of the working class through collective bargaining in the market. And indeed, scholars in America have shown that strong unions enhance the bargaining position of labor, and make extremely high executive pay less likely, flattening the income distribution (Western and Rosenfeld 2011).

But in America's highly pluralistic political system, in which interest groups play a critical role in crafting policy, labor unions also have an important influence on policy, and ultimately economic outcomes, by their electoral and lobbying activities (Radcliff and Saiz 1998; Witko and Newmark 2005). Since the decline of manufacturing, union membership has not only dropped, but has also shifted toward professional employees of state, local, and national government. So union membership in the contemporary United States refers to a more disparate class base than it did historically. Though union membership has shifted away from the manufacturing sector to service and governmental sectors, higher levels of union membership should reduce economic inequality. Because the National Labor Relations Act only guarantees nonmanagerial employees the right to organize, collective bargaining tends to promote contracts that limit the most dramatic differences between top earners and bottom earners covered by the contract, and these effects spillover to nonunion members (Fortin and Lemieux 1997; Hyclak 1980; Mosher 2007). Therefore, since labor unions appear to constrain the influence of business and high-income groups, we expect that more union membership should reduce inequality via both collective bargaining and government activity (Hyclak 1980; Radcliff and Saiz 1998; Witko and Newmark 2005). We examine this using a measure of *union density*, which is the percentage of the nonagricultural workforce represented by a union in collective bargaining.[5]

It is also necessary to again control for economic and demographic variables that influence the income distribution. We include the state's *unemployment rate* (proportion unemployed) and the overall health of, and income generated by, the economy (*per capita income*), which we expect to be positively and negatively related to inequality, respectively. We also again include the proportion of the population that is *white* and *over age 60*. Finally, as noted in our discussion above, the federal government influences inequality. Historically, when Democrats have held power in the national government and when liberal policies have been enacted in Washington, DC, inequality has been lower (Bartels 2008; Kelly 2005; 2009). Therefore, we estimate two sets of models of the effect of state government variables. First, we include only state-level determinants of economic inequality. Then we include dummy variables for whether the presidency and Congress are controlled by the Democratic Party.

HOW STATE GOVERNMENT LIBERALISM IS ASSOCIATED WITH INEQUALITY

A summary of the results of the data analysis, including the federal partisan control variables, is presented in figure 4.2, with full statistical tables again presented in appendix B in tables B.4 and B.5. We see that state government liberalism is associated with significant reductions in the Gini coefficient of income inequality, and the top 10% income share, but not the top 1% income share (for the latter, though there is a negative relationship, it is not actually statistically significant). In figure 4.2 we present the reduction in inequality associated with a standard deviation increase in state government liberalism using the three measures of income inequality. The results presented here include controls for federal political variables, which were significant determinants of inequality in the expected direction. We can see here that for certain measures, the effect of state government liberalism on inequality is substantial.

State government liberalism has very little ability to influence the share of income going to the top 1%, and only a modest ability to influence the share going to the top 10% of income earners. This relative inability to affect top incomes likely reflects, in part, that state income tax systems are quite flat and some states lack an income tax entirely, which influences the compensation practices of highly paid managers, executives, and so on, even before taxes are collected (Volscho and Kelly 2012). In contrast, the states can influence the overall income distribution, as we can see with the effect on the Gini coefficient of income inequality. Taken together, these findings suggest that the states may have a greater influence on the income distribution by affecting the wages of the poor and middle class than by influencing the income of upper-income earners. Indeed, we will see in

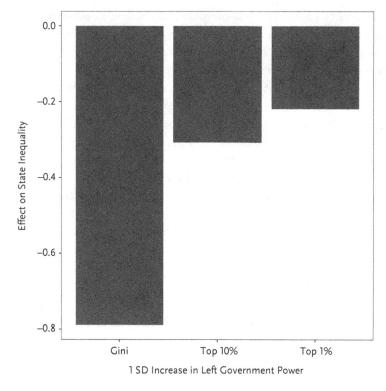

Figure 4.2: The Reduction of Inequality Associated with a Standard Deviation Increase in State Government Liberalism

Note: Estimates are based on the model results presented in appendix table B.5.

chapters 6 and 7 that awareness of inequality is important for the formation and enactment of policies designed to boost the wages of those with low income.

One finding in our analysis of this time period that contrasts with prior research at the federal and state levels is that we do not observe that stronger unions have any direct effect on reducing economic inequality. Indeed, in the model of the top 10% income share we find that states with stronger unions have a higher percentage of income going to the top 10% (and this is significant at the .10 level). This contrasts with the general finding of union influence in Kelly and Witko's (2012) study, which examined the period of 1976–2007. This may reflect that they focused only on the Gini coefficient, but it is more likely that the difference here reflects the major decline in union strength in the early 1980s, before the period of our study. Thus, unions have been relatively weak for almost the entire time period of our analysis in most states, which does not permit a good estimation of their effect on the income distribution. Furthermore, during this later time period the class composition of union membership has also changed considerably, since in 1980 the typical union member was a blue-collar worker, while in 2010 the typical union member in many states a college-educated professional in the public sector. On the other hand, as we will see in subsequent chapters, unions are still important actors for the advancement of certain egalitarian policies.

Democratic Congresses are also associated with significantly lower inequality across all three measures of state income inequality. Interestingly, we find that in the first year of a Democratic presidency income inequality increases, but this should be taken with a grain of salt given that this reflects only two years in our data set (1993 and 2009). The substantive effect of a standard deviation increase in the percentage of congressional seats held by Democrats has a larger substantive effect than state government liberalism. However, Democrats have not typically controlled the Congress in recent years, which makes this in some respects a moot point. In any case, our findings show significant effects of state government liberalism on economic inequality in the states, which is impressive considering that the states are often entirely neglected in discussions of the politics of income inequality.

CONCLUSION

We have seen in this chapter that a growing concern about inequality is associated with the growth of state government liberalism, after we control for other factors. In turn, we see that state government liberalism is associated with significantly lower Gini coefficients of income inequality and lower 10% income shares. In contrast, it does not seem that state government liberalism has much of an effect on the top 1% income share. As awareness of inequality grows, some states will choose to elect more liberal state governments, or sitting politicians will shift to the left, which results in lessened inequality in those states. This suggests that the states may provide some measure of thermostatic response to growing economic inequality, even if the federal government appears wholly unwilling or incapable of doing so.

Admittedly, in many states there is not a realistic possibility that the electorate will embrace liberal governments, nor would politicians willingly shift to the left. However, the ability of an increasingly concerned public to influence the income distribution is by no means limited to doing so through state government liberalism. Indeed, in states with the initiative, citizens concerned with income inequality can circumvent the elected branches altogether to craft policy designed to reduce inequality. In chapter 6 we examine how the initiative has been important to minimum wage increases, in even conservative states. Furthermore, not all policies that result in a more equal income distribution are resisted by conservatives—conservatives have embraced the earned income tax credit, which we consider in chapter 7. Before these two chapters, however, we consider how the initiative creates opportunities for the electorate and activists to address inequality, and how individual views toward inequality shape how the public responds to specific policy proposals designed to reduce inequality, by focusing on tax increases on the wealthy in the next chapter.

CHAPTER 5

Taxing the Rich

The Initiative, Attitudes toward Inequality, and

Washington's Proposition 1098

In the previous chapter we showed that a growing awareness of inequality is associated with growing government liberalism, which is in turn associated with lower levels of inequality. In previous chapters we relied on aggregate trends in the public's attitudes about income differences, and for good reason. This is the most appropriate way to assess how Americans have responded to *over-time changes* in economic inequality. Now that we have established a general awareness of growing inequality among the public, it is also useful to focus more specifically on how individuals view inequality and whether these views are important when people consider the role of the government in addressing unequal economic outcomes. Using Washington State's 2010 ballot measure to examine this question is ideal for a number of reasons. We summarize some of these reasons here and discuss them in more detail below. First, ballot measures typically provide a straightforward way of assessing individual policy preferences since the public is asked to vote directly on explicit proposals, as opposed to asking people for their preferences on hypothetical policies. Also, the debate surrounding the vote on Proposition 1098 regularly touched on the issue of economic inequality, meaning that views on inequality may have been relevant when deciding how to vote. Finally, this specific ballot initiative was designed to redistribute income and increase taxes on the wealthy, something fairly unusual over the last few decades. If it had passed, the measure would have created new income taxes on the rich and used the additional revenue to fund social programs in the state that benefit many other taxpayers.

Broadly speaking, the American public has one of the lowest overall tax burdens relative to other developed nations. When considering taxes at all levels of government—that is, federal, state, and local—for countries that are members of the Organization for Economic Cooperation and Development (OECD), the United States is nearly last in the amount of tax revenue it collects as a percentage of GDP (Campbell 2012).[1] While the federal tax system is viewed as mostly progressive thanks to its reliance on the income tax (Steinmo 1995), the federal income tax is not as progressive as it once was because of uneven tax cuts over the last few decades. As we show in figure 5.1, the top marginal tax rate has declined substantially since the 1970s, when it was 70%. The current top rate of just below 40% is striking when considering that the United States once had a marginal tax rate over 90% for the highest income earners. Along with the top income tax rate, the plot also shows a trend in public attitudes that are seemingly in general agreement with the decline in the income tax rate. When asked if upper-income people pay their fair share in taxes, the percentage of Americans who believe the rich pay "too little" declined from a high of 77%

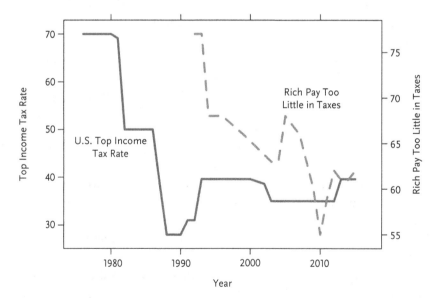

Figure 5.1: The Federal Top Income Tax Rate and the Public's View of Upper-Income People's Tax Burden

Source: Internal Revenue Service (https://www.irs.gov/uac/soi-tax-stats-historical-table-23) and Gallup (http://www.pollingreport.com/budget.htm).

in the early 1990s to a low of 55% in 2010. Yet this downward trend has reversed since 2010, and a majority of the public still believes that the rich pay too little in taxes.

We believe that the structure of tax policy and the public's views of taxation demonstrated in figure 5.1 touch on several important points about progressive taxation that are central to this chapter. The first is that US tax policy has become less progressive in recent decades (see Piketty and Saez 2007), which suggests that addressing inequality via the tax code will be a politically difficult task. While we argue below that this shift toward reducing the tax burden of the wealthy is beginning to change course, these changes are not likely to happen overnight. Second, the decline in the public's view that the rich are not paying enough in taxes is indicative of the growing division of attitudes about progressive tax policy along partisan and ideological lines, where Republicans and conservatives have become less likely to support higher taxes on the rich.[2] This means that the politics of redistribution has become much more partisan over time and that reaching a broad consensus on more progressive policies is doubtful. Finally, whether attitudes about tax policy are shaped by the public's concern for inequality will depend on the context within which policy change is considered. One explanation for the increase in those who believe the rich pay too little in taxes since 2010 (see figure 5.1) is the rise in prominence of income inequality in the United States as a result of the Great Recession and the related Occupy Wall Street movement (e.g., McCall 2013). If the issue of income inequality continues to grow as part of the political discourse surrounding policy, views on inequality will be more likely to shape the public's preferences for progressive policy.

As we discuss below, even if there is a shift among Americans toward more support for progressive tax policy, it is unlikely that the federal government will be willing or able to make such policy changes. We suggest that the states will play a large role in responding to the public's view that the wealthy should be contributing more to government programs, and that the initiative process could be crucial to state policy responsiveness.

We demonstrated in chapter 4 that the public has generally become more aware of inequality as it has grown, and government liberalism has increased in response. So why, then, is the initiative process so important if citizens appear to be changing their state governments as a reaction to rising inequality? Is it not the case that these relatively liberal state legislators will respond to the public's concern about inequality by adopting more redistributive policies? While we do show in the previous chapter that states with more left-leaning governments tend to have lower levels of income inequality, the influence of the public's policy preferences on legislative outcomes is certainly not a one-to-one relationship. Even though state governments are perhaps more responsive to public sentiment than the federal government is for a variety of reasons (see chapter 2), citizen preferences are not the only factor influencing legislative decision-making. Organized interests, lobbyists, and the personal goals and preferences of a lawmaker all have the potential to shape legislative outcomes away from the preferences of the public.

Even if public support for legislation is a main factor in determining whether a policy is enacted, politicians are not always fully informed about the public's preferences and they likely have incentives to respond to only a subset of their constituents (Gilens 2012; Flavin 2012). Additionally, a legislature's political agenda has a limited amount of space, meaning that only a small portion of existing political issues are ever addressed by the government (Kingdon 1984). The point here is that representative democracy, at any level of government, is flawed in its ability to reach democratic outcomes. This is why the initiative process is useful—it provides the public with a way to circumvent the traditional lawmaking process, and has the potential to make policy more representative of collective opinion. Currently, since many of the policies that might lessen inequality do have widespread public support but are not being pursued by many state governments, and in most cases not being pursued at all by the federal government, the initiative is playing an important role in state policy responses to inequality.

In order for the initiative to push policies in a more egalitarian direction, however, it is necessary for voters to be able to link their own economic self-interest or attitudes toward inequality to the "correct" or "congruent" policy position on actual public policies. Washington's Proposition 1098 is perfect for investigating this because it was a large tax increase on the wealthy, which made one's self-interest very clear, and was also debated with explicit reference to the role of tax policy in income inequality. We discuss the existing views on whether it is likely that the public can tie its self-interest and broad attitudes toward inequality to specific policy proposals, before discussing the specific of Proposition 1098. We begin here, however, by explaining why the initiative is important for tax policy and likely to be important for tax increases on the wealthy, in particular.

THE INITIATIVE AND STATE TAX POLICY

As the federal government cut top marginal tax rates over the last few decades, so too did some states. Table 5.1 gives a general overview of the

Table 5.1. STATE TOP INCOME TAX RATES, 1976–2012

State	Top Income Tax Rate 1976	2012	Change 1976–2012	State (cont.)	Top Income Tax Rate (cont.) 1976	2012	Change (cont.) 1976–2012
Alabama	5	5	0	Montana	11	6.9	–4.1
Alaska	14.5	0	–14.5	Nebraska	11.2	6.84	–4.36
Arizona	8	4.54	–3.46	Nevada	0	0	0
Arkansas	7	7	0	New Hampshire	0	5	+5
California	11	10.3	–0.7	New Jersey	2.5	8.97	+6.47
Colorado	8	4.63	–3.37	New Mexico	9	4.9	–4.1
Connecticut	0	6.7	+6.7	New York	15	8.82	–6.18
Delaware	19.8	6.75	–13.05	North Carolina	7	7.75	0.75
Florida	0	0	0	North Dakota	10	3.99	–6.01
Georgia	6	6	0	Ohio	3.5	5.925	+2.425
Hawaii	11	11	0	Oklahoma	6	5.25	–0.75
Idaho	7.5	7.4	–0.1	Oregon	10	9.9	–0.1
Illinois	2.5	5	+2.5	Pennsylvania	2.2	3.07	+0.87
Indiana	2	3.4	+1.4	Rhode Island	11.9	5.99	–5.91
Iowa	13	8.98	–4.02	South Carolina	7	7	0
Kansas	9	6.45	–2.55	South Dakota	0	0	0
Kentucky	6	6	0	Tennessee	0	6	+6
Louisiana	6	6	0	Texas	0	0	0
Maine	10	8.5	–1.5	Utah	7.75	5	–2.75
Maryland	5	5.75	+0.75	Vermont	17.5	8.95	–8.55
Massachusetts	5.37	5.25	–0.12	Virginia	5.75	5.75	0
Michigan	4.6	4.35	–0.25	Washington	0	0	0
Minnesota	18	7.85	–10.15	West Virginia	9.6	6.5	–3.1
Mississippi	4	5	+1	Wisconsin	11.4	7.75	–3.65
Missouri	6	6	0	Wyoming	0	0	0

Source: Book of the States (http://knowledgecenter.csg.org).

top income tax rates across the states from 1976 to 2012, and shows how top rates have changed over this period. Top income tax rates vary dramatically across the states but change relatively little over time.[3] Most states did not make considerable changes their tax rates over this nearly 40-year period. The double-digit changes seen in Delaware and Minnesota are the exception rather than the rule. But among those states that did change their taxes, most of the changes that have occurred over this period have been decreases in top rates. Nineteen states reduced their top income tax rates by one percentage point or more, while only eight states increased their rates by one or more percentage points over this period.

And this one type of tax policy does not capture all of the tax changes that have taken place in recent years. In fact, the modern "tax revolt" was led by states like California, with the passage of its Proposition 13, which slashed property taxes and limited future annual increases. Several other states enacted similar property tax limits in the ensuing years (Tolbert 2003; Magleby 1994). The initiative process was critical to these reductions in taxes. As we note in chapter 2, the use of the initiative declined after the 1930s, but, as the effects of deindustrialization, stagnant incomes, and inflation appeared, in the 1970s the initiative gained in popularity again, and was important in adjusting tax policy in the states.

As property values increased but wages remained stagnant, paying property taxes became more difficult in states like California, and some citizen groups and organized interests began to advocate for property tax relief proposals (Schrag 1998). Elected officials and powerful organized interests like unions and business associations often opposed these large property tax cuts, like Proposition 13, because they would bring dramatic reductions in revenue for programs like education, and these predictions were typically accurate (Schrag 1998). While some may argue that tax cuts were the wrong response to problems like stagnant wages, the tax revolt was a response to actual economic problems felt by the middle class, and which federal and state governments were generally failing to address. Thus, policy was out of step with perceptions of the economic self-interest of many voters, and the initiative was used to adjust policy in the direction of the preferences of voters. The antitax fervor began with state property taxes, but did not end there. Many states and the federal government also slashed income taxes substantially.

In recent years we are again seeing that the initiative is critical to addressing an emerging economic problem, growing economic inequality, which may be caused in part by the dramatic tax reductions that Proposition 13 helped to usher in. How may a tool that was so central to the tax revolt, which generally limited taxes on wealthier taxpayers, be used to pursue greater equality? The answer is that the initiative is neither liberal nor conservative per se. Instead, the initiative is an institution that can push policy in the direction of public preferences whenever they are out of line with the status quo, as discussed in chapter 2. The initiative does not lead to higher taxes and higher spending or lower taxes and lower spending—how the initiative manifests itself depends on the governing status quo at the time and the preferences of the public in a given state. Matsusaka (2004) found that during the first half of the century, when government policy was arguably more conservative than preferred by the public (it is impossible to know for sure because opinion polls are lacking), initiatives states from 1902 to 1942 spent more than non-initiative states on welfare and government services. But during the more recent period (1970–2000) the initiative was used to reduce overall spending and expenditures by state and local government. Overall, Matsusaka argues that the initiative makes government policy more responsive to citizen preferences, whether it be demands for higher taxes on the wealthy and a larger welfare state in the Progressive Era and Great Depression, or the opposite during the tax revolt in the 1970s and 1980s.

As government fails to address inequality, the initiative is being used to craft policy intended to slow or roll back growing inequality. This is most notable in the spate of initiatives raising the minimum wage as the federal minimum wage has stagnated (Freeman and Rogers 2007; Smith and Tolbert 2010). In the 2014 and 2016 elections in several states, including conservative states like Alaska, Arkansas, Nebraska, and South Dakota, used the initiative process to increase wage minimums. Despite the unpopularity of taxes, after more than 30 years of the tax revolt we are beginning to see the initiative used to try to reverse large tax cuts for the wealthy. Progressive income tax increases on individuals or corporations or both have been on the ballot or are being proposed for the ballot in states including Massachusetts, Michigan, Washington, California, and Colorado.

The initiative is likely to be important for increasing taxes on the wealthy because the wealthy are often resistant to tax increases and have a great deal of influence in the traditional policy process (Page, Bartels, and Seawright 2013). Furthermore, even liberal politicians are often worried about the implications of their support for tax increases. With the initiative, the voters can take the political blame, and politicians still get the revenue. While there is no reason to expect a frenzy of tax increases any time soon, as inequality grows we anticipate that we will see the initiative used more often to increase taxes on the wealthy. If our theories about how inequality and self-interest shape policy preferences are correct, greater concern about inequality should lead individuals to be more supportive of tax increases on the rich.

INDIVIDUAL ATTITUDES TOWARD PROGRESSIVE TAXATION AND REDISTRIBUTION IN AN UNEQUAL ERA

In order for the initiative to result in increased taxes on the wealthy, citizens must be able to tie their economic self-interest and individual attitudes toward inequality to specific tax policies. However, partisanship is a key determinant of tax policy in this highly partisan era. We discuss the ways that these factors shape individual tax policy preferences below.

The Elephant (and Donkey) in the Room

We are primarily interested in how attitudes toward inequality shape views of tax increases on the wealthy. However, perhaps the primary correlate of tax policy preferences at the mass level is simply party affiliation. The parties have become a more potent force in American politics as inequality has grown, arguably because inequality has grown (Garand 2010; McCarty, Poole, and Rosenthal 2006). Partisanship has become so important a predictor of voting and policy preferences that the importance of views on income inequality and economic self-interest may simply be swamped by the effect of party at the individual level. In fact, Lupia et al. (2007) argue that partisanship explains support or opposition to the Bush-era tax cuts better than self-interest, information, concern about inequality, or other factors. Even after controlling for preference-based predispositions to support a party, research shows that partisanship can have an important independent effect on voters' policy preferences (Lenz 2009). It is probably the case that people who are very concerned about inequality are more likely to be Democrats, but certainly not all individuals concerned about inequality are Democrats, and many Democrats are not concerned about inequality. This may weaken the relationship between attitudes toward inequality and preferences for tax increases on the wealthy.

State ballot contests, which we examine here, are officially nonpartisan, but partisanship is nevertheless an important determinant of voting on initiatives (Bowler and Donovan 1998; Smith and Tolbert 2004; Branton 2003). In fact, because voters are responsive to cues from partisan elites (Karp 1998) and organized interests that are typically associated with one of the parties (Smith and Tolbert 2001), individual partisanship is the most important predictor of voting behavior in initiative elections in the American states over time (Branton 2003; Hasen 2000). This use of partisan cues can help explain the pattern of ideological consistency in votes observed across a range of initiatives on state ballots (Banducci 1998). Campaigns in direct democracy elections target issue dimensions they believe will be most effective among partisans most likely to favor their position on the issue (Nicholson 2005; Donovan et al. 2008; Smith and Tolbert 2010). When multiple, competing frames are present in a policy debate, individuals will be more likely to accept information confirming existing beliefs (Lau, Smith, and Fiske 1991), which often means accepting information that is consistent with one's partisan predispositions (e.g., Campbell et al. 1960; Mutz 2007). Considering these facts about partisan filters and initiative voting, and that increasing polarization has accompanied increasing inequality (McCarty, Poole, and Rosenthal 2006), we expect that partisanship will directly affect support for tax increases and condition individuals' responsiveness to arguments for and against such policies.

Self-Interest and Inequality

Existing research on how economic factors shape support for policy alternatives has highlighted the role of individual self-interest and broader, societal (or sociotropic) concerns. In periods of high inequality, such as we see in the United States, either economic self-interest or these broader concerns could lead to greater support for tax increases on the wealthy. Prominent economic theories of individual behavior argue that the rise of inequality will lead to a growing demand for redistribution because more individuals stand to personally benefit from this redistribution as the highest earners become much wealthier than the median voter (Meltzer and Richard 1981). Others have suggested that the public's reaction to rising inequality will be more nuanced than this, and propose that increasing inequality will not always lead to major demands for redistribution (e.g., see Franko 2016). Instead, for a variety of reasons the public's collective desire for redistribution will be greatest at very high and very low levels of inequality (Benabou 2000). In the context of our individual-level analysis, one of the more important agreements among these perspectives is that the poor, and those with lower incomes more generally, will almost always be more supportive of redistribution out of their economic self-interest. Indeed, theorists have long argued that mass democracy will lead to higher levels of redistribution simply because most voters are not wealthy (Tocqueville 1945).

Political scientists have long raised doubts about the extent to which economic self-interest influences public opinion and policy preferences, however (Sears et al. 1980; Markus 1988). Citrin et al. (1997) show that personal economic motivations play little role in the formation of opinions on immigration, and that sociotropic concerns about the national economy are more important. Surveys reveal, however, that on economic issues high-income and low-income voters often have different preferences

(Gilens 2009; Page, Bartels, and Seawright 2013), and lower-income voters are expected to be more supportive of tax increases on the wealthy if self-interest drives policy preferences. Bartels (2005; 2008), however, finds that individuals with lower incomes were actually more supportive of the Bush tax cuts, which benefited the wealthy most. He views these results as a manifestation of "unenlightened self-interest" since, he argues, the predictable long-term consequence of the Bush tax cuts would be to increase taxes and/or lead to spending cuts in programs benefiting lower-income voters. It is unenlightened because citizens lack information about the long-term effect of the tax cuts and thus consider only their own short-term interests when passing judgment on tax policies. Perhaps this is not surprising, since broader attitudes often have a greater effect on preferences than self-interest.

Even if self-interest does not spur individuals to support higher taxes on the wealthy, because there appears to be many negative social consequences associated with income inequality (e.g., Kawachi et al. 1997), growing inequality could mean that even individuals who are personally not economically harmed by growing inequality may be against it and favor policy to lessen inequality. This is more consistent with the literature on sociotropic motivations mentioned above. Many researchers have demonstrated that the public is certainly aware of, and increasingly concerned about, economic inequality (McCall and Kenworthy 2009; Page and Jacobs 2009; Bartels 2008). And it is not only the poor who are concerned about economic inequality. In one innovative study, Doherty et al. (2006) find that lottery winners became more hostile to estate taxes, but that there was no significant wealth effect on broader attitudes toward social stratification and inequality, demonstrating that wealth per se has little influence on views toward the positives and negatives of inequality.

Using abstract survey questions about whether taxes on those with high incomes are "too low" (like those we discuss above), McCall and Kenworthy (2009) show that attitudes toward inequality are a relatively strong predictor of views on the tax burden of the wealthy. They find that moving from being very unconcerned about inequality to being most concerned is associated with an approximate increase of between 30 and 60 percentage points in the predicted probably of thinking that taxes on the wealthy are too low. But this relationship appears to have weakened over time (McCall and Kenworthy 2009). Thus, it is not clear that either self-interest or broad attitudes toward inequality will shape actual tax policy preferences.

Information, Arguments, and the Formation of Preferences for Redistribution

We think that whether individuals link their attitudes toward inequality or self-interest to the corresponding position on a tax increase proposal depends on the structure of the tax policy and the nature of the debate surrounding that proposal. Despite the research discussed above, we actually know little about whether individuals can link their economic self-interest and attitudes toward inequality to the congruent policy position in the context of actual policy debates. One major reason that we do not know much about how these factors influence views toward tax increases on the wealthy is that tax *cuts* have been the norm over the last four decades, and support for tax cuts and support for tax increases are different decisions. Even if tax cuts benefit the wealthy most in dollar terms, they usually provide some tax relief to lower-income voters. This makes determining what someone's self-interest is in a tax cut situation very tricky. Is it unreasonable to favor a small tax cut now that *might* lead to a large tax increase in the future? Is it reasonable to not prefer a tax cut simply because someone else may get a bigger one? Furthermore, in policy debates competing actors *try to confuse people* to gain their support for policies that may not be good for them. It appears that this was the case regarding the Bush tax cuts (Hacker and Pierson 2005), where politicians intentionally misled the public about distributional effects of the cuts and argued that everyone would benefit from the proposed tax changes (even though the wealthy received the largest cuts by far). Thus, it is not surprising that individuals had difficulty making a connection between inequality and the Bush tax cuts, and it is understandable that most of the public had trouble in identifying its self-interest, when considering that virtually everyone who paid taxes ended up with a lower tax burden.

In contrast, when a tax increase targets only one income group and provides benefits for all other income groups, it is much easier to separate out the self-interest of different categories of voters. If the costs and benefits of policies to different groups are clear, then it is more likely that self-interest will play a role in shaping policy preferences, so long as these costs and benefits feature prominently in the debate surrounding a policy. There is a lot of evidence that elite arguments and frames are critical in the process of policy preference formation both in the lab and in real-world policy debates (Berinsky 2007; Lau and Redlawsk 2006; Schneider and Jacoby 2005; Witko 2003; Zaller 1992). In any given policy debate there are a large number of dimensions on which policy may be evaluated, and manipulating the dimension along which a policy debate takes place is at the heart of political strategy (Schattschneider 1960). Elites have some (but certainly not complete) freedom to determine the dimensions along which policies will be debated. In any given policy debate elites make choices regarding which issue dimensions are emphasized and how these dimensions are discussed, with important impacts on preferences (Chong and Druckman 2007a, 2007b; Druckman 2001; 2004; Krosnick and Kinder 1990; Nelson and Kinder 1996; Nelson et al. 1997; Schneider and Jacoby 2005; Zaller 1992). Research on direct democracy also indicates that elite cues and media campaigns are important in issue elections (Bowler and Donovan 1998; Lupia 1994; Smith and Tolbert 2001; 2004). Initiative campaigns can prime voters to elevate certain issues, making them more salient, which can affect voting on the issues or for candidates running for office in the same election (Bowler and Donovan 1998; Nicholson 2005; Donovan et al 2008; Smith and Tolbert 2010).

Self-interest and sociotropic concerns can be primed by different arguments and frames. That is, how policy alternatives are presented and discussed by political elites can shape whether voters primarily consider self-interest or broader concerns. Chong, Citrin, and Conley (2001) demonstrate in a laboratory setting that when the effect on individuals from a policy is clear, and when they have been primed to think about personal costs and benefits of policies, self-interest becomes a more important determinant of preferences. Being primed about sociotropic matters weakens the relationship between self-interest and policy preferences, but does not eliminate it (Chong, Citrin, and Conley 2001). If this experimental evidence holds in actual debates, where the costs and benefits of redistributive tax and spending policies to different groups are clear and feature prominently in the debate over the policy, economic self-interest should significantly shape attitudes toward redistributive taxation. Similarly, if the broader impacts on social outcomes are made clear, then these attitudes can also be expected to shape support for policies.

WASHINGTON STATE'S PROPOSITION 1098

In this era of general antitax sentiment, tax increases are difficult to pursue for elected officials, which is why tax increase proposals have been so rare. Thus, it was via the initiative that a proposed tax increase entered the political debate in Washington in 2010. Though there is always some ambiguity in the costs and benefits to different groups of particular policies, Proposition 1098 is about as straightforward a policy as one could hope to find for identifying the winners and losers. Voters in Washington were able to vote on a ballot measure that would have created an income tax on the wealthy. This policy is highly progressive and redistributive, and the costs and benefits to different economic groups, as well as the broader social impact were made very clear during the course of the campaign, which was highly publicized and well funded. This led to a rich information environment, with a number of elite cues related to the tax, featuring prominent arguments about the redistributive nature of the tax and its relationship to inequality. Not surprisingly, while officially nonpartisan, Democratic elites were more supportive of 1098 than Republicans. Focusing on this single initiative is valuable for these reasons, but because other ballot items can also "prime" voters, focusing only on Washington also allows us to hold this factor constant for all voters.[4]

Washington is one of nine states lacking a general income tax. Proposition 1098 would have imposed an income tax on individuals earning over $200,000 a year ($400,000 for families), or the top 2% of households. Under the proposal, earnings up to $1,000,000 would be taxed at 5%, and earnings above this amount at 9%. The initiative would simultaneously have reduced property taxes for most families and provided some funds for small businesses. The additional revenue from the newly created tax—an estimated $2 billion a year by 2013—was to be devoted to education and healthcare programs (Garber 2010). Though the latter programs, especially education, are not geared exclusively toward the poor, on the whole there was a redistribution of income from the wealthy to others, including the middle class, by the reduction in property tax rates and expansion in government programs.

Anyone who voted would have been exposed to this information because it was stated on the ballot itself:

> This measure would tax "adjusted gross income" above $200,000 (individuals) and $400,000 (joint-filers), reduce state property tax levies, reduce certain business and occupation taxes, and direct any increased revenues to education and health.[5]

But even nonvoters were likely to be exposed to some information about the proposal thanks to the vigorous campaign surrounding the measure. Funding and promotion for each side of the issue was primarily managed by two organizations—Yes on 1098 headed support for the measure, while the Defeat 1098 committee opposed the proposed tax. These organizations were, in turn, supported and by organized interests (such as labor unions supporting Yes on 1098, and business groups supporting Defeat 1098) that are active on economic issues (Witko and Newmark 2005). In addition, notable individuals, including Bill Gates Sr. and Bill Gates Jr., the latter as of this writing the wealthiest individual in the world, supported Proposition 1098. Prominent opponents included the founder and CEO of Amazon.com and a number of other Microsoft board members, creating a well-resourced opposition media campaign. The two groups ran strong campaigns, spending large amounts for their respective sides. According to disclosure records, Yes on 1098 spent $6.42 million and Defeat 1098 spent $6.33 million, which combined is approximately $2.50 per Washington adult. This is more than what has been spent by the presidential or congressional candidates in Washington in recent elections (Tolbert, Bowen, and Donovan 2009) and is similar to spending in Governor Gregoire's hotly contested 2008 reelection campaign.[6]

Although 1098 raised taxes on wealthy Washingtonians, the debate was not fought entirely along class lines, as even some very wealthy people supported the tax out of their own broader concerns about income inequality. A *Seattle Times* article, for instance, reads, "Washington Wealthy Clash over Income Tax on the Rich" (Woodward 2010). In fact, one person given credit for the creation of 1098 is Bill Gates Sr. It is possible that having wealthy notables divided in their stances on the proposal attenuated the "class war" aspect of the public debate over 1098. Bill Gates Sr., however, was clear about one of the main purposes of the ballot measure, which was to create a more equal tax system in Washington, given the state's reliance on regressive taxation, such as the sales tax. Several months before the 2010 election Gates stated in an interview with reporters that "poor people and middle-income people are paying too much to support the state and rich people aren't paying enough. That's the starting point for me" (Robison 2010). A spokesperson for the Yes on 1098 campaign also suggested that those opposed to 1098 were "a small group of wealthy people who benefit from the current unfair system and don't want to see the status quo change" (La Corte 2010).

Supporters of 1098 also focused on how the proposed income tax would generate funds to improve the state's education and health programs, two government programs that are generally considered to be redistributive in nature (e.g., see Kelly 2009). The importance of improving the state's education and health systems was often portrayed as a way to produce long-term economic growth, as well as an investment in the futures of Washington's children (see Garber 2010; La Corte 2010; Robison 2010; Woodward 2010). With our data set we cannot directly examine how exposure to competing frames about self-interest and inequality shaped attitudes, but economic self-interest and economic inequality were central components of the ballot measure campaign. With the unusually high levels of advertising and public interest—the survey data we analyze showed that only 11% of voters did not follow the debate at least somewhat closely—as much as any other policy debate we can assume that most people in our sample were exposed to these arguments for and against 1098.

Since partisanship may have a direct effect on preferences on 1098 and also condition the acceptance of specific arguments on 1098, it is important to consider pro and con arguments. The Defeat 1098 campaign made two main arguments to counter the claims made by proponents of the ballot measure. The first argument suggested that if 1098 were passed, the income tax would eventually be expanded to lower tax brackets. After the first two years of the newly implemented income tax on the rich, Washington legislators would have the ability to extend the tax to other income groups with a majority vote (Woodward 2010). This was a clear attempt to blunt the pro-redistribution argument since opponents argued that all taxpayers would eventually have to pay state income tax, which has long been unpopular among Washington voters (Garber 2010). The other objection to 1098 was based on the potential negative effects of the tax on economic growth. The Defeat 1098 campaign argued that establishing an income tax on the rich would discourage new business owners from moving to the state, and that a new tax on the wealthy would further slow an already struggling economy. Opponents of 1098 often referred to the proposition as a "job-killing tax" that would hurt the economy (e.g., see La Corte 2010; Robison 2010). It is clear that redistribution was one of the highlighted dimensions of the policy debate.

This brief overview provides the types of issue frames and arguments used in the debate over the proposed income tax.[7] Based on our discussion in the previous section we expect that lower-income voters and voters more concerned about economic inequality would be more likely to support Proposition 1098. In a high-information environment such as this, even relatively inattentive voters may successfully link their interests and values to congruent policy positions. However, work by Bartels (2005; 2008) and Lupia et al. (2007) shows that attention is important in aligning one's economic status and views on inequality with preferences on redistributive taxation. Therefore, we also examine how attentiveness may condition the ability of voters to link their self-interest and broader values and preferences with congruent tax-increase positions.

Although the campaigns for each side of the proposal were not directly supported by the Democratic or Republican parties, individuals are often able to connect ballot measures to the party they identify with, which allows them to vote according to their underlying political preferences (Lupia 1994; Bowler and Donovan 1998). Thus we expect that Democrats would have been more supportive of 1098. In addition to this direct effect on preferences, partisanship may filter competing arguments (frames) about the proposed tax policy. Therefore, we also examine how partisanship conditions the effect of one's economic position, attention, and attitudes toward inequality on support for 1098. Because inequality was not the only dimension of this policy or debate, we control for how important a variety of other issues were to voters. Note that thinking an issue is important does not imply a directional preference, and indeed, we consider whether partisanship may condition the effect of issue importance on support for Proposition 1098.

To test the expectations discussed above, we use data from a random digit-dialed telephone survey gathered on a sample of likely Washington State voters. The survey was conducted by the Washington Poll (University of Washington) in October 2010. The survey asked the following:

> Now I'm going to read a statewide ballot initiative that will appear on the November ballot: Initiative 1098 would institute an income tax on individuals earning more than $200,000 or households earning more than $400,000, and reduce state property taxes by 20 percent and also reduce the business and occupation tax and direct the increased revenues to education and health.

Respondents were then asked whether they voted (if they voted early) or planned on voting (if they had not yet voted) yes or no. In the following analyses, this question is used as our dependent variable, where 1 indicates support for 1098 and 0 indicates opposition to the proposal. The format of this question also ensures that all individuals surveyed would be familiar with the basic redistributive nature of 1098 even if they were not familiar with all competing arguments.

Although the survey data used in this analysis does not provide direct measures of the kinds of elite cues respondents were exposed to, most survey participants reported following the debates related to the 1098 campaigns. When asked how much attention they paid to information about the proposal, 11% of our sample said they did not pay close attention, meaning almost 90% did follow the debate at least slightly closely (with moderately closely, very closely, or extremely closely being the other options). The variable *Attention* (coded 1 for extremely closely or very closely and 0 for all others) measures how much attention individuals paid to the debate over this policy.[8] Forty-three percent of the sample was coded as high attention. Though attention may have a direct effect on support for 1098, we are mostly concerned with how it conditions the relationships between our main variables of theoretical interest and support for 1098. Based on previous research, we expect that high-attention individuals will be more likely to choose the "correct" position given their self-interest and ideology.

We examine the effect of attitudes toward inequality, partisanship, and personal income (proxy for economic self-interest) on support for 1098, and whether more attention to the debate may strengthen the effect of these variables. The survey includes measures for each of these concepts. Respondents were asked whether the growing difference in the incomes of the rich and poor is a good thing, bad thing, or neither good nor bad.[9] Those who think that income inequality is a "bad thing" are coded as 1 and all others are coded as 0 (variable *Inequality Bad*). We expect Democrats to be more supportive of Proposition 1098, and *Party Identification* is measured using a three-point scale with Democrat = 3, independent = 2, and Republican = 1.

Though almost everyone in our sample would be exempt from the tax simply because very few individuals earn over $200,000 per year, the wealthier may have a greater expectation of eventually earning over $200,000 a year or fear being the next group taxed. The survey originally measured income using a seven-point scale. Given the importance of economic interest, we measure income three different ways and estimate separate models with the three measures of income. A variable *Lower Income* is used to determine how economic self-interest may influence views toward redistribution. We use a dummy variable indicating whether respondent's family incomes are below $60,000 coded 1, with family incomes over $60,000 coded 0. We selected this income range because it approximates the Washington State median family income and theoretical models predict greatest support for redistribution among those with incomes below the median (Meltzer and Richard 1981). To make sure our results are not dependent on how we account for self-interest, we also measure income using three categories, with two binary variables for low income ($40,000 or less) and high income ($100,000 or more) with middle incomes ($40,000–$100,000) as the reference category. Finally, we measure family income using five categories, with binary variables for low income ($40,000 or less), middle ($40,000–$60,000), high ($80,000–$100,000) and very high ($100,000 or more), with income in the $60,000–$80,000 category as the reference. As noted, we also consider how the effect of one's income group and belief that inequality is bad may be conditioned by attention to the ballot measure campaign and party identification.

Because the redistributive aspects of the policy were only one dimension on which this policy was debated, we control for individuals' concerns about other issue areas affected by this proposition. We are uncertain of the direction of the effect of a concern about specific issues because a concern for an issue like taxes could indicate that someone thinks they are either too high or too low. And as we will see, the effect of a concern for the economy can lead different individuals to have different preferences on Proposition 1098. To measure whether respondents believed these were important issues, we use answers to an open-ended question about the most important issues.[10] Since education, healthcare, taxes, and the economy were all discussed in the context of the ballot measure, we consider how a belief that any of those issues was most important influenced support for 1098 by using a series of dummy variables. Because they are open-ended, these questions do not necessarily tap what was considered to be the most important factor affecting support for 1098, and thus these variables also control for broader attitudes and predispositions.[11] Finally, we include controls for government approval, ideology (conservative or liberal), education, age, home ownership (because of the property tax cut in the bill), and gender.[12] With our binary dependent variable all models are estimated using logistic regression.

SUPPORT FOR 1098: INEQUALITY, ECONOMIC SELF-INTEREST, AND PARTISANSHIP

We begin our discussion by noting the differences in support for 1098 depending on party, position in the income distribution, and views on inequality, which leads to the initial conclusion that citizens can translate these factors into congruent tax policy positions. What is striking in this bivariate context is the very large difference in support for redistributive taxation based whether one thinks inequality is bad, a 40-percentage-point difference (61.4% versus 21%). The difference for the income groups is in the expected direction, but much smaller, at around a five-percentage-point gap (49.0 for lower income versus 44.1 for the wealthier). However, the largest difference in support of 1098 is found among adherents of the different parties; 74% of Democrats supported it, while only 18% of Republicans did. As noted above, we are interested in the additive effects of these variables on support for redistributive taxation (shown in appendix table B.7), as well as how these effects differ based on attention to the competing 1098 campaigns (shown in appendix table B.8) and an individual's party identification (shown in appendix table B.9), since attention to an issue may help people better align their preferences with policy positions, and party can also condition receptivity to different arguments and frames.

Regardless of how personal income is measured, we see clear evidence that people who think inequality is bad and people in the lower income groups are more likely to favor raising taxes on the wealthy; the effects are positive and statistically significant. Interestingly, our results clearly show that upper-middle- and high-income voters, with incomes of $60,000–$100,000 and up, were not less likely to vote for the ballot measure, but those with incomes of $40,000 or less were significantly more likely to vote yes (and those in the $40,000–$60,000 range were more supportive, though the *p*-value was just above .10). Thus, the effect of income does not appear to be linear. But an important contribution of this study is that poorer people do vote for higher taxes on the wealthy (when there is an informed debate) based on their economic self-interest. Democratic partisanship is also significant predictor of support in all of our models.

Figure 5.2 graphs the change in the probability of favoring redistributive taxation varying attitudes about inequality, personal income, and partisanship. Holding other variables in the model constant at mean values, varying attitudes about inequality from "not bad" to a "bad thing" increased the probability of supporting Proposition 1098 by .20, or 20 percentage points, whereas moving from a not low-income citizen to the lower-income group increased support for the ballot measure by 15 percentage points. These are independent effects that, combined, would increase the probability of supporting the tax proposal by about a third. However, the influence of economic self-interest and attitudes about inequality are comparatively smaller than the effect of party identification. Democrats were more than 30 percentage points more likely to favor the initiative than Republicans, with other factors held constant. Since none of the 95% confidence intervals cross zero, we can be confident that attitudes about inequality, self-interest, and partisanship had significant effects on support for the ballot measure. These findings hold if we control for a range of issue concerns, homeownership, and demographics.

Economic Interest, Inequality, and Party Conditioned on Attention

Our analysis also provides estimates of our key independent variables of theoretical interest—economic self-interest, perceptions of inequality, and party identification—when conditioned on attention to the 1098 campaign using the binary measure of income (see appendix table B.8). The results show that, on average, more attention is associated with greater opposition to 1098. This is consistent with findings that voters tend to be risk averse when voting on economic initiatives (Bowler and Donovan 1994) and that opposition arguments and spending may be more effective than those in support of the initiative (Gerber 1999). However, high-attention,

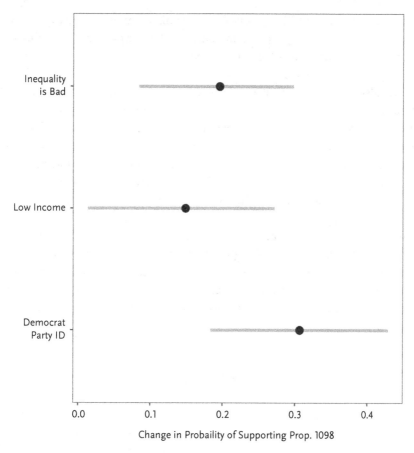

Figure 5.2: Change in the Probability of Supporting Redistributive Taxation
Note: Change in the probability of supporting Proposition 1098 when changing attitudes about inequality ("not bad" to "bad thing"), individual income ("not low" to "low income"), and party ("Republican" to "Democrat") with other variables in appendix table B.7, model 1 held constant at mean values. Bars represent 95% confidence intervals.

low-income voters were not significantly more or less likely to favor 1098 than their less informed, lower-income counterparts. Similarly, individuals who think inequality is bad are more likely to favor 1098, but more attention did not significantly strengthen this relationship. These findings are, on the one hand, surprising in that more attention can be expected to lead to the "correct" position. However, the findings are consistent with our argument that when policy proposals are straightforward and the distributional consequences are clear, it is easier even for people who do not pay close attention to link their interests and attitudes to congruent policy preferences. In contrast, increased attention strengthened the effects of partisanship, with informed Democrats more likely to favor the measure and Republicans less likely. This finding confirms previous research that partisans are able to link positions on officially nonpartisan proposals to the "correct" party, but it appears to require a bit more attention than in openly partisan debates.

We also see evidence that which issues voters thought were most important influenced opinions on Proposition 1098. Individuals who are mostly concerned about the issue of taxation were less likely to support the ballot measure. This result suggests that, on average, the Defeat 1098 campaign's decision to focus on the possibility of income taxes expanding to all Washington residents was a salient factor for voters who were concerned about taxes. Respondents stating that the economy is the most important issue do not appear to be for or against 1098. Both campaigns focused on the influence the new income tax would have on the economy, with proponents of Initiative 1098 arguing for a positive effect and opponents suggesting the economy would be negatively influenced by the tax. Individuals concerned about education were more likely to support 1098, though it was not quite significant at the .05 level. Concerns about healthcare did not have any significant effect.

Economic Interest and Inequality Conditioned on Party

Given the centrality of partisanship in contemporary American politics and in attitudes toward Proposition 1098, and the way that party identification can filter information, we next examine whether the strength of relationships between a concern for inequality and one's economic position varied by party identification (see appendix table B.9). Thinking inequality is bad was positively related to the likelihood of support for all groups. The effect of one's income group was not conditioned by party identification but, for Democrats thinking that inequality was bad, led to much higher levels of support than for independents or Republicans. Figure 5.3 shows the conditional effect of believing that inequality is bad on support for Proposition 1098 by partisanship.

Finally, we test whether arguments (frames) made by the campaigns for and against 1098 were more effective with Democratic or Republican partisans. We see that the interactions between believing taxes are the most important issue and partisanship and the economy issue and partisanship are also positive and significant. Because even Democrats who were most concerned with taxes were less supportive of 1098, it seems that for many people a concern with taxes is synonymous with a concern that taxes are too high. But the difference in a concern about taxes in reducing support

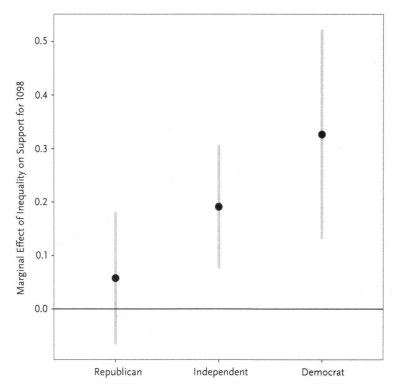

Figure 5.3: Marginal Effects of Attitudes about Inequality on Support for Proposition 1098 by Partisanship

Note: Estimates are based on the model results presented in appendix table B.9. Bars represent 95% confidence intervals.

for 1098 between Democrats and Republicans shows that campaign arguments/frames were viewed through partisan lenses.

Figure 5.4 plots the estimated marginal effects of considering that taxes and the economy (those issues with significant partisan interaction terms) were the most important issues on support for 1098, by party. We see in the top panel that people who thought taxes are the most important issue were less supportive of 1098, regardless of party. In line with our expectations, however, we see that the negative effect of this variable is much smaller for Democrats. Comparing those who believed taxation was the most important issue decreased the probability of support for 1098 by .15 for Democrats and .22 for Republicans, all else equal. Results for viewing the economy as the most important issue are even more striking. Republicans who thought that the economy was the most important issue were less supportive (30% decrease), while Democrats who thought it was the most important issue were more supportive (20% increase),

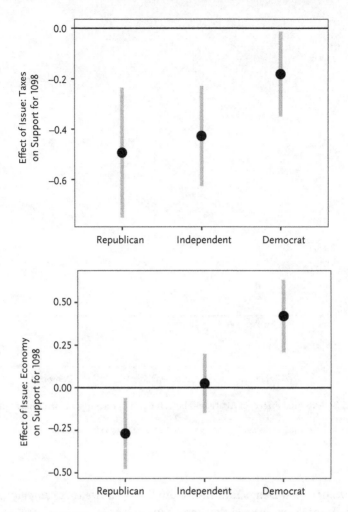

Figure 5.4: Marginal Effects of Issue Importance on Support for Proposition 1098 by Partisanship

Note: Estimates are based on the model results presented in appendix table B.9. Bars represent 95% confidence intervals.

reflecting the powerful effect that party has on mediating elite messages, and ultimately redistributive preferences. Thus, framing the policy in terms of the economy was salient among members of both parties, but each group reached different conclusions about the policy's economic effects, demonstrating the important role of partisan filtering in such debates.

BROADER LESSONS FOR TAX REFORM: CALIFORNIA'S
PROPOSITION 30 AND THE CONTEXT OF STATE INCOME TAXES

We focused on how individual attitudes shapes views on tax increases on the wealthy in Washington, but our findings have implications well beyond this single state. Progressive tax increases have been on the ballot or are in the signature-gathering stage in many states. In Massachusetts, liberal activists are attempting to get a personal income tax increase on the ballot, while in Michigan groups are attempting to place a corporate tax hike on the ballot. In Colorado, Proposition 66, which would have replaced the flat income tax with a progressive tax increase, was placed on the ballot in 2015. Like Washington's 1098, Proposition 66 was defeated. As noted, even where these tax initiatives are defeated, they focus the public and policymakers on the possibility of tax increases and may lead to less "extreme" tax increase proposals in the future even where they go down to defeat (Gerber 1999).

At this point one of the few successful progressive tax increases enacted via initiative was enacted in California. California is often a bellwether in tax policymaking, and the initiative process is central to this bellwether status. After the failure of Proposition 1098, tax increases on the wealthy seemed doomed for failure. But just two years after the defeat of 1098, California voters enacted Proposition 30, which did the following:

- Increased marginal tax rates for seven years: by 1% for income between $250,000 and $300,000; 2% for income between $300,000 and $500,000; and 3% for income over $500,000 (twice these amounts for couples)
- Increased the state sales tax by ¼ cent for four years
- Used revenue to fund public safety, K–12 education, and community colleges

This constituted an approximately 30% tax increase on earnings above $1 million. At the time, California was facing a multi-billion-dollar budget deficit, which would have required large cuts in public services, especially higher education. The California state public employee unions and the California Democratic Party were the main supporters of the measure.

Proposition 30 was opposed by the Small Business Action Committee and the Howard Jarvis Taxpayers Association (Soley-Cerro 2012), the same organization that had sponsored Proposition 13 three decades earlier. Opponents argued the measure did not reform the process that led to large deficits in the first place, that there was no guarantee that the money would be spent on education since the legislature could simply shift different funds out of education, and that the money will be wasted, as in the past. The groups against the measure also argued that Proposition 30 only increased taxes on the very wealthy since only couples with income above $500,000 would pay additional taxes (or individuals earning more than $250,000), so the merely affluent were getting off too easily (KCET 2012). It is notable that even opponents did not generally claim that the wealthy paid too much in taxes, which would likely not attract much sympathy after the financial crisis. Interestingly, big-business groups (like the California Chamber of Commerce) that often oppose tax increases stayed neutral. Some large firms actually endorsed the measure, including Bank of America, AT&T, and Kaiser Permanente, citing the need to invest in the state's schools to produce an educated workforce (Buchanan 2012).

The public was provided with an opportunity to become familiar with the arguments for and against Proposition 30 with a well-funded ad campaign. Data gathered from the National Institute on Money in State Politics show that Proposition 30's supporters raised over $72 million dollars, while opponents of the measure donated over $76 million, amounts that add up to almost $4 per voter; this is more than was spent per voter in recent presidential elections in the state. As we have mentioned, proponents and opponents of Washington's Proposition 1098 spent nearly $2 per voter. Both ballot contests were characterized by greater information and more extensive mass-media campaigns than during national debates over the Bush tax cuts in 2001.

Proposition 30 passed in the 2012 November election with 55.4% of the vote. Advocates of Proposition 30 seemed to have learned from the failure of Proposition 1098 and the general unpopularity of tax increases, and structured the policy accordingly. First, the tax increase was temporary though not short term. This helped to reduce the opposition to tax increases. Second, the additional revenue was earmarked for specific, popular programs. Third, provisions included in Proposition 30 were intended to avoid a common criticism of tax increases—that the government will waste the money and that tax increases allow the government to continue the loose spending ways that drive fiscal problems in the first place. Proposition 30 prevented new money from being spent on administration (as opposed to instruction, for example) and required independent auditing of how money was spent to ensure this requirement was being met. Voters can go online and track the expenditures of the Proposition 30 revenue (http://trackprop30.ca.gov/). More recently, the tax increase was extended for another 12 years through 2028 via Proposition 55, which was approved by the voters with 63% of the vote in November 2016.[13] Thus, this tax increase has proven very successful and highly popular. Considering this outcome, other liberal states with the initiative may be likely to pursue such plans in the future.

We have argued that the use of the initiative to increase taxes on top income earners is a relatively new phenomenon that could reverse the trend started several decades ago in which citizens used the initiative process to cut taxes. Of course, we will know much more about the direction of state tax policy in the years to come. But in this section we briefly consider whether cross-state variation in income tax rates is related to some of the state factors that have been central to our study to this point—for instance, the public's awareness of inequality and the public's policy mood. The relative stability of top income tax rates in the states noted at the outset of this chapter (see table 5.1) implies that change in this area is difficult (which is evident from the case of Washington's Proposition 1098) and also suggests that the recent expansion of income inequality has not led to increases in taxes in most states.

However, against a backdrop of general tax cutting, if states do not reduce their relatively high income taxes, this would provide evidence that attitudes toward inequality and other factors have prevented tax increases. It is notoriously difficult to determine why things do not happen. But if states more aware of inequality did not cut taxes during this period, we should observe that variation *between* the states can be at least partially explained by state characteristics that we have argued are important when considering how changes in inequality have influenced state policymaking. While we are unable to examine every potential tax change in every state in the same detailed manner with which we studied Washington's proposed tax increase, we can use the aggregate measures of state characteristics that were introduced in earlier chapters to make inferences about why some states have more progressive tax policy than others. For instance, our measure of the public's awareness of growing inequality can be used to approximate a general concern about inequality, and we can use measures of the public's policy mood and the ideology of state governments to get a sense of the political resources available in the states to make progressive policy changes.[14]

Several straightforward bivariate analyses of state top income tax rates and several other variables are presented in figure 5.5. Since, as we showed toward the beginning of this chapter, top tax rates do not vary much over time, we examine the state averages for each variable between 1987 and 2012 (these are the years our measure of inequality awareness is available). For the most part, the state factors we assess here are associated with top

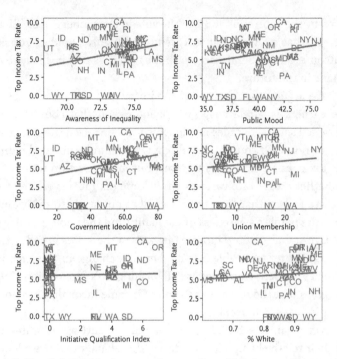

Figure 5.5: The Relationship between Average State Top Income Taxes and State Characteristics

tax rates as we would expect. States with greater awareness of inequality, those with more liberal publics and governments, and states with higher union membership all tend to have maintained higher top income tax rates.[15] Indeed, the state awareness of inequality has the strongest bivariate relationship (i.e., steepest sloped line) of any of the variables. States with the initiative do not appear to have higher tax rates, but, as we discussed earlier in this chapter, the presence of the initiative is not expected to lead to more progressive policy on its own, and these tax increases initiatives are just starting to appear on ballots.[16]

CONCLUSION

In order for the public's concern about inequality to result in policy change, we must observe that voters link their concerns about inequality and economic self-interest to congruent policy positions. On taxes, we should see that lower-income voters and those concerned about inequality are more supportive of higher taxes on the wealthy. Washington State's Proposition

1098 allowed us to examine these questions. And we find that in the context of this debate, which made the effects of this policy clear, each of these factors influenced support for this tax policy. It seems that increasing taxes on the wealthy would be an obvious response to increasing inequality, and theoretical models predict such policies in times of growing inequality. But Proposition 1098 was actually defeated, and handily at that.

This reflects that partisanship is a critical determinant of support for specific policies in today's environment—Republicans and independents (who are more disposed to support the arguments against the policy) were overwhelmingly against 1098. But an important subset of Democrats was also against it. In particular, a concern about taxation in general led both Democrats and Republicans to oppose 1098, though it had less of an effect on reducing support among Democrats. In addition, voters in direct democracy elections tend to be risk-averse (Bowler and Donovan 1994; 1998), so spending by opponents of a proposition increases the likelihood that citizens will prefer the status quo and vote no on Election Day, while proponents' spending is less likely to change the outcome (Gerber 1999; Bowler, Donovan, and Tolbert 1998). Furthermore, initiatives are less likely to pass during recessions (Bowler and Donovan 1998). All of these factors contributed to the defeat of Proposition 1098, with 65% voting no.

On the other hand, we find solid evidence that even before Occupy, many citizens were able to link their attitudes toward inequality and economic self-interest to specific redistributive policy preferences. This probably reflects that the elite debate surrounding Proposition 1098, as well as the quite simple structure of the policy proposal itself, made it easier for the public to translate broad attitudes toward inequality and their own economic self-interest into consistent policy preferences. Our research shows that if tax policy is simply structured and redistribution is a central theme of the policy debate, at least some citizens can make better-informed decisions that are in line with their attitudes and interests. The results provide evidence in favor of experimental findings that self-interest becomes important when the personal costs and benefits of a particular policy proposal are prominent frames in the debate surrounding the policy (Chong, Citrin, and Conley 2001). The results also challenge a general assumption in the literature that economic self-interest and attitudes about inequality do not influence preferences on redistributive taxation. While Proposition 1098 failed, the results suggest that future attempts to raise taxes on the wealthy may succeed if they are openly debated in redistributive terms. Because Washington does not have any income tax, enacting an entirely new tax was difficult. But in states that already have an income tax merely raising tax rates should be substantially easier, as in California.

Even in defeat, initiatives can put issues on the agenda in other states where voters and activists take note. Indeed, in the 2012 election California voters adopted Proposition 30, which raised taxes on the wealthy to avoid major budget cuts to government programs. This is substantively important for residents of California, who as a result of Proposition 20 do not have to experience dramatic cuts in government services, but it is also symbolically important because California sparked the antitax revolt of the late 1970s with Proposition 13. Just as the states led the tax revolt in the 1970s, a handful of states are beginning to pursue tax increases on the wealthy. Federal policymakers can also learn from Proposition 30. Though the initiative is not a tool available in Washington, DC, the specific structure of tax increases can affect their popularity, which can in turn affect the odds that elected officials will support them. Admittedly, any tax increases are highly unlikely while Republicans control Congress.

Though tax increases on the wealthy are likely to spread among the states and even localities, there are likely to be limits on the use of high taxes on the wealthy to address growing inequality, simply because this is such a highly partisan issue. And because many states lack the initiative and have conservative governments and voters, this will not be an equally viable approach to addressing inequality throughout the country. Tax increases are unpopular among conservatives and Republicans, and information about the effect of tax cuts is filtered through a partisan lens, making it hard to convince individuals who would objectively economically benefit from tax increases on the wealthy that they should support them. This is not the case with other policies that will lessen inequality, some of which elicit bipartisan mass support. In the next chapters we examine how state policymaking on the minimum wage and the earned income tax credit have responded to action and inaction in federal policymaking, and how the initiative and other factors have influenced their adoption.

CHAPTER 6

State Responses to Federal Inaction and Growing Inequality

The Case of the Minimum Wage

Using a salient instance of the consideration of new taxes on the rich, we have shown the importance of public attitudes about inequality for tax policy preferences at the individual level. In this chapter we shift back toward a look at aggregate data in the 50 states, and we also consider policy changes that are not likely to be limited to the most liberal states. Furthermore, we consider policies that influence the distribution of income in a way that is different from, but complementary to, increasing taxes on the wealthiest Americans. Instead of focusing on the aspect of redistribution that takes resources from the rich to give to the poor and middle class, we look at government programs designed to bolster the incomes of those at the bottom of the income distribution by examining state minimum wage laws and state earned income tax credit (EITC) programs, in chapters 6 and 7, respectively.

To understand state responses to growing economic inequality amid the broad backdrop of federal inaction, these policies are particularly ideal to study for two reasons. The first is that both policies have a clear influence on the distribution of income. Discussed in more detail below, minimum wage laws influence the market income (i.e., preredistribution) of workers, that is, they are market-conditioning policies. The pretax incomes of low-wage workers—those at the bottom of the income distribution—are improved without using public funds to supplement the incomes of those with low earnings. Unsurprisingly, then, the declining value of the US minimum wage over the past several decades has been associated with the expansion of economic inequality (Lee 1999; Slonimczyk and Skott 2012). This means that increasing the minimum wage is one way to reduce economic inequality. The EITC, which we examine in the next chapter, also boosts the incomes of low-wage workers, but does so through more traditional redistribution, and thus affects the post-tax, post-transfer income distribution.

The second reason we focus on the minimum wage and EITC is that both policies exist at the federal level, yet states share policy authority with the federal government, and a number of states have passed their own versions of these laws that expand on federal policy. Although the states do not have many options to reduce the benefits provided through the national minimum wage and federal EITC program, states that believe the benefits are not generous enough can pass state legislation that sets their minimum wage above the federal level, or they can create their own EITC program at the state level that increases the amount of aid offered to low-wage earners.

One major difference between the EITC and the minimum wage is that the latter was pioneered by the states during the Progressive Era and later adopted by the federal government during the New Deal era, while the EITC emerged out of the period of federal government activism in the decades after World War II, when the federal government took the lead in reducing inequality and poverty, and in expanding opportunity. The EITC, therefore, allows us to examine how states have built off of federal policies designed to reduce inequality in this period of relative federal inaction, while the minimum wage allows us to understand how states continue to use a policy that they have pioneered in these circumstances.

In this chapter we examine how a public awareness of inequality, government liberalism, and the initiative shaped the adoption of higher minimum wages in the states. Because the minimum wage is jointly controlled by the federal government and state governments, we can also explicitly model how federal failures to raise the minimum wage to keep even with the rate of inflation influence state choices regarding raising the minimum wage. As in previous chapters, we find that a public awareness of inequality is associated with more activity to reduce inequality, in this case higher minimum wages. We also find that liberal state governments are associated with higher minimum wages, identifying one policy mechanism that translates state government leftism into a flatter income distribution, which we observed in chapter 4. In addition, we find that the initiative is associated with growing state minimum wages, especially as the length of time since the last federal minimum wage increase grows. While at the elite level there is polarization on the issue of the minimum wage, it is broadly popular among the public. Thus, the initiative can be used to bring government policy in line with overwhelming public preferences for a higher minimum wage, even as polarization and Republican control of Congress prevent federal minimum wage increases.

THE FEDERALIZED MINIMUM WAGE

The minimum wage is a policy that is "federalized," or in other words, jointly controlled by the federal and state government. The history of the minimum wage policy is similar to many of the other policies intended to mitigate the threats associated with modern industrial capitalism, like old-age pensions and unemployment insurance. As we discuss in chapter 2, many such policies were first advanced by the states during the Progressive Era, and only later adopted by the federal government, typically not until the Great Depression of the 1930s.

The Progressive movement provided the basic philosophical foundation for minimum wages. A central tenet of Progressivism was the concept of the "public good," which suggested that we should consider the community as a whole when assessing whether social outcomes are justifiable. Progressives recognized the value of individual achievement and its ability to lead to satisfactory political and economic outcomes, but they also believed in the necessity of distinguishing a more general public good from the simple aggregation of individual circumstances (Kloppenberg 1986). In the context of the changing economy during this time period, this meant that collective economic gains brought on by industrialization were not automatically ideal if certain groups in society were suffering. This does not imply that Progressives were necessarily hostile toward industrialization or capitalism more broadly. In fact, they largely accepted the newly forming industrial society, but they also believed that government action was required to preserve the market (e.g., by eliminating monopolies) and to make it more humane (Kloppenberg 1986).

The incredibly low wages earned by some in the industrial economy was a cause for concern to many Progressive reformers (Leonard 2015), and the minimum wage was advanced as one solution to this problem. The minimum wage offers a straightforward way to improve the well-being of those who were not benefiting from the newly forming economy, and it stems from the view that all working members of a community should have their basic needs met through the support of a standard living wage. How to define a "standard wage" was not easily settled then, and is still debated today, but Progressives were able to borrow from Australia's minimum wage standards—which were the world's first, established in 1896—to demonstrate that a large number of Americans fell below these basic measures of need (Waltman 2000).

Though today we tend to think of unions as supporters of a minimum wage, labor leaders were initially uncertain whether to support minimum wages, as they wanted such questions to be reserved for collective bargaining, and were concerned that minimum wages might function as maximum wages (Grossman 1978). The women's movement played a key role in the early advancement of the minimum wage because manufacturing sweatshops were largely staffed by women. This led to the formation of numerous women's rights groups that lobbied for a minimum wage (Aktas 2015). The women's movement was central to the development of the minimum wage in part because of the legal environment during this time period. Although the Supreme Court was generally hostile to labor regulation, in 1908 the Court upheld an Oregon law that set a ceiling on the number of hours women could work in a day. Progressive leaders viewed the Court's apparent patriarchal leanings as an opportunity to further expand workers' rights through a minimum wage policy that would apply to women. Indeed, in 1912 Massachusetts passed the first minimum wage law in the United States, which covered women and working children (Aktas 2015). Women's groups and Progressive activists played key roles in advancing minimum wage laws.

Following the lead of Massachusetts, eight states adopted minimum wage laws in 1913, and six more passed wage minimums over the next 10 years (Whitaker et al. 2012). The US Congress joined the state minimum wage movement in 1918 and adopted a policy for the District of Columbia, over which Congress has legal authority. These new laws did not go unchallenged, however, and intense pressure from business interests led a number of states to repeal their wage standards in the 1920s. This backlash, along with the Supreme Court's decision to invalidate DC's law, left only a few states with minimum wage policies in place by 1930, and these existing regulations were often weakly enforced (Waltman 2000). Nevertheless, these minimum wage fights showed that such policies were relatively easily implemented and clearly spurred the federal government to consider a minimum wage. Finally, in the midst of the Great Depression and New Deal, in1936 the Supreme Court ruled that Washington State's general minimum wage law was constitutional, clearing the path for several other states and the federal government to enact such laws with the knowledge that they would not be struck down by the courts at some later date (Waltman 2000). By this time, most of organized labor was on board with the idea of minimum wage legislation (Grossman 1978).

Following this ruling, the federal government pursued a general minimum wage law for the entire country. The national Fair Labor Standards Act (FLSA) of 1938 established a federal minimum wage that all states must abide by, for the types of employees covered by the FLSA (Tritch 2014). Several states never adopted a minimum wage law, and the minimum wage in these states is governed solely by the FLSA. Some other states with a minimum wage law set the minimum wage equal to the federal government's. Some states set their minimum wage above the federal government's through periodic increases. Other states have increases above the federal minimum wage that automatically follow a federal minimum wage increase, while others still are indexed to increases in the cost of living or general wages, which is a fairly recent innovation in US minimum wage policy. The result is that federal government action on the minimum wage is important for establishing overall minimum wage policy in the United States. However, as we will see, states do have quite a bit of discretion over the minimum wage, and they have been using it to combat growing inequality and sluggish wage growth for the working poor in recent years.

During the time period of decreasing income inequality and a federal government focus on reducing poverty between World War II and roughly 1980, the federal government routinely expanded both the numbers and types of workers covered under the FLSA and the amount of the minimum wage to keep up with, and at times rise faster than, the rate of inflation. From 1950 to 1980 the federal minimum wage was raised 12 times, or once every 2.5 years (https://www.dol.gov/whd/minwage/chart.htm). Initially, the FLSA minimum wage provision covered only employees engaged in interstate commerce or production of goods for interstate commerce. But over the decades the types of employees have expanded considerably, so that by 1990 approximately 70%–80% of the workforce was covered by the FLSA minimum wage (Volscho 2005).[1] Despite the increasing coverage of the FLSA minimum wage provisions, a substantial percentage of employees remains uncovered, which is why state minimum wage policy is still important even when the federal government routinely increases the minimum wage. At times when the federal government is not routinely raising the minimum wage, state laws become even more important because they are a means by which the vast majority of minimum wage workers and other low-wage workers may receive a pay raise.

As American politics shifted to the right, the federal government failed to raise the minimum wage to keep even with inflation after the 1970s (Bartels 2008). This reflected a more general preference for less government intervention in the economy among certain scholars and politicians, who, supported by industries that rely on low-wage workers, argued that the minimum wage did more harm than good. Of course, workers at the bottom of the income distribution will experience wage increases when the minimum wage is raised, but economists have debated whether increasing the minimum wage decreases overall employment for "unskilled" workers, which may decrease their average wages if the effects are bad enough (Bartels 2008). A growing literature, however, suggests minimum wage laws play an important role in boosting incomes for low-income families, and that typical increases in the minimum wage barely have a discernible effect on employment (Card and Krueger 1995; Lee 1999; Morris and Western 1999; Schmitt 2013).

Another common argument against raising the minimum wage is that minimum wage workers are often teenagers who do not really need the money, and thus the minimum wage imposes costs on business, with little benefit for wage earners who are supporting themselves. But studies examining increases in the federal minimum wage in 1990 and 1991 show that individuals influenced by the minimum wage are often the sole income providers for their families (Card and Krueger 1995; Morris and Western 1999). This suggests that minimum wage policy is consequential for the overall economic well-being of many families, and not simply increasing wages for secondary sources of income. In terms of wage equity, this same research estimates that the minimum wage expansion in 1990 decreased the growth of income inequality in the 1980s by 30%. The overall effect of the federal government's stagnant minimum wage policy has been to reduce the real earnings of low-income individuals (Bartels 2008; Morris and Western 1999; Schmitt 2009).

Overall, then, the typical minimum wage increase has minimal negative effects on employment while boosting the pay of low-wage workers who need the money. Despite the lack of evidence supporting the idea that the minimum wage has a negative influence on the economy, this belief is widespread within the Republican Party. As one Republican senator stated in the buildup to the eventual failure of a bill introduced to increase the minimum wage in 2014, "Most of the Republicans are pretty united on this. It's bad for the economy. It's bad for jobs" (Bolton 2014). Bartels's (2008) detailed analysis of the partisan politics surrounding US minimum wage policy suggests this sentiment is historically common among conservative politicians. In addition, while business is powerful within both parties, it is safe to say that industries that rely on low-wage workers have more influence within the Republican Party, as unions provide a counterbalance to these interests within the Democratic Party.

The antipathy toward minimum wage laws by conservatives and business groups has led to a lack of increases in the minimum wage by the federal government because these actors have gained more power since the late 1970s. In contrast with the period from the 1950s through the 1970s, when the minimum wage was increased once every 2.5 years on average, from 1981 to 2006 the federal minimum wage was raised only five times, or once every five years—half as often as it was between 1950 and 1980. The minimum wage increased in 1981 (before Ronald Reagan was inaugurated), 1990, 1991, 1995, and 1996. With unified Republican control of government after the 2000 election, the minimum wage was not increased again until the Democrats regained control of the Congress in 2007. Thus there have been long spells when the federal government did not increase the minimum wage at all, which was unprecedented before recent decades.

This failure to increase the minimum wage alongside growth in the cost of living means that the real value of the minimum wage, that is, what it can buy in goods and services, has declined dramatically over time. Figure 6.1 provides an image of the trajectory of federal minimum wage policy in the postwar era (https://www.dol.gov/whd/minwage/chart.htm) with the minimum wage adjusted for the inflation rate facing urban consumers. Looking at the figure, it is clear that from the late 1940s through the late 1960s the minimum wage rose faster than the rate of inflation. The value of the minimum wage peaked in 1968. Despite a number of minimum wage increases in the 1970s, high inflation led to a declining real value of the minimum wage during this decade. But a dramatic decline in the real value of the minimum wage is seen during the 1980s, as the federal government did not even attempt to keep it even with inflation. The value was partly restored by minimum wage increases in the early and mid-1990s, before again plummeting in the late 1990s and early 2000s as the federal government again failed to increase the minimum wage.

Overall, from 1979 to 2006 the value of the minimum wage (in inflation-adjusted dollars) declined by approximately one-third, taking a great deal of money out of the pockets of low-wage workers. The minimum wage increases after the Democrats regained the control of Congress following the 2006 election did not restore the value of the minimum wage to its 1970 levels. Even with the most recent increase to $7.25 in 2009, the value of the minimum wage is considerably lower than it was in 1968 (about $10.90 in 2014 dollars). Even prior during the Obama administration there did not seem to be much political support in Washington, DC, for raising the minimum wage back to late 1960s levels, despite the president's call for raising the minimum wage substantially in his 2013 State of the Union Address. And while relatively few workers earn the minimum wage, increases in the minimum wage may have a "ripple effect" on the pay of other low-wage employees who earn just above the minimum wage (Card

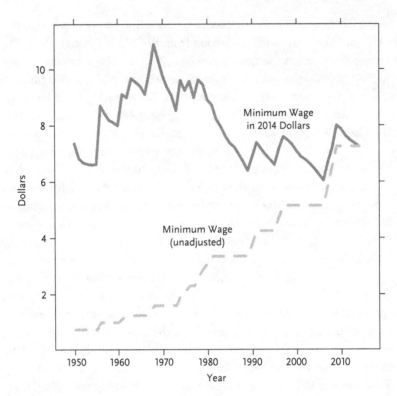

Figure 6.1: The Value of the US Minimum Wage in Real and Nominal Dollars
Source: US Department of Labor.

and Krueger 1995). Thus, the minimum wage has important consequences for economic inequality since a lower minimum wage reduces the income of many workers at the lower end of the income scale. Research has shown that the decline of the minimum wage has contributed to growing inequality in recent decades (Kelly and Witko 2012; Lee 1999; Slonimczyk and Skott 2012).

The failure of the federal government to increase the minimum wage as inflation ate into its value is a perfect example of what Hacker and Pierson (2010) call policy "drift." Rather than through action, by inaction, the federal government lessened the value of the minimum wage, and in the process worsened inequality. But it would be incorrect to view the failure to raise the minimum wage as the result of federal inaction alone. Very hard work and skilled argumentation by a small number of conservative ideologues and businesses that are reliant on low-wage workers was critical to undermining support for the minimum wage in Congress.

Not increasing the minimum wage is also a great example of a minority faction preventing the will of the people from being enacted, since a large majority supports raising the minimum wage. Bartels (2008) states that in the late 1990s and early 2000s, when the value of the minimum wage was rapidly eroding, support for increasing the minimum wage was nearly unanimous among the poor and above 70% for the wealthy. A 2011 national survey showed that two-thirds of voters supported an increase in the minimum wage from $7.25 to $10.00 per hour, and majorities of nearly every demographic group supported this proposal, including Democrats and Republicans (Thomson-DeVeaux 2011). This level of agreement is unusual in our polarized era, but as of now a large federal minimum wage increase is not a realistic possibility. However, because minimum wage policy is federalized, the states can use their policy authority to partly counter federal inaction. And as the federal government has allowed the minimum wage to erode, many states have used their authority to increase the value of the minimum wage, a process that we consider in more detail below.

THE STATES TAKE ACTION

In a study of income inequality in the states, the Center on Budget and Policy Priorities (a liberal advocacy group) blamed the falling value of the minimum wage for the increasing income inequality found in the states (Bernstein and Parrott 2014). Thus, advocates for the poor and those concerned about income inequality view the minimum wage as an important means of reversing this trend. As a result, in recent years activists and politicians concerned about inequality have embraced the minimum wage as a way to fight growing inequality because it is a simple policy that has a great deal of public support.

Agitation for a higher minimum wage has not been limited to state capitols. Fight for 15 is a group funded mostly by the Service Employees International Union and backed by religious leaders and poverty advocates that is focused on increasing minimum wages for fast-food industry workers and providing them with the right to union representation. They have been successful in raising the minimum wage to $15 per hour in San Francisco, Seattle, and New York and $13 per hour in Kansas City and Chicago (Greenhouse 2016). In contrast with early debates about the minimum wage in American history, labor organizations are leading the fight for increased minimum wages as a way to demonstrate the value of unions to low-wage workers and increase union organizing.

The local drives to increase the minimum wage have been important since many workers are employed in these large cities, but here our focus is on the state governments, and we have seen similar movement in the state capitals. For instance, when the governor of Massachusetts signed a bill to increase the state's minimum wage to the highest in the country in 2014, he stated that the states was showing the nation that "opportunity can and must be spread outward, not just upward" (Morath 2014). New Jersey Policy Perspective (a progressive advocacy group) senior policy analyst Raymond Castro wrote in a press release, "There appears to be no end in sight in growing inequality in New Jersey—unless state policies are established to address this trend," as a prelude to his group's recommendation to raise the minimum wage (Kalet 2012). Attempts to raise the minimum wage are typically opposed by sectors that employ low-wage workers, such as the retail and hospitality industries. Right-leaning organizations funded largely by business such as ALEC (the American Legislative Exchange Council) and Americans for Prosperity, the Koch brothers organization that is active in many states (Hertel-Fernandez et al. 2016), have also opposed minimum wage increases on economic and ideological grounds.[2]

In the spring of 2016 California, Oregon, and New York all enacted legislation committed to raising the minimum wage to $15 in phases by the early 2020s (Siders 2016; Theen 2016). In each state, these represent an increase of 50% or more. Because inflation is quite low, even when these wage increases are fully phased in they will still represent large real increases.

Indeed, since the national minimum wage has remained rather stagnant over the last few decades, many states have passed legislation establishing wage floors that are higher than the federal level. No states have created entirely new minimum wage laws where none existed before. Instead, states have raised the previously legislated minimum wage. Even in some conservative states, given the opportunity to vote on minimum wages, the public has supported higher minimums. For example, in 2014 voters in South Dakota approved a minimum wage increase via ballot initiative, and in 2016, 71% of the voters in South Dakota rejected an initiative to reduce the minimum wage for younger workers.[3]

To get a more comprehensive sense of which states have adopted higher minimum wages, figure 6.2 highlights states that as of 2014 had passed a minimum wage above the federal minimum (which was $7.25).[4] Of course, the map simplifies the laws by only looking at whether a state has enacted a minimum wage higher than the federal level—some states have higher wage minimums than others—but it provides a straightforward overview of state actions related to wage standards. The figure shows that 23 states have minimum wages higher than the federal minimum wage.

No Min. Wage Min. Wage Above Fed

Figure 6.2: State Minimum Wage Adoptions, 2014
Source: US Department of Labor.

In addition to passing new legislation to increase minimum wages, in recent years a number of states have added provisions to their minimum wage law that index the minimum wage to inflation or average wages. This means that the minimum wage automatically increases with a given metric, usually either cost of living or wages. This puts policy "drift" to work on behalf of low-wage workers since a future legislature does not need to enact new legislation to increase the minimum wage—in the face of inaction the wage will keep pace with the rate of inflation or earnings. It would require entirely new legislation to increase minimum wage increases, which given the popularity of the minimum wage, is unlikely to happen. The first state to index its minimum wage to inflation was Washington, which began to do so in 1998. Over the next several years, eight other states (Colorado, Florida, Missouri, Montana, Nevada, Oregon, and Vermont) have indexed their minimum wages to inflation (US Department of Labor 2012). Because the value of the minimum wage in most states declined so dramatically prior to the adoption of such "indexed" laws in the last decade or so, this indexing does not entirely fix the problem of federal inaction on the minimum wage over the last few decades, but it prevents further erosion in the value of the minimum wage, and the legislature can still increase the minimum wage above current levels, as many have done periodically over the years. Next we turn to an examination of why some states have raised the minimum wage.

Perceptions of Inequality and Increases in the State Minimum Wage

Why have some states increased their minimum wages and others have not? Some of the qualitative discussion above indicates that for some activists and politicians concerns about inequality are a key motivator for wanting to raise the minimum wage. More generally, and in keeping with our broader argument, this suggests that where concern about economic inequality is greater, we should expect to see larger increases in the minimum wage. As we show in chapter 3, when state inequality increases, so does the public's awareness of growing income differences. If people are aware of changes in inequality, this suggests the possibility that the public will also change its preference for egalitarian policies as the gap between the rich and the poor grows larger, as we explored in the context of tax policy preferences in the last chapter.

A growing awareness of inequality ought to translate into stronger preferences for egalitarian policies for a few reasons. Most political economy literature takes economic self-interest as its starting point, and an awareness of growing inequality probably makes voters more cognizant of the gaps that exist between their own income and those of the very rich. Theoretical models and common sense lead to the expectation that this would increase the demand for policies that reduce the gap between rich and poor, simply because most people are not rich (Meltzer and Richard 1981; Shapiro 2002). But individual self-interest is not the largest predictor of policy attitudes. Growing awareness of inequality can cause all individuals to place more importance on their beliefs about equality when evaluating their policy preferences (McCall 2013; McCall and Kenworthy 2009). Studies that examine the relationship between growing inequality and a growing preference for redistribution produce mixed results, with a number of studies finding a positive relationship (Kenworthy and Pontusson 2005; Lupu and Pontusson 2011) but others finding no or even a negative relationship (Alesina and Glaeser 2004; Kelly and Enns 2010). But explicit redistribution is not very popular in America, whereas the minimum wage policy has broad public support. Furthermore, while tax policy preferences are highly partisan and most Republicans oppose redistribution under any circumstances, there is not nearly as much polarization in mass opinions about the minimum wage. Thus, we expect that as public concern about inequality grows in a given state, that state should be more likely to increase its minimum wage.

Even though we have reason to believe that on average the public's attitudes about inequality should influence state policy decisions, in particular about the minimum wage, awareness of inequality is not the only factor that will shape whether a state is likely to raise its minimum wage. Some publics are just more liberal than others as a baseline situation, and it is more likely that the minimum wage will be raised in states with high levels of public opinion liberalism. We therefore include the Enns and Koch (2013) measure of public opinion liberalism in our model of increases in the state minimum wage.

In addition, the extent to which lower-income groups have the political resources available to affect government action will shape how egalitarian policy is. From the perspective of what is known as power resources theory, which we discussed in chapter 4 (Kelly 2009; Kelly and Witko 2012), people belonging to the working and middle classes support different policies than the wealthy. To achieve their policy goals, which typically involve greater government redistribution, the lower classes have to use political organization to overcome the power advantages held by the rich (much of this advantage is related to their wealth and social status). Two key resources for the disadvantaged are the ability to elect left-leaning parties into office and the presence of strong labor organizations.

To maintain their elected positions liberal politicians will favor the enactment of more egalitarian programs, and labor unions have incentives to bolster the wages of low-income citizens—both members and nonmembers—by supporting government policies that assist the less well off (Hicks, Friedland, and Johnson 1978). Altogether this suggests states with more liberal governments and those with a stronger labor union presence will be more likely to adopt minimum wage policies. We have seen qualitative evidence that unions are playing a key role in campaigns to increase the minimum wage, but we examine whether there is a systematic relationship. The states with the largest increases in their minimum wages, California, Oregon, New York, and Massachusetts, are all states with quite liberal governments. We use the Berry et al. (2013) state government ideology measure. For union strength we use state union density, which is the percentage of nonagricultural workers in a union (Hirsch and MacPherson 2003).

Another institutional factor we expect to play an important role in the state adoption of inequality-limiting policies is the ability of citizens to introduce and pass legislation. This is broadly referred to as direct democracy, but the ballot initiative can be particularly influential to the policy process (see chapter 5). The initiative allows the electorate to control the policymaking process from writing the legislation to a popular vote on the proposal to determine the future of the policy. This allows residents of the 24 states that have the initiative process to use this political tool to circumvent their legislatures if they are unresponsive to public demands. The ability of the public to act on its own can be consequential when concern about economic inequality continues to grow and neither the federal nor state government is willing to address the problem. Furthermore, because public support for the minimum wage is high, but low among conservative elected officials, we should see that the initiative is an important factor in minimum wage increases. For instance, the relatively conservative state of Missouri's minimum wage law was enacted via the initiative.

In addition to the initiative process giving citizens direct control over policy outcomes, the initiative has also been shown to have an indirect effect on the actions of state legislators. This indirect effect is the result of the public simply having the ability to create and pass legislation without input from the legislature. The idea is that legislatures in states with the initiative will move their policies closer to the preferences of the public in order to maintain control over the policy process and to avoid having the citizens of the state adopt a policy that is too far from the legislature's own preferences. In both California and Oregon union-funded campaigns began to try to place initiatives to increase the minimum wage to $15 on the November ballot in 2016, but these campaigns were ended once state governments enacted these laws in the spring of 2016. Very clearly, policymakers enacted minimum wage laws because of the threat of initiatives that would have increased the minimum wage more rapidly than the legislation that was finally enacted (Siders 2016).

To examine both the direct and indirect effects of the initiative process we use a variable that measures how difficult it is to qualify legislation for the ballot, using Bowler and Donovan's (2004) measure. This allows us to distinguish among states that make the initiative more accessible to citizens (and therefore the initiative is more regularly used) and those states that have an initiative process that is rarely used because qualifying an initiative to appear on the ballot is quite difficult.[5]

Finally, the minimum wage offers a unique opportunity to directly model how state minimum wages respond to federal policy inaction. As minimum wage increases at the federal level become less common, we expect that increases at the state level become more common and that more states will seek to increase their minimum wage above that federal minimum. And, more specifically, we expect that the longer it has been since the federal government has increased the minimum wage, the more likely it will be that the states will adopt higher minimum wages in their laws. In contrast, in a year when the federal government has increased the minimum wage, it will be less likely that states will increase the minimum wage.

In addition to these variables of theoretical interest, we control for the state poverty rate, the difference between the federal and state minimum wage, and whether the state has adopted the EITC policy, which might make it less likely for states to use preredistribution approaches to raising the wages of low-income earners (in other words, the EITC and the minimum wage substitute for one another).

Similar to the analyses presented in previous chapters, we use statistical modeling techniques that allow us to assess the effect of public attitudes about inequality and political context on the adoption of state minimum wage policies while accounting for a variety of additional state characteristics.[6] Our models include nearly all states and examine over-time changes in state decisions to enact minimum wage laws that set state minimums above the federal level from 1986 to 2012.[7] To assess the extent to which states offer a higher wage minimum than the floor set by the federal government, we use a measure that captures the difference between each state's minimum wage and the federal minimum. A state with a minimum wage of $8.00 in 2012, for example, would be recorded as $0.75—that is, the difference between $8.00 and $7.25 (the federal minimum in 2012). States without a minimum wage, or a state minimum that is less than or equal to the federal minimum, will simply have a difference of zero.[8] A summary of the measure is presented in table 6.1, which shows the average minimum wage difference for each state over the 25-plus years being studied. On average, state minimums were about $0.20 higher than the federal level over the time period. Some states, however, have consistently had much higher wage minimums than others. For instance, the state minimum wage in Oregon and Washington has averaged over $1.00 higher than federal law, while states like Alabama and South Carolina have never had a minimum wage set above the federal minimum.

Although it is not clearly evident in table 6.1, the evolution of state wage minimums differs substantially over time, which is taken into consideration using time-series analysis when we model the development of state minimum wage policy.[9]

EXPLAINING STATE INCREASES IN THE MINIMUM WAGE

The complete results of our analyses of state wage minimums can be found in appendix table B.11. After taking into account a number of state factors, one of the most important relationships we find is that increases in public concern about income inequality make it more likely that a state will have a wage minimum above the federal level, which provides evidence supporting our claim that citizen attitudes about growing inequality do influence state policymaking, pushing it in a more egalitarian direction. This suggests

Table 6.1. AVERAGE STATE MINIMUM WAGE POLICIES, 1986–2012

State	Average above Federal Level ($)	State	Average above Federal Level ($)
Alabama	0.00	Montana	0.08
Alaska	0.79	Nebraska	0.00
Arizona	0.14	Nevada	0.15
Arkansas	0.06	New Hampshire	0.07
California	0.73	New Jersey	0.31
Colorado	0.15	New Mexico	0.09
Connecticut	0.85	New York	0.24
Delaware	0.39	North Carolina	0.05
Florida	0.18	North Dakota	0.00
Georgia	0.00	Ohio	0.16
Hawaii	0.58	Oklahoma	0.00
Idaho	0.00	Oregon	1.08
Illinois	0.37	Pennsylvania	0.11
Indiana	0.00	Rhode Island	0.62
Iowa	0.17	South Carolina	0.00
Kansas	0.00	South Dakota	0.00
Kentucky	0.00	Tennessee	0.00
Louisiana	0.00	Texas	0.00
Maine	0.40	Utah	0.00
Maryland	0.05	Vermont	0.75
Massachusetts	0.77	Virginia	0.00
Michigan	0.16	Washington	1.02
Minnesota	0.10	West Virginia	0.08
Mississippi	0.00	Wisconsin	0.09
Missouri	0.10	Wyoming	0.00

that the expansion of economic inequality has not gone unnoticed by the public, and that in response people are willing to support policies that can reduce the gap between the rich and the poor.

Additionally, we can see that political support for the working and middle classes by way of more left-leaning governments can affect the adoption of state minimum wage laws. Specifically, states with more liberal governments are more likely to have wage floors above the federal level. Unsurprisingly, we find that states with more liberal public opinion are also more likely to raise the minimum wage. Somewhat surprisingly given the importance of unions to minimum wage campaigns of recent years, we do not observe any relationship between union strength and a higher state minimum wage. Perhaps it is the case that a certain threshold of union strength is necessary, but beyond that, additional strength is not essential.

To get a sense of the relative effects of some state factors that are central to our analysis, we present the estimated effect of increasing several variables by a standard amount (i.e., by one standard deviation) on state minimum wage law (figure 6.3). While each of the variables shown in the plot has a statistically significant influence on minimum wage policy, the effect of inequality awareness appears to be substantively stronger than the effect of public mood and the state initiative. This is not entirely surprising, as the minimum wage is quite popular even among conservatives.

Another factor that appears to drive increases in state minimum wage increases is the inaction of the federal government. That is, our findings provide convincing evidence that as the length of time since the last federal minimum wage increase grows, states become more likely to increase their own minimum wage. In addition, we observe that the initiative is significantly associated with a higher likelihood of increasing the minimum wage.

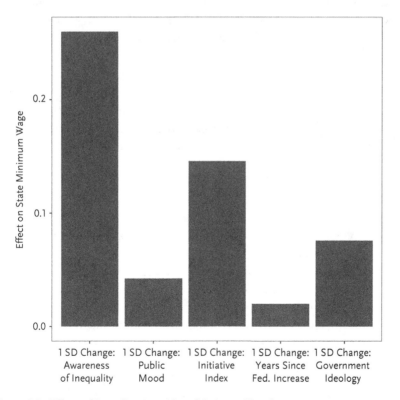

Figure 6.3: Effects of State Factors on State Minimum Wage Laws
Note: Estimates are based on the model results presented in appendix table B.11.

Several studies provide evidence suggesting that initiative states do tend to have policy outcomes that are closer to the public's attitudes about a number of political issues when compared with non-initiative states, even when the initiative process is not used to adopt the policies (Gerber 1996; 1999; Matsusaka and McCarty 2001), and we see evidence of this in the most recent minimum wage fights.

Furthermore, the initiative is particularly valuable in pushing this policy change when the states face federal inaction.

As we demonstrated in figure 6.1, there have been several instances where the federal minimum wage has gone unchanged for a number of years. From 1997 to 2007, for example, the federal minimum was stagnant at $5.15 per hour. Using the number of years the federal wage floor did not change during the period under analysis, we examined whether initiative states were more likely to take action when the national minimum wage had gone unchanged for long stretches of time. The results are presented in figure 6.4, which shows the effect of the initiative process on state wage levels at different durations of federal inaction. The plot suggests that the initiative process becomes more important in increasing the minimum wage during periods when there are no changes in the wage minimum at the national level. For example, at only two years without a federal minimum wage increase the initiative's effect is indistinguishable from 0 (since the error bar overlaps 0), while at four years or more the effect is significant and increasing. This evidence indicates that the initiative may provide an important avenue for policy change when policymakers in Washington, DC, are unwilling to address the issue of rising inequality and when there may even be significant opposition among state elected officials.

CONCLUSION

In this chapter we have demonstrated the important role of the states in taking steps to limit economic inequality as the federal government does little to address the issue. This state action is even more consequential when considering the unequalizing effect Congress has had on the distribution of income. Recent studies have shown that congressional inaction has contributed to the expansion of inequality by allowing the political and economic factors that lead to an expanding income gap to go unchecked (Enns et al. 2014; Hacker and Pierson 2010). In other words, by doing nothing, the government has been instrumental in the growth of economic inequality. Not raising the minimum wage has allowed for an erosion of the income of the lowest-paid workers.

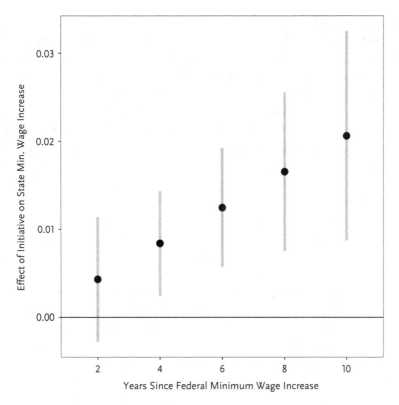

Figure 6.4: Effect of the Initiative Process on State Minimum Wage Increases by Years since the Last Federal Increase

Note: Estimates are based on the model results presented in appendix table B.11. Bars represent 95% confidence intervals.

In contrast to the federal government, a number of states have been relatively active in developing policies that reduce income inequality. In particular, the minimum wage has been used to combat growing economic inequality driven in part by stagnant wages at the low end of the income distribution, an effort that has been found to boost the incomes of low-wage workers (Card and Krueger 1995) and reduce state-level inequality in other studies (Kelly and Witko 2012). The fact that the minimum wage is jointly controlled by the federal government and state governments allows us to examine how states respond to federal government inaction, and it also allows us to examine how perceptions of inequality and other factors shape the adoption of higher minimum wages. But, despite its popularity, not all states have increased their minimum wage during this era of growing inequality.

Consistent with a core argument of the book, public perceptions of the gap between the rich and poor play a key role in whether the states address inequality. As residents of a state become more concerned about growing inequality, the state becomes more likely to enact a minimum wage increase. Of course, public opinion on inequality is only one factor that leads states to enact policies aimed at income redistribution. Others include the ideological composition of a state's government and the ability of citizens to directly affect state policy through the use of the initiative process. Both of these factors are significantly related to higher wage minimums. Additionally, initiative states appear to be the most active in adopting strong minimums during long spells of inaction on the part of the federal government. This builds on our findings from chapter 5 that suggest the initiative process can lead to more egalitarian political debates and sometimes outcomes. While tax increases will always be somewhat unpopular, because the minimum wage is quite popular, the initiative can help to increase minimum wages in the states, particularly as the federal government fails to increase the minimum wage.

Although a strong minimum wage can mitigate growing income differences, these programs alone are not enough to reverse the rapid expansion of inequality observed over the last 35 years. If the United States wants to address inequality, it will require a combination of federal and state actions that allow all Americans to benefit from the economic system. If recent trends in the productivity of the federal government are an indicator of future policymaking, however, those concerned about inequality will have to rely on the states, and perhaps new state innovations, to reverse the resilient trajectory of growing income disparities. In the next chapter we consider how state governments have used more explicit redistribution to boost the income of low-wage workers to respond to growing income inequality in the form of the earned income tax credit.

CHAPTER 7

Building on Success

The Case of the Earned Income Tax Credit

As we have argued throughout the book, the role of government in addressing expanding economic disparities in the United States is largely a story about the national government being unable or unwilling to respond to the new economic reality of concentrated incomes and some state governments taking action to address a growing public concern about inequality. Broadly speaking, public policies have the potential to reduce inequality by reducing top incomes via regulation or asking those at the top of the income ladder to pay more taxes, or by increasing the incomes of those at the bottom of the income distribution. Of course, there are a number of policy choices available to accomplish these goals. Focusing on two prominent policy options that address both kinds of egalitarian policy, we have shown that the states play a central role in responding to inequality through policy action. In the cases of higher income taxes on the rich (chapter 5) and the adoption of the state minimum wage (chapter 6), we found that the public's understanding of and concern about income inequality, the initiative option, and liberal governments are important for the development of government programs that are expected to lead to more equal economic outcomes.

In this chapter we again explore a policy that is designed to increase the incomes of those at the bottom of the income distribution, the earned income tax credit (EITC). Like the minimum wage, the EITC is an interesting policy to study for our purposes since it has a direct effect on income inequality. The EITC aids workers with low earnings by offering a credit to offset paid income taxes, and in some cases family incomes are supplemented through the program beyond the amount of their income tax liability. Unlike the minimum wage, the EITC influences postredistribution incomes since the program provides a tax refund from the government (also known as a tax expenditure) and direct cash aid above taxes paid for those who qualify. Like the minimum wage, evidence suggests that the EITC is an effective way to reduce income inequality (Hungerford 2010).

The story of the EITC is different from the minimum wage in that the federal government created the program and it grew steadily through the 1980s and 1990s (Ventry 2000). The growth of the EITC over time is in, part due, to a handful of extensions initiated through congressional legislation, but it is also a result of program benefits being indexed to inflation and an increase in the number of people who are eligible for the credit (Falk and Crandall-Hollick 2014). Unlike the other policies that we have examined, states followed the lead of the federal government in establishing EITC programs. By 2014, 25 states had state versions of an EITC, building on this federal policy innovation.

There are many potential explanations for why some states have chosen to extend the benefits of the federal EITC to the state level. We, of course, investigate the role that awareness of inequality plays, along with the other factors we examined in the previous chapter. However, government liberalism may not be an important predictor of EITC adoptions at the state level because, unlike the minimum wage and tax increases on the wealthy, conservative have traditionally embraced the EITC (Hungerford and Thiess 2013). The EITC is also a version of indirect government spending via the tax code, which has typically been the favored policy approach taken by the Republican Party (Faricy 2011). The possibility that the EITC is used even by more conservative state governments in the face of awareness of inequality would show that it is not only the most liberal state governments that respond to this concern.

In addition, as we will show, examining state EITCs does demonstrate the limitations of the initiative process in circumventing legislative inaction. An important difference between the minimum wage and the EITC is that the minimum wage has consistently been a much more prominent issue across the country, while the EITC tends to get substantially less attention. This difference is likely due to the complexity of the EITC when compared with the minimum wage, which minimizes the direct role of the public in policymaking on this issue.

The United States has a long history of favoring social policy focused on encouraging work over a perceived dependency on government, with welfare programs that are viewed as providing "handouts" often being the easiest targets of those who want to reform or eliminate poverty assistance policies altogether. A long line of literature suggests that most Americans value the idea of individual responsibility and view those who benefit from welfare programs as being lazy or undeserving (Gilens 1999; Katz 1990; Kluegel and Smith 1986). These attitudes about the welfare state have made it particularly difficult for those interested in addressing poverty to build a consensus on the kinds of government programs needed to tackle the issue. This established welfare debate is the backdrop for the creation of the EITC.[1]

Conservatives have championed the EITC as an alternative to the New Deal welfare state programs, but its roots lie in the period of federal activism in addressing inequality, poverty, and a lack of opportunity from the 1930s to the 1960s. The EITC emerged from a plan within Lyndon Johnson's administration to establish a negative income tax (NIT), as part of his broader 1964 War on Poverty (Ventry 2000). At the time, the NIT was viewed by some as a viable alternative to traditional welfare policies that offered cash assistance to the less fortunate, but were easily attacked by those who claimed that the policies disincentivized work and contributed to government dependency. The basic idea of an NIT is that it would provide a government payment to working individuals whose taxable incomes fell below a specified amount. The NIT proposal under the Johnson administration argued for a tiered system that would phase out at higher levels of income. Unlike the cash assistance programs being used in the 1960s (e.g., Aid to Families with Dependent Children [AFDC]), NIT payments would slowly decline as wages grew rather than making a family ineligible for the program once a set income level was reached. This aspect of the NIT was thought to limit work disincentives, and in some situations could promote work. Additionally, since an NIT program could be simply implemented through the tax code, and did not require additional large bureaucracies, taxpayers would save on costs related to the administration of most existing cash assistance programs that would no longer be necessary if they were replaced by the NIT (Ventry 2000).

In the end, even with the apparent benefits and simplicity of the NIT and a national poverty rate approaching 19%, around two-thirds of the American public was opposed to the NIT (Holtz and Scholz 2003). Johnson eventually abandoned the proposal and instead favored programs that were more consistent with the country's tradition of promoting opportunity by, for instance, offering job training. In other words, though the NIT promoted work more than traditional programs like AFDC (Aid to Families with Dependent Children), LBJ ultimately wanted to promote policies that could more easily be identified as "pro-work" (Hotz and Scholz 2003).

Although Johnson focused on the pro-work aspects of the policies he advanced, government spending on the AFDC cash assistance program grew larger than ever in the late 1960s and early 1970s. Once Richard Nixon was elected in 1968, he vowed to dramatically change the federal welfare system and replace it with a program that would encourage work while assisting those in poverty. Nixon's Family Assistance Plan (FAP) proposed replacing the existing AFDC, food stamps, and Medicaid programs with what essentially amounted to a negative income tax (Passell and Ross 1973). Nixon's NIT plan would have provided payments to those who fell below certain income thresholds, and a graduated phase-out as income increased, with work requirements for most potential beneficiaries. As Ventry (2000) describes it, however, both liberals and conservatives criticized the Nixon plan. Those on the right were concerned about the cost of the program, and while the policy attempted to include work incentives, it was unclear how well they would work. On the left, many were worried that the proposed FAP benefits were not generous enough to replace the cuts that would have been made to other poverty assistance programs.

Nixon's FAP was not pursued by Congress. Watered-down versions of the FAP were regularly revisited by politicians in the following years as a type of work bonus for low-income earners, but none of these attempts gained enough support to lead to a policy change until a slumping economy emerged in 1974. Filling in for Nixon after his resignation, Gerald Ford proposed tax reductions as a way to stimulate economic growth and to avoid a deep recession. As part of the tax cuts, Congress adopted a temporary EITC for workers with low incomes that was intended to partially offset payroll taxes and prevent higher rates of unemployment (Ventry 2000).

The EITC, which somewhat resembled the NIT and work bonus plans that preceded it, was temporarily renewed by Congress in each of the next three years and was made a permanent part of the tax code in 1978. With the benefits initially being relatively modest, few people viewed the EITC as playing a potentially significant role as a social welfare program. President Carter saw the opportunity the program offered to assist with his welfare reform initiative, but he was unable to expand the EITC, and it remained mostly unchanged until 1986. Similar to the circumstances surrounding the stagnant federal minimum wage policy we discussed in chapter 6, the real value of the EITC declined substantially during this period because it was not indexed to inflation. In addition to a declining minimum wage, the tax burden was also being disproportionately increased on the lowest-income earners because of cuts in corporate tax rates and increases in payroll taxes. To make matters worse, a number of social programs were being defunded as a part of the welfare reform movement in the 1980s under the Reagan administration (Piven and Cloward 1982).

The financial hardship being experienced by the lower and working classes led to general concern among many, and the EITC eventually became central to Congress's approach to addressing the problem. The Tax Reform Act of 1986 expanded the EITC in important ways. First, it increased the maximum benefit levels and the phase-out income levels. Perhaps more importantly, the reform indexed the EITC levels to inflation, meaning that the value of the program would no longer decrease as a consequence of future lawmakers simply ignoring the policy (Ventry 2000). Policy drift was put to work for low-income taxpayers, unlike the minimum wage. The ability to substantially expand the program was not only due to the general perception that the poor were being unfairly burdened by taxes, but the EITC was also viewed as a welfare alternative that could incentivize work (Hotz and Scholz 2003).

The program was again expanded in 1990 and 1993. However, by the early 1990s Republican support for the EITC had dissipated. President Clinton's proposed expansion in 1993 passed, but the bill did not receive one vote from the Republican Party. Some view this as a pivotal moment in the history of the EITC, marking the beginning of the once bipartisan policy being tied to the Democratic Party (Hotz and Scholz 2003). Some Republicans suggest the EITC had grown into an "income-redistribution program that serves many who are not poor" (Snyder 1995). In recent years criticisms of the poor not paying enough in taxes have become even louder, most notoriously in Republican presidential candidate Mitt Romney's statement about 47% of the public not paying taxes (Cook 2012). Though Romney's statement about 47% not paying taxes was inaccurate, since all wage earner pay payroll taxes and other types of taxes, it is true that a large percentage of Americans do not pay income taxes, and child tax credits and the EITC are the main reason that the working poor do not pay income taxes (Williams 2011).

As discussed above, one reason that proponents of antipoverty efforts see the EITC as an alternative to the minimum wage and other traditional welfare programs is that expanding the EITC was more politically possible than expanding other policies, particularly as the federal government moved to the right starting in the 1970s. More recently, however, conservatives have raised concerns about the growth of the program and the number of people that receive benefits. It is against this backdrop that some states also developed EITC programs since the 1970s.

STATE EARNED INCOME TAX CREDIT PROGRAMS

Figure 7.1 shows which states had adopted an EITC as of 2014. The map does somewhat simplify state EITC adoption since some programs are more generous than others, but it provides a straightforward overview of state actions related to the EITC. The figure shows that nearly half (24) of states have adopted their own version of the EITC, and that these adoptions are relatively spread out across the country. The main exception to this dispersal is that very few southern states have adopted an EITC (Louisiana is the only Deep South state that has a state EITC). To get a comparative sense of how state EITC adoption is related to state minimum wage adoption, table 7.1 provides a straightforward cross tabulation of the two policy adoptions. The table suggests states that have adopted one of the policies are more likely to enact the other, and vice versa. Some states have certainly decided to adopt either a minimum wage (seven states) or an EITC (nine states), but for the most part the

No EITC   State EITC

Figure 7.1: State EITC Adoptions as of 2014
Source: Tax Credits for Working Families.

Table 7.1. STATE MINIMUM WAGE AND EARNED INCOME TAX
CREDIT POLICIES, 2014

State Minimum Wage above	State Earned Income Tax Credit		
Federal Minimum	No	Yes	Total
No	18	9	27
Yes	7	16	23
Total	25	25	50

states appear to favor establishing both a wage increase and an EITC (16 states) or neither of the two policies (18 states). Thus, rather than the EITC replacing the minimum wage or vice versa, it appears that these have been used as complementary approaches to reducing poverty and inequality. We also find little evidence suggesting that there is a chronological ordering to the adoption of the two policies in states that have both higher wage minimums and an EITC. In other words, states with both policies do not tend to increase their minimum wage first and then adopt an EITC after, nor is the inverse true.[2]

One of the states with the highest levels and most rapidly growing inequality over the last few decades, Massachusetts, exemplifies these dynamics. We already discussed in the previous chapter how the state has one of the highest minimum wages in the country. But as inequality has grown, the government of Massachusetts has sought a number of ways to try and reduce inequality. Senate president Democrat Stanley Rosenberg made fighting inequality the centerpiece of his leadership when he assumed that position in 2015, and the EITC was an important part of his agenda (Miller 2015). When asked about the plan, one Massachusetts state senator said, "There's a real push this session on how do we address inequality, and EITC is a proven tool that puts money in the pockets of poor families" (Johnston 2015). In April 2015, Republican governor, Charlie Baker, signed an expansion of the EITC into law that will increase the size of the program by around 50% for the average beneficiary (Baker Press Office 2015). And Baker alluded to growing inequality as a reason to support the EITC when he said the expansion would "extend the benefits of a growing economy to more individuals across the Commonwealth." This linking of growing inequality with the EITC has not been limited to Massachusetts. Legislators from California argued that implementing a state EITC would prevent many families from falling "deeper into debt and poverty as the rest of the state prospers" (Atkins and Weber 2015).

As national-level conservatives have turned against the EITC, we also see growing controversy surrounding the EITC in the states. Though moderate Republican Baker supported a major expansion of the EITC in Massachusetts, conservative politicians and advocacy groups in the states, in particular ALEC, have begun to push for the repeal of earned income tax credit provisions in more conservative states, like Kansas, Oklahoma, Nebraska, and North Carolina (Williams and Johnson 2013). Even against this backdrop, Nebraska expanded its EITC. However, North Carolina, which has become something of a petri dish for experimenting with policies favored by conservative activists in recent years, did repeal its EITC in 2013 (Weisbecker 2013). Thus far, few states have repealed their EITCs, and it is clear that this will not happen in liberal states like Massachusetts. Though conservative states have generally not repealed their EITCs, the growing calls to do so by conservative activists may lead more conservative states to do this in the future. We see that the politics of the EITC have become increasingly complex, as conservatives have turned against it.

What are the circumstances, then, that have led 25 states to adopt the inequality-reducing EITC state expansion? Once again, we examine whether the public's awareness of growing inequality and the ability of the public to further its policy goals by way of more liberal governments and organized labor will influence whether states are able to pass local EITC programs. We also consider whether the initiative process plays a role with the EITC like that we found with the minimum wage.

Since in other chapters we have extensively discussed the importance of whether the public is aware of growing economic inequality for how people develop preferences for redistributive policy, we give a brief summary of our expectations here. To the extent that the EITC is identified as a policy that reduces inequality, we expect that a growing awareness of inequality among the public will be associated with a greater likelihood of a state adopting the EITC. The relatively complexity of the EITC may attenuate this relationship, however, compared to easier-to-understand policies like the minimum wage or high taxes on the rich.

Of course, even if the public's concern about inequality has grown along with income differences, there is no guarantee that these attitudes will translate into more redistributive policy. Instead, we typically rely on our representatives in elected office to pursue our policy goals. While politicians are broadly responsive to the aggregate preferences of the public (Erikson, Mackuen, and Stimson 2002; Page and Shapiro 1992), this responsiveness is by no means a one-to-one relationship. Many factors can influence how closely lawmakers follow the public's view on an issue, and it is not always easy for politicians to know exactly what the public wants. Even when the constituent preferences are clear, policy change can still be difficult because of institutional constraints that often make it difficult to create new policies (Krehbiel 1998). Furthermore, legislators are often inundated with diverging preferences from a number of groups, and some interests will inevitably win out over others. This means that political groups will regularly attempt to influence the decisions made by our elected officials. Groups with greater levels of political resources—for example, the ability to contribute to a campaign—are more likely to have their preferences represented (Gilens 2012). In the state of North Carolina the power of conservative activists has grown dramatically in recent years, as a wealthy funder of conservative causes, Art Pope, has become chief of staff to the state's governor, Pat McRory, and also helped to bankroll the conservative Republican majority in the state (Gold 2014). In contrast, lower-income groups have traditionally relied on ideologically left-leaning parties and labor organizations, which are the groups we focus on here.[3]

On the one hand, the EITC has traditionally been viewed as a bipartisan, somewhat conservative approach to the welfare state. But it is increasingly viewed as a progressive policy that redistributes wealth. Thus, we investigate whether states with a stronger presence of liberal governments and labor unions will be more likely to adopt EITC programs. Although the EITC effectively redistributes income to those with fewer resources, studying this program provides an interesting test case since the EITC has sometimes had bipartisan support. So it is possible that government ideology will have a attenuated effect on the expansion of the EITC at the state level. At the same time, the unique politics surrounding the EITC may also mean that lower-income groups have to rely more on labor organization to push for the redistributive policy, meaning we can expect the independent influence of state union membership to be relatively strong. Unlike North Carolina, where unions are notoriously weak, unions are strong in states like Massachusetts and California, where the EITC has been embraced.

In chapter 6 we argued that the initiative is an important policy tool at the state level that can be used by the public when governments are not responsive. In the case of minimum wage policy, we demonstrated that states providing greater access to the initiative were more likely to adopt wage floors above the federal level, particularly during periods when the federal minimum wage had gone unchanged for a number of years. The reason for this is that the initiative allows citizens to circumvent the typical legislative process by giving them the ability to pass laws by directly voting on legislation. Additionally, scholars have shown that initiative states tend to have state policies that more closely correspond to public preferences even when the initiative was not used to enact these policies (Gerber

1996; 1999; Matsusaka and McCarty 2001). This is referred to as an indirect effect of the initiative process, which is a result of state legislators wanting to maintain control of lawmaking. From the perspective of elected officials, it is more desirable to address public concerns via the state legislature so that the public does not use the initiative to create policies that deviate too much from the preferences of state lawmakers.

An exception to the influence of the initiative on policy outcomes is that initiative states appear to more closely reflect citizen demands when the issue being considered is salient and relatively uncomplicated (Arceneaux 2002). The limited relationship between public opinion and policy outcomes in initiative states when looking at less salient and more complicated issues is likely due to the inability of state representatives to gauge the preferences of the public, making it difficult and less essential to incorporate citizens' views on the topic (Matsusaka and McCarty 2001). This is especially important to consider when studying the effect of the initiative on state EITC programs. While the EITC and minimum wage are targeted at similar groups and both are intended to raise the incomes of the lowest-paid workers, the two policies do differ when taking into account how much public attention is given to the minimum wage and the EITC and the level of understanding people have of the policies.

For the most part, the mechanics of the minimum wage are straightforward. A wage minimum simply sets the lowest dollar amount an hourly employee can legally be paid. The simplicity of the policy is perhaps one of the main reasons the minimum wage is so popular among the public, with nearly three out of four Americans supporting a wage increase.[4] Unlike the minimum wage, the EITC is notorious for its complexity. Program benefits can depend on family income, marital status, and number of dependents, and claiming the credit requires completing pages of additional paperwork when filing tax returns (Hungerford and Thiess 2013). The complexity of the program may provide some insight into why the EITC is not a widely known policy among the public. In the most recent poll that asks about knowledge of the topic, nearly 40% of respondents said they did not know what the EITC was or had never heard of the program (Bartels 2008).

There are also differences in the amount of attention the minimum wage and the EITC receive in the news. Figure 7.2 shows the number of articles published in the *New York Times* that mention the two policies from 1985 to 2014.[5] The plot shows that the minimum wage is much more prominent in media discussions since the 1980s. On average, the minimum wage is mentioned in almost 200 more articles per year than the EITC. This evidence is important when studying the state adoption of the EITC, since it has implications for why public opinion and the initiative process may have

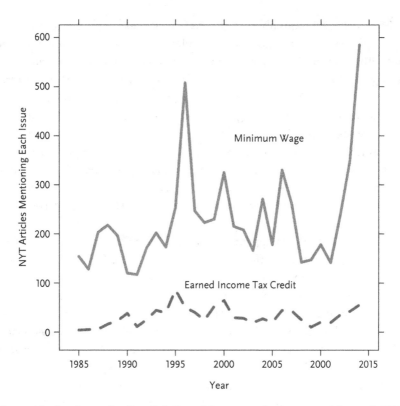

Figure 7.2: Articles in the *New York Times* Mentioning the Minimum Wage and EITC, 1985–2014

a more limited effect on EITC adoptions relative to its effects on minimum wage policy demonstrated in chapter 6.

This salience and complexity may also weaken the relationship between public opinion and adoptions of the EITC, as briefly noted above. On the other hand, it is not always necessary for the public to have detailed information about the EITC or to regularly discuss the program in order to develop meaningful attitudes about the policy that are consistent with their broader political preferences. Scholars have demonstrated that people are able to form policy preferences on a wide range of issues, oftentimes without being able to provide specific details about how they arrived at their opinion. Rather than attempting to have a comprehensive understanding of some set of political issues, individuals often rely on information shortcuts that provide enough knowledge to develop attitudes that are consistent with their political interests. These shortcuts can take the form of something as simple as an individual reading a comment about an issue from a trusted politician or public figure (Lupia and McCubbins 1998).

So we believe it is possible for citizens to have meaningful attitudes about the EITC even if the program is not regularly discussed and is not a salient issue. To examine this possibility more carefully, we use a survey question asking about support for the EITC in a 2007 poll, which is the most recent question we could find on the EITC. The question asks respondents about their opinion on whether the program should be changed.[6] A plurality of interviewees, nearly 43%, supported expanding the program, and another 28% wanted the EITC to remain the same. Only 7% of respondents wanted to reduce the scale of the credit, with just under 9% responding that they favored eliminating the program altogether. A moderate portion of people, just over 13%, did say they were unsure. More importantly for the purpose of our study, when examining those who supported expanding the EITC we find that individuals do appear to have attitudes that are consistent with preferences for redistribution more generally. Figure 7.3 shows the level of support for expanding the program by partisanship (the top panel) and income (the bottom panel). First, we can see that Democratic identifiers are much more likely to support expansion, by a margin of over 30 percentage points, than Republicans. This is what we would expect in the period following Clinton's EITC extension in 1993. Additionally, if self-interest is at work, individuals with lower incomes should have higher levels of favorability for the EITC, which is what we observe. Those in the bottom income quartile are over 10 percentage points more likely to support EITC expansion than individuals in the third or fourth quartile. This provides some basic support for the claim that the public does have reasonable attitudes about the EITC even with its reputation as a relatively complex policy. Furthermore, ultimately politicians take the vague and blunt demands of the public and turn them into specific policy proposals. Even if the public never clamors for the EITC, politicians can take the general growing concern about inequality and channel that into expansions of the EITC.

WHICH STATES ARE MORE LIKELY TO ADOPT THE EITC?

We once again use statistical modeling to better understand state decisions to adopt their own versions of the EITC. Our models include nearly all states and examine whether an EITC is adopted and the timing of the adoption from 1986 to 2012.[7] In table 7.2, we list the year each state passed an EITC when appropriate—states without an EITC program are left blank.[8] From 1986 to 2012 about half of the states (24 to be exact) enacted their own versions of the EITC that build on the benefits families receive from the tax credit program at the federal level. It should be noted

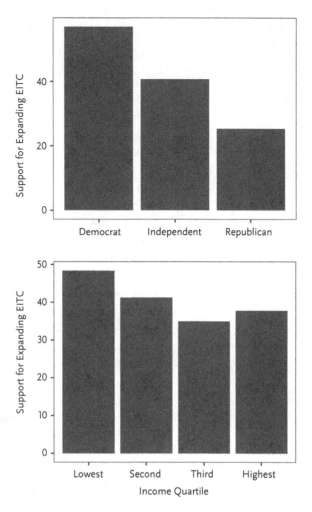

Figure 7.3: Public Support for Expanding the EITC
Source: Cooperative Congressional Election Study (http://projects.iq.harvard.edu/cces/home).

that the timing of these state EITC adoptions varies, with some states creating programs in the 1980s and others enacting an EITC more recently.
Our analysis takes the timing of these adoptions into account by using
time-series cross-sectional methods designed to capture these over-time
dynamics.[9]

In addition to the local factors expected to influence the adoption of
EITCs discussed above—that is, public awareness of inequality, government liberalism (Berry et al. 2010; 2013), union membership (Hirsch
and MacPherson 2003), and the initiative process (Bowler and Donovan
2004)—we account for several additional state characteristics. Public

Table 7.2. STATE ADOPTION OF THE EITC, 1986–2012

State	EITC Adoption Year	State	EITC Adoption Year
Alabama		Montana	
Alaska		Nebraska	2006
Arizona		Nevada	
Arkansas		New Hampshire	
California		New Jersey	2000
Colorado	1999	New Mexico	2007
Connecticut	2011	New York	1994
Delaware	2005	North Carolina	
Florida		North Dakota	
Georgia		Ohio	
Hawaii		Oklahoma	2002
Idaho		Oregon	1997
Illinois	2000	Pennsylvania	
Indiana	1999	Rhode Island	1986
Iowa	1989	South Carolina	
Kansas	1998	South Dakota	
Kentucky		Tennessee	
Louisiana	2007	Texas	
Maine	2000	Utah	
Maryland	1987	Vermont	1988
Massachusetts	1997	Virginia	2004
Michigan	2006	Washington	2008
Minnesota	1991	West Virginia	
Mississippi		Wisconsin	1989
Missouri		Wyoming	

Source: Tax Credits for Working Families.

mood capture the public's general support for redistribution beyond concern about inequality (Enns and Koch 2013). We also include measures of each state's poverty rate and the percentage of total state revenue that comes from income taxes. These variables account for the fact that some states will have a greater need for the EITC than others, above and beyond inequality. States with higher rates of poverty might want to provide assistance to those with lower incomes, and state with higher income taxes could potentially want to offset these higher taxes with the tax credit. The percentage of the population that is white is also included in our models, along with an indicator for whether a state has also adopted a state minimum wage. Finally, we consider the effect of two potential forms of policy diffusion: the total number of states that have adopted the EITC and the proportion of neighboring states that have the policy.[10]

The complete results of our analyses of EITC programs can be found in appendix B. After taking into account a number of state characteristics, we once again find that the public's awareness of inequality makes it more likely that a state will adopt a local version of the EITC. This supports our argument that the public can play an important role in pushing state governments to implement more redistributive policies. Even when it comes to the relatively complex EITC, public officials appear to be aware of and are responding to the public's heightened concern about growing income differences. Interestingly, our results do not show that more liberal governments are more likely to adopt state EITC programs. The relationship between liberal governments and EITC adoption is positive, but we cannot be confident in the estimate at traditional levels of statistical significance. State union membership, however, does have a positive and significant effect on state tax credit adoption. In fact, along with changes in public awareness of inequality, the influence of labor is one of the strongest in our model. We present the comparative influence of both inequality awareness and union membership in figure 7.4. When awareness and union membership change from their values at the 10th percentile to their values at the 90th percentile, a state has about a 1.2 percentage point, and a 1.5 percentage point, increase in the probability of adopting a state EITC, respectively, in a given year.

As expected, there is also a divergence in the effect of the initiative process on policy adoption when comparing the EITC to the minimum wage. As in chapter 6, we use a standard measure of the state initiative process that takes into account whether citizens have the option of using the initiative in a state and the rules that govern how the initiative process is used (Bowler and Donovan 2004). This allows us to distinguish among states that make the initiative more accessible to citizens (and therefore the initiative is more regularly used) and those states that have an initiative process that is rarely used because qualifying an initiative for the ballot is difficult.[11] Unlike the case of state minimum wage policy, we cannot say with statistical certainty that the initiative leads to more state tax credit programs. This finding is likely related to the EITC being more complex and less salient than the minimum wage, and the initiative process tends to have a stronger effect on policies when the public gives more attention to them. This greater complexity of the EITC also probably explains why unions are more important to the adoption of the EITC. Almost all voters are familiar with and supportive of the minimum wage, thus unions have relatively little to add. In contrast, union lobbying for the EITC (and union

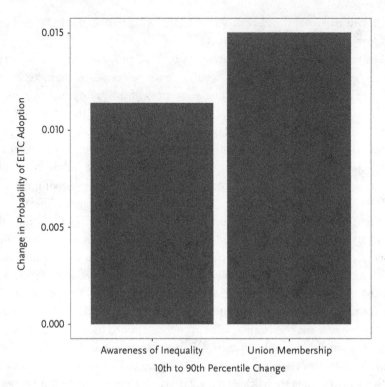

Figure 7.4: Effect of Public Awareness of Inequality and Union Membership on Likelihood of State EITC Adoption

Note: Estimates are based on the model results presented in appendix table B.12.

support of antipoverty groups that do the same) are critical to creating the conditions for adopting the EITC.

CONCLUSION

The earned income tax credit is an effective policy that has been implemented by both the federal and state governments. It has been shown to reduce poverty, curtail income inequality, and boost overall levels of employment (Eissa and Hoynes 2006; Hungerford 2010). The idea behind the EITC is to limit the income tax liability of workers who are already struggling financially, and in some cases to offer a direct cash payment to those with low earnings. Similar to the reasoning behind examining the minimum wage in chapter 6, the EITC is an inequality-reducing program that has been adopted by a number of state governments. These features of the EITC allow us to ask why some states have chosen to adopt the redistributive policy while others have not, while emphasizing the importance of public's growing concern about inequality and political organization of the lower classes.

Consistent with our findings in previous chapters, we show that the public's awareness of expanding income differences influences whether the states adopt their own versions of the EITC. Specifically, states are more likely to have an EITC expansion when public perceptions of inequality increase. This finding makes an important connection between economic inequality, the public's understanding of inequality, and government redistribution. Some scholars have argued that Americans are unable to link their concern about inequality with their preferences for redistributive policy and that government is largely unresponsive to public opinion in any case (e.g., Bartels 2008). But the EITC (and the minimum wage examined in the previous chapter) show that where inequality is perceived as greater, democratically elected governments provide more inequality-reducing policies. Additionally, the analysis in this chapter highlights the essential role of labor organizations in pushing for more equitable economic outcomes. When the presence of union membership is at a high level, we find that states have a higher likelihood of adopting a state EITC, which differs from the minimum wage, where unions were relatively unimportant (though they appear to be becoming increasingly important in recent years). Interestingly, though labor is often leading the charge for the minimum wage, labor seems more essential to the enactment of EITC programs, perhaps because of their greater complexity and less familiarity among the public.

In chapters 5 and 6 we argued that the state initiative process has provided citizens with a tool that allows them to circumvent the legislative process when government is unresponsive. This is seemingly the case when considering proposals to raise taxes on the rich, and our study of state minimum wage policy also substantiates this claim. When examining the EITC, however, the limitations of the initiative process are evident. Unlike wage minimums in the states, the initiative has no apparent effect on the adoption of state EITCs. We argue that this is largely due to the complexity and lower salience of EITC programs. Compared to the minimum wage or taxes on the wealthy, the EITC is still a relatively young policy that has the potential to become more prominent under the right circumstances, but the policy's complexity means that it may never have levels of familiarity and support as high as the minimum wage.

As we mentioned in the conclusion to chapter 6, a single state policy— whether it is higher taxes on rich, the minimum wage, or the EITC—is unlikely to transform American inequality on its own. The combination of policies like these, however, might influence the income distribution in ways that create a substantial shift in who benefits from the economic system. We can see clearly that states do not choose between these policies—states like Massachusetts and California have higher taxes on the wealthy, higher minimum wages, and generous EITCs. In contrast, states like North Carolina and Texas have lower taxes on the wealthy and more regressive tax systems, low minimum wages, and do not have the EITC (at least recently in North Carolina). Thus, the new economic populism has not hit all states, let alone the federal government. However, even some very conservative states like Missouri, South Dakota, and Nebraska have adopted minimum wage or EITC programs in recent years. Furthermore, if the adoption of these populist policies proves to be popular and successful, the likelihood that they will spread to what are now less hospitable states and the federal government will grow over time. We turn to this and other concluding thoughts in the final chapter.

CHAPTER 8

The New Economic Populism and the Future of Inequality in the United States

The United States has traditionally been a world leader in many things, and in recent years this has included leading the industrialized world in income inequality. We are bombarded almost daily with media stories about the growth of inequality in the United States and the socioeconomic consequences of this trend. Even the 170-year-old *Scientific American*, hardly a left-wing propaganda outlet, recently proclaimed in a headline, "Economic Inequality: It's Far Worse Than You Think" (Fitz 2015). As inequality worsens, its effects pervade virtually all aspects of American life. Just before Halloween in 2015 the chocolate and candy company Hershey's reported weaker-than-expected earnings and pointed to the "bifurcated" consumer market as the culprit (Reuters 2015). As income inequality has increased, higher-end consumers are willing to shell out big bucks for specialty chocolate, while for an increasing number of consumers who have faced stagnant wages, the simple Hershey bar is becoming an expensive luxury. More generally, companies that cater to the low and middle classes are struggling across the country, while those that cater to the rich are performing very well (Schwartz 2014).

These dynamics have led observers to worry about the long-term health of the American economy. Consumer spending has driven the growth of America's economy for over a century, but if most consumers lack increasing wages, where will the new growth come from? Median income growth was strong in 2015 (Tankersley 2016), but this has been unusual in recent years. Credit and speculative bubbles have been the normal route to increased consumer spending over the last few decades, but the dot-com boom and the housing bubble had painful consequences once they burst. The aftermath of the housing bubble is still being felt, as wealth has been permanently destroyed for many households and homeownership rates are at their lowest in decades. Though the wealthy still have growing incomes, it is not clear that they can provide broad economic growth, since even if the very wealthy spend a great deal of their income on consumer products, they can buy only so many products because they are relatively few in number. There is continuing debate about whether inequality leads to stunted growth, but there is accumulating evidence that it does (Organization for Economic Cooperation and Development 2014).

What happens if the economy stagnates for decades? Or if an increasingly dispirited majority with limited economic prospects observes the growing wealth of the few? History suggests that social and political unrest is likely. The nature of the relationship between economic inequality and political instability may be one of the oldest areas of inquiry in political science, as observers of the political world have considered this topic since the time of Plato. Scholars increasingly compare the American political system to a relatively benign plutocracy, where the rich get what they want and the poor and the middle class rarely win in the policy process when their preferences oppose those of the wealthy (Gilens 2012; Gilens and Page 2014; Winters and Page 2009). Such a situation is objectionable to most Americans, and it is hard to believe that it is sustainable in an ostensible democracy over the very long run. Yet it does not appear that the growth of inequality will be slowed in the near future, let alone reversed.

While many hoped that the election of a Democratic president in 2008 and again in 2012 would reverse this situation, this has not proven to be the case. In fact, as with the last Democratic administration—Bill Clinton's—during the Obama administration inequality continued to get considerably worse. In truth, the modern Democratic Party sometimes pursues the interests of the wealthy arm in arm with the Republicans, as when the Clinton administration pursued tax and regulatory policies that made Wall Street bankers even richer (Witko 2016). But the reality is that it is very difficult for a president to reduce income inequality because laws passed by Congress stack the deck in favor of the wealthy and against the poor and middle class (Hacker and Pierson 2010). Because the president cannot change such policies unilaterally, for the federal government to effectively confront economic inequality congressional action is needed. But with rare and important exceptions (like the Affordable Care Act), Congress has shown no ability to tackle America's major problems in recent years, and has routinely failed or nearly failed to complete even basic tasks, like passing a budget bill or raising the debt ceiling. With this level of dysfunction in Congress it is hard to envision the body enacting major policy changes that would reverse over three decades of rising income inequality. This congressional inaction allows existing economic arrangements to remain undisturbed, and contributes to the seemingly inexorable march of growing inequality (Enns et al. 2014).

Many people who voted for Donald Trump in 2016 did so because they are deeply dissatisfied with the status quo and wanted to blow up the system in Washington, DC. Trump was elected president in 2016 on a wave of populist rage, of precisely the type that might be expected as the public becomes angrier about economic inequality and its component parts. More than most candidates in recent years, and certainly more than any Republican in decades, Donald Trump made explicit appeals to those who have been left behind by the postindustrial economy, and targeted the winners of this period of growing inequality. He criticized insiders and fat-cat bankers who were "getting away with murder" and routinely railed against trade deals that had cost hard-working Americans their middle-class jobs. In an election eve speech Trump said that day was "the day the American working class is going to strike back" (Parker 2016). Whether these class-based appeals were decisive to his victory will take a while to figure out. It seems clear that ethnic, racial, and gender divisions also played a key role in earning him the support of enough voters to win the Electoral College. But, regardless of the populist tone of his campaign speeches, Trump's victory cemented the hold of the Republican Party on the House and Senate, and the party has not shown itself to be very concerned with inequality in recent years. Indeed, among the first proposals to be discussed after the election were tax cuts with disproportionate benefits for the wealthy, and cuts to safety net programs like Medicaid, policies very likely to make inequality worse. Thus, while Trump's governing agenda remains something of an enigma, given his relative inexperience compared to congressional leaders, more of the same neglect or exacerbation of inequality from DC is almost certain. This is troubling to Americans concerned about growing economic inequality.

Yet, as with the problems of slavery, the first Gilded Age and the Depression, we think American democracy will provide the tools needed to address the problem of growing inequality, and even Congress will probably act eventually to tackle the growing problem of inequality. It is not only that America usually does the right thing after all other alternatives have been exhausted (a comments that is sometimes attributed to Winston Churchill). As we have shown in the pages of this book, state governments and organized interests are not waiting for the Congress or other entities in Washington, DC to act. The states are already responding to growing economic inequality in a variety of ways depending on their specific political and institutional context. Though not all states are taking such steps, many are. And while the more liberal states have been more likely to act, even conservative states are sometimes doing things like raising their minimum wage and expanding the EITC. What we have called the "new economic populism" is becoming more widespread and, if history is a guide, this movement contains the seeds of an even broader and more concerted national response to growing economic inequality in the coming years.

THE ROOTS OF THE NEW ECONOMIC POPULISM

For most of the last few decades. as inequality has increased, there has been little response to inequality by any level of government. Theory would lead us to expect that in a representative democracy government will most aggressively move to address a problem when the public is more concerned about that problem. The American public prefers more equal economic outcomes, even while it dramatically underestimates the true extent of economic inequality (Norton and Ariely 2011). This underestimation of true inequality cannot be entirely surprising since, unlike the unemployment rate or economic growth, there are not generally accepted, widely disseminated, and well-understood indicators of economic inequality. While the unemployment rate is simple to understand, the Gini coefficient is much more difficult to comprehend. Though top income share data are much simpler to interpret, until recently these have not been widely disseminated in the media.

Despite these obstacles to understanding changes in inequality for the mass public, as inequality has grown the public has, in fact, become more aware of growing economic inequality (Kelly and Enns 2010). But as we show here, public responsiveness to growing inequality is by no means uniform across the states. In part, this reflects that the timing and severity in the growth of inequality has varied greatly across states, and as we showed in chapter 3 the variation in the degree of public awareness of inequality is related to changes in the objective percentage of income going to the highest earners. In the states where inequality is worse, people are more aware of economic inequality. Yet, even after controlling for objective levels of inequality, there is still variation in public concern about this phenomenon among states. This reflects that other economic and political factors, particularly mass partisanship and ideology, shape the public's awareness of income inequality. Democrats and liberals are simply predisposed to be more concerned about economic inequality, and are thus more aware of growing inequality regardless of how severe this growth actually is. This is important since, whereas the public as a whole has become more Republican and conservative over the last few decades, there is extensive variation in the states. Some states, like California and Vermont, have shifted toward the Democratic Party. This variation in state mass partisanship means that some state populations will be more responsive to growing inequality than others and than the national electorate, opening up the possibility of state responses to this problem. Regardless of the precise causes of a growing awareness of inequality, which are partly objective and partly subjective, we have seen in the preceding chapters that public awareness of inequality is associated with a number of changes in government and public policies in the states that can be expected to produce more equal economic outcomes.

FORMS OF NEW ECONOMIC POPULISM

What we have called the new economic populism can in some ways be seen as a coherent, rational response to growing inequality. A public concern about inequality is associated with objective levels of inequality. This awareness of inequality then pushes the government to the left, and some policies are crafted to address concerns about inequality. However, the new economic populism also reflects a diverse set of governing and policy arrangements. For instance, some conservative politicians may support the EITC because they want to reduce taxes for everyone, and the initiative can be used in even fairly conservative states to get more egalitarian policy outcomes.

Government Liberalism

Over the last few decades state governments have probably been growing more conservative in general, but we showed in chapter 4 that where inequality is perceived to be a greater problem, governments are more liberal or left-wing than would otherwise be expected after controlling for these broader, secular shifts toward conservatism found in public opinion. Considering the large amount of comparative literature indicating that such governments will preside over more equal economic outcomes, we expected to see that more liberal state governments were also associated with lower-than-expected levels of economic inequality, which is precisely what we observed in our data, including different variables and covering a different time period than past studies. Thus, in some states, the growing perceptions of inequality are associated with more liberal governments, which contribute to lower inequality.

The Initiative

The institutional variation found in the states also creates some space for the development of policies to address inequality, which does not exist at the federal level. The initiative is one such institution, which allows for more majoritarian control over public policy. Some policies, such as tax increases, are viewed as politically very dangerous, and even liberal politicians may not want to touch these "third rails." In states with conservative governments and generally conservative citizens some egalitarian policies—like an increased minimum wage—are popular, but elected officials won't enact them because of the preferences of their core constituents. Where politicians fear these third rails or their core constituents and interest group backers do not support egalitarian interventions supported by the general public, some policies will be out of step with the majority's preferences. Under such conditions, the initiative is a tool that can be used to bring policy back into line with the preferences of the mass public (Matsusaka 1995). Indeed, states adopted this institution during the Gilded Age, when it was perceived that state governments were dominated by big business and the wealthy, as we described in chapter 2. And we see that at least in some cases the initiative can be important for higher taxes on the wealthy and for minimum wage increases.

Raising Taxes on the Rich

Over the last few decades, proposing a tax increase or voting to increase taxes has become a third rail for politicians. Almost nothing could be worse than being viewed as a "tax and spend" liberal. Yet surveys show that most Americans support increasing taxes on the wealthy to reduce inequality (Page, Bartels, and Seawright 2013). But even very liberal politicians are hesitant to propose tax increases after many decades when taxes have been given a bad name. Under these circumstances the initiative can move tax policy closer to voter preferences. In chapter 5 we examined support for a ballot initiative in Washington State, Proposition 1098, which would have created an income tax for high-income earners. Proposition 1098 also allowed us to see how individual attitudes toward inequality shape specific policy preferences. We saw that growing economic inequality featured prominently in the debate over this issue and that individuals who were more concerned with growing inequality were more likely to support Proposition 1098, suggesting that as inequality grows, the potential for tax increases will also. Furthermore, just a couple of years later a similar initiative passed in California, producing a large budget surplus and none of the projected negative economic consequences that critics of tax increases on the wealthy predict. More broadly, we showed that a greater public awareness of inequality is associated with higher top income tax rates. Given the apparent success of this policy in California and the growing awareness of inequality, other states may emulate California's new policy, just as they did Proposition 13 in the 1970s.

Redistribution and Market Conditioning to Raise Incomes of the Poor

Admittedly, tax increases on the wealthy are unpopular among conservatives and therefore unlikely to take place in conservative states, though the multidecade refusal to consider tax increases does seem to be coming to an end, even in some conservative states (Niquette and Newkirk 2015). But other egalitarian policies, including some redistributive policies, do have high levels of support from the public. In chapters 6 and 7 we examined the minimum wage and the earned income tax credit (EITC), two egalitarian policies that have widespread public support, and which have sometimes been enacted even in conservative states in recent years.

The minimum wage is an example of an egalitarian "market-conditioning policy," that is, one that shapes the income distribution before taxation and government spending. The minimum wage originated in the states, and several states adopted minimum wages well before the federal minimum wage law was enacted in the 1930s. Now the federal government and state governments jointly control the minimum wage, but Republican control of the federal government and of some state governments has prevented increasing minimum wages. We again saw in the analysis of the state minimum wage that it tends to be higher in states where the public's awareness of inequality is higher. And we also saw direct evidence that as the federal government failed to raise the minimum wage over a number of years, the states were more likely to do so. Liberal governments were especially likely to raise minimum wages, but even in a number of conservative states (Alaska, Arkansas, Nebraska, and South Dakota) they have recently been increased by ballot initiative. The initiative seems to be a particularly useful means of raising the minimum wage, particularly when it has been a long time since the federal government has raised the minimum wage. This policy nicely demonstrates how the initiative can help some states to overcome government nonresponsiveness to concerns about inequality, whether the state or federal government is not responding.

The EITC is an example of redistributive tax policy, since low-income earners can receive more money back in the form of a tax credit than they pay in income taxes. The roots of the EITC can be found in LBJ's War on Poverty, but this policy was also championed by conservatives in the 1970s and 1980s. Indeed, Reagan's 1986 tax reform law included a major expansion of the EITC. More recently, we have seen conservative politicians and advocacy groups like ALEC turn against the EITC. We have also seen, however, that in this era of growing inequality and growing federal inaction in the face of inequality, a large number of states have adopted an EITC. We observe that where perceptions of inequality are greater, the EITC has been more likely to be adopted. Though this was more likely to take place in states with strong unions, government liberalism was unrelated to the adoption of state EITC laws, meaning that liberal and conservative state governments have been about as likely to adopt an EITC. Because of the structure of the policy, even conservatives can traditionally get behind the EITC as a means of combating inequality, which is part of the reason that this policy was actually expanded during the 1980s. Though there are renewed attempts to do away with the EITC, they have been largely unsuccessful thus far.

With both the EITC and the minimum wage, we see relatively old policies pursued in different ways by different states as the federal government has failed to expand and update these existing policy tools (at least in the case of the minimum wage) to tackle growing inequality. We do not directly examine the effects of these policies on subsequent levels of inequality in this research since we focus on the factors that cause some states to pursue these policies, but existing research shows that the minimum wage and the EITC do in fact reduce levels of economic inequality (Hoynes and Patel 2015; Kelly and Witko 2012; Lee 1999). The continued enactments of minimum wage increases and EITC programs even as the country shifts to the right suggests that, moving forward, policy entrepreneurs should search for other egalitarian policies that can attract the support of a broad ideological coalition, are relatively easy for the public to understand, and encourage work. Such policies are likely to continue to have high levels of public support, regardless of any broader changes in the political environment. Even in this highly polarized era, there is a broad middle ground of agreement on some policies that can reduce inequality.

THE FEDS AND THE NEW ECONOMIC POPULISM

Thus far, as we note at the outset of this chapter, the federal government's response to growing economic inequality has been limited. This is why the new economic populism is occurring in the states in the first place. But federal inaction in the face of emerging economic problems is nothing new, as we discussed in chapter 2. Throughout history, the federal government has repeatedly failed to lead in the fight against emerging economic problems, with few exceptions (such as the Great Society programs of the 1960s). There are a variety of institutional reasons for this slow federal response, ranging from the structure of federal institutions, which are designed to make it hard to get much done, to the power of economic actors in the party and interest systems who prefer the status quo. These actors can control at least one of the many institutional veto points. Thus, though it is frustrating to many, we should not, based on the historical record, be entirely surprised that the federal government has failed to address growing economic inequality in the short term.

Nevertheless, this federal inaction is still problematic. The states can do much to combat economic inequality, as we have seen. But there are things that the states cannot do. For instance, the federal government has sole or primary control over monetary policy, interstate commerce issues like regulating the financial industry, and trade policy. And interstate competition for jobs and business investment can make it difficult for the states do things like bolster unions, whereas the federal government has the ability to set a level playing field for all 50 states. Indeed, a number of states have taken steps to weaken unions in recent years, ostensibly to make their states more attractive to business investment. Even in policy realms where the states can act, the federal government has many more resources with which to influence economic outcomes. Finally, though many states have acted to address growing economic inequality, many others have not. This means that a state-by-state approach to combating growing economic inequality will inevitably leave some Americans behind and leave pockets of growing inequality even as the growth of inequality is reduced or even reversed elsewhere. Just as federal action was ultimately critical to address slavery, industrialization, and the Great Depression, federal action will be needed to fully address growing inequality.

Thus, we should not view state action as a substitute for federal action. Fortunately, it is often a precursor to federal action. We showed in chapter 2 that state policy innovations and experimentation have historically diffused horizontally across states, but then also vertically up to the federal government. While the federal government was ultimately critical in addressing economic problems like developing infrastructure to create a national economy, eliminating slavery to reduce oppression and establish freer labor markets, and confronting the problems of industrial capitalism during the Progressive Era and Great Depression, almost all of the policies embraced by the federal government to combat these problems were first developed and demonstrated in the states. We expect to see a similar pattern with income inequality.

State policy experimentation does two important things. First, it demonstrates novel or innovative policy tools that can be used to effectively combat economic problems. The policies that we examine in detail in these chapters are not truly novel; in some ways they are old ideas made new again. Tax increases on the wealthy have been rare in recent years, as states and the federal government have been cutting taxes for most of the last few decades. When states pursue and adopt such policies as tax increases on the wealthy or increasing minimum wages, it gets policymakers elsewhere used to the idea that this is a viable option to consider. Because the US government has reduced inequality before and many other countries have lower levels of inequality right now, there are a number of policy tools that can be used to reduce inequality with a high degree of certainty.

There are also likely to be completely new policy tools formulated to address inequality in the coming decades that we cannot yet foresee but that politicians and thinkers are beginning to explore. For instance, in 2016 Portland enacted a surtax on companies that pay their CEO more than 100 times their average worker. The author of this provision on the city council borrowed the idea from a bill that was introduced a couple of years before in the California State Senate, even though this bill was never enacted (Erb 2016). We can expect to see more similarly creative ways to directly address income inequality in the future. If successful and popular, such policies will also diffuse to other states and the federal government, and even localities, as the Portland example shows.

Though the idea of a tax increase is itself hardly new or innovative, we saw that proponents of tax increases on the wealthy in California creatively used the ideas of a temporary tax increase, allocation to designated popular programs, and strict auditing of expenditures to gain public support for this proposal. Though temporary, a follow-up initiative enacted in 2016 extends the tax increase for an additional 12 years. Including similar provisions in tax increases, along with the current success of this policy in California, will presumably make tax increases more attractive in other states, and perhaps ultimately the federal government.

But just as important as providing policy examples for other jurisdictions, the experimentation in the states also indicates which policies are politically palatable, feasible, and even popular. For instance, once it is demonstrated that citizens in many states are comfortable with raising taxes on the wealthy and that these policies do not produce disastrous political or economic consequences (and can even lead to budget surpluses, as in California), other state or federal politicians will be more likely to advocate for such policies than they would be in the absence of these political and policy experiments. If nothing else, successful policy examples strengthen the ability to argue for a particular policy. Or perhaps it will be demonstrated that such tax increases are rarely popular and are ineffective, in which case activists should pursue other policies, like increasing the minimum wage or expanding tax credits for the working poor. Whether these state policy actions succeed or fail, they provide opportunities for learning.

Realistically, it seems like a remote possibility that the federal government will engage in massive efforts to reverse growing economic inequality in the future. But we have also seen this before. In 1931 it did not appear at all feasible that the federal government would take steps to limit the human suffering of the Great Depression, but of course it did this within a short number of years. On the eve of the 1930s, income inequality was as high as it is now. Admittedly, by wiping out many large fortunes the Great Depression did much to reverse this inequality, and the crisis of the Depression and the experience of World War II changed people's view of the proper role of government. Nevertheless, policies were put in place to make the economy function better for most people for several decades even after these crises had passed. Given that we will (hopefully) not experience anything as extreme as the Depression and a world war, it is unlikely that government action will be as swift to reduce inequality this time. It will be more of a long-term response of adopting policies to address inequality, much as Progressive Era reforms were adopted from the 1890s through the 1930s. In short, we think it is likely that the federal government will get serious about combating economic inequality in the coming decades.

We are already seeing the initial signs of this. Discussions of economic inequality have moved from the political left and intellectuals to the mainstream. Conservatives no longer deny the existence of any problem with inequality, and indeed, Republican presidential candidates have accurately criticized the growth of inequality under recent Democratic presidents and highlighted this issue on the stump (Gold 2015). Congress has yet to focus very much on economic inequality, let alone making it a major policy priority. However, it is clear that some Democratic members of Congress are concerned with economic inequality, as Bernie Sanders and Elizabeth Warren have made economic inequality the centerpiece of their campaigns for the Senate and Democratic presidential nomination in recent years.

Republicans appear less focused on economic inequality, which makes some sense considering their wealthier constituency. Yet, even within the Republican base, first in the Tea Party movement and now in the "Trumpistas," we see a strongly populist strain that is deeply suspicious of some of the political power brokers like Wall Street investment bankers, who have pushed many of the policies that have contributed to growing economic inequality (Keller and Kelly 2015; Witko 2016). After all, many Republican members of Congress voted against the Wall Street bailout after the 2008 financial crisis, urged on by their Tea Party constituents. And Donald Trump tapped into this vein of anger at economic elites within the Republican Party in his 2016 campaign. Admittedly, this current manifestation of right-wing populism may appear unlikely to be turned into a political force to stop the growth of inequality, thanks to its apparent objection to any constructive role for government in the economy and society, and its contempt for many categories of Americans who are suffering economically. Yet, as signs reading "Keep the government out of my Medicare" at Tea Party rallies attest, not all populist Republicans object to government action to combat economic problems. Donald Trump has shown that, even within the Republican Party, a large portion of voters will accept proposals that increase government's role in labor markets and trade policy and are anything but laissez-faire capitalism. It seems doubtful based on continuing Republican leadership in Congress that Trump's victory will lead to attempts to roll back inequality, as noted above. But it is possible in the future that a skillful and more experienced political leader can exploit this bipartisan dissatisfaction with the growing power of Wall Street and other economic elites and turn federal government policymaking in an egalitarian direction.

As we have shown, growing inequality matters for opinion and policy. As the public becomes more aware of existing economic disparities and the trajectory of inequality further establishes that only an elite few are benefiting from the current economic system, it is possible that our most salient political questions will more frequently be debated along class lines. A shift to a more class-based form of politics is no guarantee, particularly when considering that Americans who could be identified as lower or working class have supported recent national policies that benefit the rich at the expense of the poor (e.g., see Bartels 2008). Some have attributed this apparent disconnect between economic status and political attitudes to a "false consciousness" that exists among those from the lower classes (Pines 1993). This view suggests that rather than seeing greater support for government intervention among those at the bottom of the income ladder as a way to create more equal outcomes, the status quo is justified through the belief that economic elites are successful because of their individual efforts and that this success represents an example of the American dream being alive and well. It is also possible that rather than class inequalities becoming a more salient feature in American politics, the racial and ethnic divisions exploited by Donald Trump in his 2016 campaign will become more central, muffling class-based demands for a more equitable income distribution.

As income inequality grows, however, the public may find it increasingly difficult to support a system that leads to prosperity for few people, whether they are white, black, or brown. If Americans are generally aware of these growing income differences, is it plausible that inequality is more clearly defining economic winners and losers and emphasizing the flaws of the system? We believe this is a realistic possibility. In fact, the public's beliefs about financial success and the fairness of the economic system have changed in recent years. For instance, opinion polls show a decline over the past two decades in the number of people who believe hard work leads to success (Kohut 2015). Over a similar period, the percentage of people who agree that "there's plenty of opportunity" to get ahead in America today has declined from 81% in 1998 to 52% in 2013 (Dugan and Newport 2013). Of course, it is difficult to say whether these changes are a direct response to growing inequality, but it is telling that so many people have altered their views on what it takes to be successful, which may be a precursor to changes in how the public views the role of government in shaping economic outcomes.

In any event, the older, whiter, more affluent, and more conservative voters who are the backbone of the Republican Party and propelled Donald Trump to office in 2016 will become a smaller slice of the vote in the coming decades, meaning that groups that are, for the moment, less hostile to government action to address economic problems, favor more egalitarian policy interventions, and who have historically gotten the short end of the economic stick—women and racial and ethnic minorities—will almost certainly have more political power in the coming decades. The liberalism of African Americans is well known, but rapidly growing groups like Asian Americans also favor a more expansive role for government in society (Edsall 2015). Though many groups are trying to make it harder for younger voters and immigrants to exercise their political rights (Franko,

Kelly, and Witko 2016), and Trump seems likely to attempt to increase voter suppression, over the long run there is no doubt that the electorate will become less white and, as a result, probably less affluent. This will likely lead politicians running for state or federal office to the embrace more egalitarian policies.

Whether these predictions about the future of federal action are confirmed in the next couple of generations will remain to be seen. But American history teaches us that, despite the many flaws and imperfections of the system, there is a tendency toward self-correction and improvement. Though we think that it is likely that the federal government will take action to reverse inequality as it has in the past, this is not an invitation to sit back and wait patiently for this to happen. Our abstract model of the new economic populism makes this process seem somewhat mechanistic, almost inevitable. But the process of economic change that we envision is anything but that. Indeed, in some states powerful organized interests and politicians are pursuing policy changes, such as tax cuts for the wealthy, weakening unions, and cutting social programs, that are almost certain to increase inequality. Federal action to address emerging economic threats and problems only arose in the past thanks to the agitation and impatience of activists and politicians, often outside of the federal government in the states, unhappy with the status quo. As we have outlined in this book, this agitation is already happening in many states. These states will continue to fight economic inequality in the ways that we have examined, and they will also undoubtedly introduce other policy tools to the fight in the future. This means that as long as economic inequality continues to grow, which appears to be a certainty in the near term, the new economic populism is here to stay.

APPENDIX A
Measurement and Methodology

MEASURING THE PUBLIC'S AGGREGATE AWARENESS
OF INCOME INEQUALITY OVER TIME IN THE STATE

The most common approach to measuring state opinion in the absence of polls specifically designed to sample state populations (which are quite rare) is to use some form of disaggregation. Disaggregation generally involves combining many national surveys and then disaggregating responses by state. Since the common sample size of a national survey is around 1,000 respondents, the main drawback of this method is that a large number of surveys are required in order to produce accurate estimates of state opinion. Disaggregation is particularly problematic for this study since not nearly enough polls asked the rich-poor question to measure state opinion over time for every state. Recent advances in public opinion estimation, however, have given researchers an alternative to disaggregation when studying attitudes at the state-level. Multilevel regression and poststratification (MRP) is a measurement strategy that allows for the estimation of state opinion using typical national opinion polls. Research has shown that MRP provides accurate estimates of state and local opinion even when using a single national survey (Lax and Phillips 2009a; 2009b; 2012; Park, Gelman, and Bafumi 2006). This is the approach taken here to create a unique measure of state-level awareness of growing economic inequality (also see Franko 2017). Table A1 provides information on the collection of survey data we use to estimate inequality awareness, including the polling organizations that conducted the surveys and the years the surveys were conducted, the exact question wording, coding, and sources.[1]

Estimating opinion using MRP involves two steps. The first is to model individual responses to the survey question of interest—in this case, whether the individual agrees or disagrees with "the rich are getting richer and the poor are getting poorer" statement—using multilevel regression. These models include basic demographic and geographic characteristics of the survey respondents. Similar to pervious work, this study uses the following characteristics to model awareness of inequality: race (black, white, or other), gender (female or male), age (18–29, 30–44, 45–64, or 65+), education (less than high school graduate, high school graduate, some college, or college graduate), state of residence (all 50 states and DC),[2] the percentage of Republican Party identifiers in each state, the year of the survey (more on this below), and an indicator for each survey used to account for any potential differences across polls.

The results of the model are then used to predict the probability of agreeing that inequality is growing for every possible individual type (e.g., a white female who is 30–44 years of age with some college education living in Ohio), resulting in a total of 4,896 predicted values. These probabilities are then used in the second step of the estimation, which is poststratification. Poststratification is the process of weighting each individual type probability estimate by the actual proportion of each type in the population using data from the US census.[3] This part of the procedure adjusts for any differences between the individuals surveyed in each state and the true state population.

The strategy for creating the over-time state opinion estimates developed here departs slightly from previous studies using MRP to measure attitudes over time. One potential strategy to account for change in opinion over time using MRP is to complete the steps described above for each year under analysis (see Enns and Koch 2013). This approach is most useful when the questions used to measure opinion are asked several times every year so that enough respondents from smaller states are used to have more precise over-time estimates. While the "rich are getting richer" question is asked regularly, it is only asked more than once in a given year on a few occasions. When the survey questions being examined are not asked multiple times on an annual basis, an alternative option is to increase state sample sizes by combining surveys across multiple years. Rather than estimating state opinion for every year, surveys are pooled over specified blocks of time (e.g., a three- or five-year window) to increase the amount of information used when modeling opinion (see Pacheco 2011).

This study expands on these methods by using a completely pooled approach to estimate state opinion over time. In other words, all available survey questions for all available years are included in a single model of individual opinion (i.e., the first step of MRP). The procedure is relatively straightforward and only requires researchers to add a time component to their multilevel model. An indicator of time (in this case, the year the survey was conducted) is interacted with state of residence so that a random effect is allowed for every state-year combination.[4] This allows for unique estimates of opinion for each state over time by using all available information in one model. The result is a series of aggregate state opinion from 1987 to 2012 indicating the percentage of the public agreeing with the "rich are getting richer" statement. This variable is used throughout the book to account for the public's aggregate awareness of inequality. Additional details about the measure, along with a number of validity checks, can be found in Franko (2017).

Table A.1. SURVEY QUESTIONS USED TO ESTIMATE AGGREGATE STATE
AWARENESS OF ECONOMIC INEQUALITY

Polling Organization & Question Wording	Year of Survey	Coding
ABC News: I'm going to read a few statements, for each, please tell me if you agree or disagree with it . . . The rich are getting richer and everyone else is getting poorer.	1996	1 = agree; 0 = disagree
CBS News: These days, do you feel that the rich are getting richer and everyone else is getting poorer, or is that not the case?	2011	1 = rich getting richer; 0 = not the case
CBS News / New York Times: These days, do you feel that the rich are getting richer and everyone else is getting poorer, or is that not the case?	2011	1 = rich getting richer; 0 = not the case
Harris Poll: Now, we want to ask you about some things some people have told us they have felt from time to time. Do you tend to feel that . . . The rich get richer and the poor get poorer?	1991, 1996, 1997, 2002–2005, 2007–2009, 2011	1 = yes, feel this way; 0 = no, don't feel this way
Marttila & Kiley: Now I am going to read you a series of statements that will help us understand how you feel about a number of things. Please tell me whether you completely agree, mostly agree, mostly disagree, or completely disagree with each statement I read . . . Today it's really true that the rich just get richer while the poor get poorer.	1992	1 = completely agree or mostly agree; 0 = mostly disagree or completely disagree
Pew Values Survey: I'm going to read you some more statements on a different topic. Please tell me how much you agree or disagree with each of these statements . . . Today it's really true that the rich just get richer while the poor get poorer. Do you completely agree, mostly agree, mostly disagree, or completely disagree?	1987–1989, 1991, 1992, 1997, 1999, 2002, 2003, 2007, 2008 (Social Trends Survey), 2009, 2012	1 = completely agree or mostly agree; 0 = mostly disagree or completely disagree
Princeton Survey Research Associates: Here are some statements on a different topic. Please tell me how much you agree or disagree with each of these statements . . . Today it's really true that the rich just get richer while the poor get poorer.	1991, 1992 (5)	1 = completely agree or mostly agree; 0 = mostly disagree or completely disagree

Source: The Harris Poll surveys were accessed through the Odum Institute's data archive (http://www.odum.unc.edu/odum/). The Pew Values Survey is available through the Pew Research Center's website (http://www.people-press.org/values-questions/). All other surveys were accessed using the Roper Center's iPOLL Databank (http://www.ropercenter.uconn.edu/data_access/ipoll/ipoll.html).

Note: The Harris Poll also asked the question in 1992 (2), 1993, 1994, 1999, and 2000, and the Pew Values Survey asked the question in 1990 and 1994. The question could not be used for these particular survey years, however, because state-of-residence identifiers are not included in the data.

Table A.2. STATE TIME-SERIES VARIABLES LIST AND DATA SOURCES

Variable Name	Source	Link
Top 10% Income Share	Frank (2009)	http://www.shsu.edu/eco_mwf/inequality.html
Top 1% Income Share	Frank (2009)	http://www.shsu.edu/eco_mwf/inequality.html
Gini Coefficient	Frank (2009)	http://www.shsu.edu/eco_mwf/inequality.html
Poverty Rate	US Census	http://www.census.gov/
Union Membership	Union Membership and Coverage Database	http://www.unionstats.com/
Per Capita Income	US Census	http://www.census.gov/
Partisanship (Dem. – Rep.)	Enns and Koch (2013)	http://thedata.harvard.edu/dvn/dv/Enns
State Government Ideology	Berry et al. (2013)	https://rcfording.wordpress.com/state-ideology-data/
Public Mood	Enns and Koch (2013)	http://thedata.harvard.edu/dvn/dv/Enns
% White	US Census	http://www.census.gov/
% Age 60+	US Census	http://www.census.gov/
Unemployment Rate	Bureau of Labor Statistics	http://www.bls.gov/
Minimum Wage	Department of Labor	http://www.dol.gov/whd/state/stateMinWageHis.htm
Initiative Qualification Index	Bowler and Donovan (2004), Table 1	n/a
State EITC Adoption	Tax Credits for Working Families	http://www.taxcreditsforworkingfamilies.org/earned-income-tax-credit/states-with-eitcs/

ESTIMATING STATISTICAL MODELS FOR TIME-SERIES CROSS-SECTIONAL DATA

While many of the relationships we assess in this book focus on the importance of variation across the states, we also have to consider the fact that economic inequality in the United States has grown dramatically in recent years and that the dynamics of this growth have played quite differently among the states (see chapter 3). This means that a number of the statistical analyses we estimate must account for variation both across states and over time. In other words, the data we are modeling to assess some of our questions involve repeated measures of state characteristics over multiple years. This kind of data structure is often referred to time-series cross-sectional (or TSCS) data, and, therefore, a modeling approach for TSCS data is needed when we are analyzing this type of data. When modeling TSCS data researchers must be aware of issues related to repeated measures over time (e.g., nonstationarity and autocorrelation) as well as the clustered nature of the data (e.g., over-time measures grouped by state), and a number of strategies have been proposed to address these common methodological obstacles (Beck and Katz 1995; 1996; Wilson and Butler 2007). Similar to the approach used by numerous scholars, error correction models (ECMs) are used to estimate the models in the book that require the use TSCS data. The following equation, which includes only a single independent variable for clarity, is used to model variables that vary over time among the states:

$$\Delta Y_{jt} = \gamma_0 + \alpha_1 Y_{j(t-1)} + \beta_1 \Delta X_{1jt} + \beta_2 X_{1j(t-1)} + u_j + e_{jt}$$

The ECM is employed here since it is one of the most general time-series models and allows researchers to account for both long- and short-term effects over time (De Boef and Keele 2008; Kelly and Enns 2010). In the above equation each observation is a particular state j in a given time period t. The first difference of the dependent variable, Y, is regressed on a lagged version of the dependent variable and a lagged and differenced version of each explanatory variable. The effect of the independent variable on the dependent variable is represented by β_1 and β_2, with the former being an estimate of the short-term effect of the variable. The α_1 estimate—also referred to as the error correction rate—together with the β_2 coefficient provides the long-run effect of the variable. The total effect, or long-run multiplier, is estimated as $(\beta_2 / -\alpha_1)$. The main distinction to make between short- and long-term effects is that short-term effects occur immediately, while long-term effects are distributed over time. When the effect of a variable is distributed over time, the long-run multiplier provides an estimate of the total effect of the variable for all periods.

All of the ECMs in the book are estimated using linear regression analyses that allow the intercept for each state to vary randomly (represented by the u_j term) as a way to account for any unexplained cross-sectional heterogeneity. Additionally, Hadri Lagrange multiplier stationarity tests were conducted for the main dependent variable used in the analyses. While a number of tests indicate evidence of nonstationarity in the levels of our dependent variables, the differenced version of the variables—that is, the version used in all of the models estimated for the book—demonstrate no signs of nonstationarity. Although time-series models that include a lagged version of the dependent variable as a regressor (as all of our models do) tend to have very low, if any, serial correlation of the errors (Beck and Katz 2011), we attempt to limit any remaining serial correlation by including time indicators in the models to account for any trending in the first-differenced dependent variable. Specifically, a set of time variables estimating a second- or third-order polynomial are included in each analysis.

APPENDIX B
Data and Results

Table B.1. THE EFFECT OF INCOME INEQUALITY ON PUBLIC
AWARENESS OF INEQUALITY

	Δ Awareness of Inequality		
	(1) b / (se)	(2) b / (se)	(3) b / (se)
Awareness of Inequality$_{t-1}$	−0.459***	−0.479***	−0.489***
	(0.024)	(0.024)	(0.024)
Δ Top 10% Income Share	31.898***		
	(6.067)		
Top 10% Income Share$_{t-1}$	−0.999		
	(2.545)		
Δ Top 1% Income Share		23.815***	
		(4.260)	
Top 1% Income Share$_{t-1}$		1.971	
		(2.416)	
Δ Gini Coefficient			0.638
			(4.832)
Gini Coefficient$_{t-1}$			0.242
			(2.284)
Δ Poverty Rate	0.078*	0.069*	0.070*
	(0.034)	(0.034)	(0.034)
Poverty Rate$_{t-1}$	0.035	0.023	0.027
	(0.027)	(0.027)	(0.028)
Δ Union Membership	−0.065	−0.064	−0.152+
	(0.080)	(0.079)	(0.080)
Union Membership$_{t-1}$	−0.041	−0.027	−0.005
	(0.047)	(0.047)	(0.047)
Δ Per Capita Income	−0.037	−0.048	0.026
	(0.083)	(0.082)	(0.082)
Per Capita Income$_{t-1}$	−0.019	−0.040+	−0.031
	(0.024)	(0.022)	(0.021)
Δ Partisanship (Dem. − Rep.)	0.097***	0.100***	0.104***
	(0.010)	(0.010)	(0.010)
Partisanship (Dem. − Rep.)$_{t-1}$	0.088***	0.094***	0.092***
	(0.009)	(0.009)	(0.009)
Constant	36.026***	37.546***	37.934***
	(1.986)	(1.848)	(2.153)
N	1200	1200	1200
Log-Likelihood	−2405.388	−2404.108	−2419.775

+ p < .10, * p < .05, ** p < .01, *** p < .001.
Note: Each model includes a set of time variables estimating a second- or third-order polynomial
to account for any remaining trend in the first-differenced dependent variable (these estimates
are not included in the table).

Table B.2. THE EFFECT OF INCOME INEQUALITY ON PUBLIC AWARENESS
OF INEQUALITY, CENTERED VARIABLE MODEL SPECIFICATION

	Δ Awareness of Inequality		
	(1) b / (se)	(2) b / (se)	(3) b / (se)
Awareness of Inequality$_{t-1}$	−0.497***	−0.506***	−0.537***
	(0.024)	(0.024)	(0.024)
Δ Top 10% Income Share	34.527***		
	(6.363)		
Top 10% Income Share$_{t-1}$	12.081*		
	(4.755)		
Δ Top 1% Income Share		21.370***	
		(4.259)	
Top 1% Income Share$_{t-1}$		1.506	
		(2.915)	
Δ Gini Coefficient			−1.311
			(4.672)
Gini Coefficient$_{t-1}$			9.236**
			(3.193)
Δ Poverty Rate	0.082*	0.083*	0.080*
	(0.037)	(0.037)	(0.038)
Poverty Rate$_{t-1}$	0.040	0.055	0.051
	(0.043)	(0.043)	(0.043)
Δ Union Membership	−0.086	−0.106	−0.211**
	(0.079)	(0.078)	(0.078)
Union Membership$_{t-1}$	0.064	0.021	0.047
	(0.061)	(0.061)	(0.059)
Δ Per Capita Income	−0.079	−0.048	0.016
	(0.080)	(0.079)	(0.078)
Per Capita Income$_{t-1}$	0.006	0.002	0.016
	(0.036)	(0.035)	(0.036)
Δ Partisanship (Dem. – Rep.)	0.078***	0.085***	0.086***
	(0.011)	(0.011)	(0.011)
Partisanship (Dem. – Rep.)$_{t-1}$	0.053***	0.066***	0.059***
	(0.013)	(0.012)	(0.012)
Constant	3.810***	3.400***	3.798***
	(0.549)	(0.533)	(0.570)
N	1200	1200	1200
Log-Likelihood	−2373.000	−2374.632	−2382.683

$+ p < .10,$ $^* p < .05,$ $^{**} p < .01,$ $^{***} p < .001.$
Note: These models are replications of the estimates presented in table B.1 with the only difference
being that the variables in these models have been mean-centered as an alternative way to account
for heterogeneity across states and over time. Each model includes a set of time variables estimating a second- or third-order polynomial to account for any remaining trend in the first-differenced
dependent variable (these estimates are not included in the table).

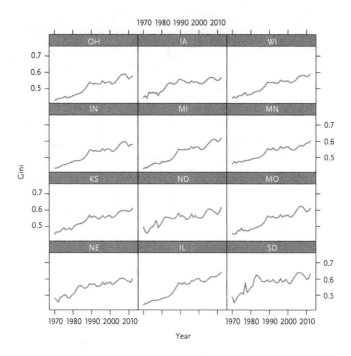

Figure B.1: Income Inequality Trends in Midwestern States (Gini Coefficient), 1970–2012

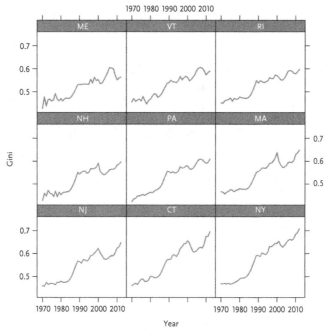

Figure B.2: Income Inequality Trends in Northern States (Gini Coefficient), 1970–2012

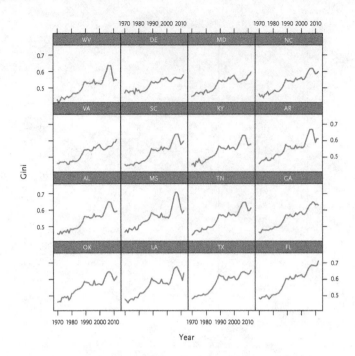

Figure B.3: Income Inequality Trends in Southern States (Gini Coefficient), 1970–2012

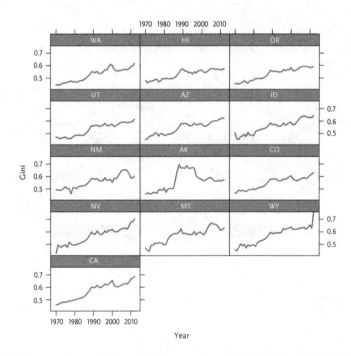

Figure B.4: Income Inequality Trends in Western States (Gini Coefficient), 1970–2012

Table B.3. THE EFFECT OF AWARENESS OF INEQUALITY
ON STATE GOVERNMENT IDEOLOGY

	Δ State Government Ideology	
	B	se
State Government Ideology$_{t-1}$	−0.114***	(0.013)
Δ Awareness of Inequality	0.418**	(0.133)
Awareness of Inequality$_{t-1}$	0.606***	(0.120)
Δ Public Mood	0.477***	(0.124)
Public Mood$_{t-1}$	0.098	(0.068)
Δ % White	−0.909	(0.823)
% White$_{t-1}$	0.084**	(0.033)
Δ % Age 60+	3.332	(2.326)
% Age 60+$_{t-1}$	0.114	(0.145)
Δ Per Capita Income	−0.011	(0.307)
Per Capita Income$_{t-1}$	0.119+	(0.068)
Constant	−53.791***	(10.251)
N	1200	
Log-Likelihood	−4307.248	

$+ p < .10$, $* p < .05$, $** p < .01$, $*** p < .001$.
Note: Each model includes a set of time variables estimating a second- or third-order polynomial to account for any remaining trend in the first-differenced dependent variable
(these estimates are not included in the table).

Table B.4. THE EFFECT OF STATE GOVERNMENT IDEOLOGY ON
STATE INEQUALITY

	Δ Gini b / se	Δ Top 10% b / se	Δ Top 1% b / se
Gini$_{t-1}$	-0.090***		
	(0.012)		
Top 10%$_{t-1}$		-0.227***	
		(0.018)	
Top 1%$_{t-1}$			-0.201***
			(0.017)
Δ State Government Ideology	-0.007*	-0.004	-0.003
	(0.004)	(0.003)	(0.004)
State Government Ideology$_{t-1}$	-0.004*	-0.004*	-0.002
	(0.002)	(0.002)	(0.002)
Δ Union Membership	-0.031	-0.025	-0.049
	(0.035)	(0.027)	(0.038)
Union Membership$_{t-1}$	0.001	0.029+	0.010
	(0.008)	(0.016)	(0.014)
Δ Unemployment Rate	-0.189***	-0.275***	-0.364***
	(0.048)	(0.035)	(0.052)
Unemployment Rate$_{t-1}$	0.092***	0.036	0.045
	(0.027)	(0.024)	(0.033)
Δ Per Capita Income	0.175***	0.245***	0.337***
	(0.050)	(0.038)	(0.054)
Per Capita Income$_{t-1}$	0.016	-0.025	0.024
	(0.010)	(0.015)	(0.016)
Δ % White	-0.015	0.039	0.028
	(0.101)	(0.077)	(0.111)
% White$_{t-1}$	-0.005	-0.028**	-0.005
	(0.004)	(0.011)	(0.008)
Δ % Age 60+	-0.306	-0.811***	-1.464***
	(0.286)	(0.238)	(0.337)
% Age 60+$_{t-1}$	-0.005	-0.041	-0.013
	(0.018)	(0.037)	(0.033)
Constant	6.897***	11.947***	2.600**
	(0.839)	(1.343)	(0.943)
N	1200	1200	1200
Log-Likelihood	-1822.319	-1516.336	-1937.044

+ $p < .10$, * $p < .05$, ** $p < .01$, *** $p < .001$.
Note: Each model includes a set of time variables estimating a second- or third-order polynomial to account for any remaining trend in the first-differenced dependent variable (these estimates are not included in the table).

Table B.5. THE EFFECT OF STATE GOVERNMENT IDEOLOGY AND
FEDERAL PARTY CONTROL ON STATE INEQUALITY

	Δ Gini b / se	Δ Top 10% b / se	Δ Top 1% b / se
Gini$_{t-1}$	−0.075***		
	(0.013)		
Top 10%$_{t-1}$		−0.250***	
		(0.021)	
Top 1%$_{t-1}$			−0.263***
			(0.021)
Δ State Government	−0.001	−0.001	0.001
Ideology	(0.003)	(0.003)	(0.003)
State Government	−0.003	−0.004*	−0.003
Ideology$_{t-1}$	(0.002)	(0.002)	(0.002)
Δ Union Membership	0.016	0.006	0.021
	(0.035)	(0.026)	(0.035)
Union Membership$_{t-1}$	0.006	0.023	0.043*
	(0.008)	(0.016)	(0.021)
Δ Unemployment Rate	0.097	−0.134*	−0.092
	(0.071)	(0.055)	(0.073)
Unemployment Rate$_{t-1}$	0.114***	0.081*	0.047
	(0.031)	(0.031)	(0.042)
Δ Per Capita Income	0.536***	0.655***	0.678***
	(0.071)	(0.054)	(0.072)
Per Capita Income $_{t-1}$	−0.061***	0.010	−0.164***
	(0.012)	(0.022)	(0.026)
Δ % White	−0.069	−0.031	0.068
	(0.095)	(0.072)	(0.096)
% White$_{t-1}$	−0.007+	−0.025*	−0.008
	(0.004)	(0.010)	(0.013)
Δ % Age 60+	−0.092	−0.019	−0.701*
	(0.306)	(0.260)	(0.348)
% Age 60+$_{t-1}$	0.020	−0.011	0.029
	(0.018)	(0.039)	(0.052)
Δ Democratic President	0.491**	0.811***	0.829***
	(0.151)	(0.118)	(0.160)
Democratic President$_{t-1}$	−0.219	−0.142	−0.382+
	(0.190)	(0.145)	(0.200)

Table B.5. CONTINUED

	Δ Gini b / se	Δ Top 10% b / se	Δ Top 1% b / se
Δ % Democrats in Congress	−12.933***	−8.470***	−7.141***
	(1.446)	(1.060)	(1.406)
Democrats in Congress$_{t-1}$	−14.559***	−15.481***	−14.898***
	(1.368)	(1.118)	(1.497)
Constant	14.894***	19.466***	12.486***
	(1.112)	(1.388)	(1.614)
N	912	912	912
Log-Likelihood	−1258.649	−1014.490	−1283.402

+ $p < .10$, * $p < .05$, ** $p < .01$, *** $p < .001$.
Note: Each model includes a set of time variables estimating a second- or third-order polynomial to account for any remaining trend in the first-differenced dependent variable (these estimates are not included in the table).

Table B.6. WASHINGTON POLL SURVEY QUESTION WORDING AND VARIABLE CODING

Variable	Question Wording	Coding
Support for 1098	Now I'm going to read a statewide ballot initiative that will appear on the November ballot: Initiative 1098 would institute an income tax on individuals earning more than $200,000 or households earning more than $400,000, and reduce state property taxes by 20 percent and also reduce the business and occupation tax and direct the increased revenues to education and health. Will you vote yes or no on initiative 1098? [Did you vote yes or no on initiative 1098?]	1 if respondent voted (if respondent voted early) or planned on voting yes, 0 if voted or planned on voting no.
Inequality is Bad	There is some talk these days about how the difference in incomes between rich people and poor people in the United States has continued to grow in the past 20 years. That is, rich people are getting richer, and poor people are getting poorer. Do you think this is a good thing, a bad thing, neither good nor bad, or haven't you thought about it?	1 for those who think that income inequality is a "bad thing," 0 otherwise.
Income	What was your total combined household income in 2009 before taxes. This question is completely confidential and just used to help classify the responses. Just stop me when I read the correct category. Less than $20,000; $20,000 to less than $40,000; $40,000 to less than $60,000; $60,000 to less than $80,000; $80,000 to less than $100,000; $100,000 to less than $200,000; More than $200,000	See text for discussion of various coding strategies used.
Party Identification	Generally speaking, do you think of yourself as a Democrat, a Republican, an independent, or what? [Follow up for those with no initial party affiliation:] Even though you do not consider yourself a Democrat or Republican, which of these parties do you feel closer to? Democrat, Republican, Independent/Other.	3 for Democrat, 2 for independent, and 1 for Republican.

(continued)

Table B.6. CONTINUED

Variable	Question Wording	Coding
Attention to 1098	How closely have you paid attention to information about ballot measure 1098, the proposal to establish a state income tax on the wealthy and reduce other taxes? Would you say extremely closely, very closely, moderately closely, slightly closely, or not closely at all?	1 for extremely closely or very closely, 0 otherwise.
Issue: [Education, Health Care, Taxes, and Economy]	Thinking ahead to the November 2010 elections, what general issues are most important to you as you decide how you will vote? [What general issues were most important to you as you decided how you would vote?]	A separate variable is used for each issue (Education, Health Care, Taxes, and Economy). For each variable, 1 for those who stated the issue was most important, 0 otherwise.
Government Approval	Now I'm going to read you a list of names of public officials and public organizations, and for each one, I want you to tell me whether you have a very favorable, somewhat favorable, somewhat unfavorable, or strongly unfavorable view of that person or organization. [List is randomized.] How about the state legislature in Olympia? Do you have a very favorable, somewhat favorable, somewhat unfavorable, or strongly unfavorable view of the state legislature in Olympia?	4 for very favorable, 3 for somewhat favorable, 2 for somewhat unfavorable, and 1 for strongly unfavorable.
Liberal	When it comes to politics, do you usually think of yourself as a Liberal, a Conservative, a Moderate, or haven't you thought much about this?	1 for Liberal, 0 otherwise.
Conservative	When it comes to politics, do you usually think of yourself as a Liberal, a Conservative, a Moderate, or haven't you thought much about this?	1 for Conservative, 0 otherwise.

Table B.6. CONTINUED

Variable	Question Wording	Coding
Education	What is the highest level of education you completed? Just stop me when I read the correct category—Grades 1–8, some high school, high school graduate, some college or technical school, college graduate, or post-graduate.	4 for post-graduate, 3 for college graduate, 2 for some college or technical school, and 1 for high school graduate or less.
Age	In what year were you born?	Age in years calculated from response.
Male	[Not asked; coded by interviewer.]	1 for male, 0 for female.
Homeowner	Do you currently own or rent your home?	1 for own, 0 otherwise.

Table B.7. LOGISTIC REGRESSION MODELS OF SUPPORT FOR PROPOSITION 1098 (TAXES ON THE WEALTHY)

	Income Binary		Income 3 Categories		Income 5 Categories	
	b	(se)	b	(se)	b	(se)
Inequality is Bad	0.835***	(0.248)	0.873***	(0.249)	0.830***	(0.251)
Income: 2 Category						
Less than $60k	0.604*	(0.260)				
$60k+ (reference)						
Income: 3 Category						
Less than $40k			0.602*	(0.295)		
$40–$100k (reference)						
$100k+			0.101	(0.267)		
Income: 5 Category						
Less than $40k					0.937*	(0.401)
$40–$60k					0.652	(0.409)
$60–$80k (reference)						
$80–$100k					0.068	(0.436)
$100k+					0.362	(0.367)
Income missing	−0.425	(0.318)	−0.522	(0.317)	−0.216	(0.415)
Party Identification	0.651***	(0.148)	0.665***	(0.147)	0.661***	(0.149)
Attention to 1098	−0.530*	(0.217)	−0.541*	(0.217)	−0.531*	(0.218)
Issue: Education	0.772+	(0.437)	0.721+	(0.436)	0.836+	(0.446)
Issue: Health Care	0.023	(0.362)	0.031	(0.364)	0.024	(0.365)
Issue: Taxes	−1.288***	(0.297)	−1.259***	(0.295)	−1.302***	(0.298)
Issue: Economy	0.467+	(0.282)	0.505+	(0.285)	0.505+	(0.287)
Government Approval	0.366***	(0.090)	0.365***	(0.090)	0.366***	(0.091)
Liberal	0.669**	(0.253)	0.679**	(0.253)	0.668**	(0.254)
Conservative	−0.733*	(0.299)	−0.679*	(0.299)	−0.712*	(0.302)
Education	0.280*	(0.116)	0.239*	(0.115)	0.274*	(0.117)
Age	−0.014+	(0.007)	−0.011	(0.007)	−0.013+	(0.007)
Male	−0.859***	(0.211)	−0.893***	(0.210)	−0.869***	(0.211)
Homeowner	−0.075	(0.286)	−0.096	(0.290)	−0.036	(0.294)
Constant	−2.489***	(0.669)	−2.483***	(0.675)	−2.749***	(0.706)
N	733		733		733	
Log-Likelihood	−317.333		−317.943		−316.344	
Pseudo R^2	0.374		0.373		0.376	

+ $p < .10$, * $p < .05$, ** $p < .01$, *** $p < .001$.

Table B.8. LOGISTIC REGRESSION MODEL OF SUPPORT
FOR PROPOSITION 1098, CONDITIONAL ON ATTENTION
TO BALLOT MEASURE

	Conditional Model: Attention	
	b	(se)
Inequality is Bad	0.942**	(0.321)
Income: Less than $60k	0.519+	(0.311)
Income: $60k+ (reference)		
Income missing	−0.445	(0.326)
Party Identification	0.186	(0.181)
Attention to 1098	−3.185***	(0.768)
Inequality is Bad × Attention	−0.403	(0.539)
Income: Less than $60k × Attention	−0.103	(0.451)
Party ID × Attention	1.242***	(0.298)
Issue: Education	0.631	(0.440)
Issue: Health Care	−0.005	(0.369)
Issue: Taxes	−1.275***	(0.304)
Issue: Economy	0.441	(0.290)
Government Approval	0.346***	(0.093)
Liberal	0.680**	(0.256)
Conservative	−0.974**	(0.320)
Education	0.277*	(0.118)
Age	−0.011	(0.007)
Male	−0.913***	(0.217)
Homeowner	−0.111	(0.285)
Constant	−1.458*	(0.730)
N	733.000	
Log-Likelihood	−306.657	
Pseudo R^2	0.395	

$+ p < 0.10,$ $^* p < 0.05,$ $^{**} p < 0.01,$ $^{***} p < 0.001.$

Table B.9. LOGISTIC REGRESSION MODELS OF SUPPORT FOR PROPOSITION 1098, CONDITIONAL ON PARTY IDENTIFICATION

	Cond. Model (1): Party ID		Cond. Model (2): Party ID	
	b	(se)	b	(se)
Inequality is Bad	−0.136	(0.601)	0.847**	(0.257)
Income: Less than $60k	0.934	(0.585)	0.692**	(0.267)
Income missing	−0.476	(0.330)	−0.345	(0.337)
Party Identification	−0.075	(0.292)	0.338+	(0.178)
Attention to 1098	−3.344***	(0.736)	−0.555*	(0.222)
Inequality is Bad × Party ID	0.483+	(0.281)		
Income: Less $60k × Party ID	−0.202	(0.234)		
Attention × Party ID	1.186***	(0.279)		
Issue: Education	0.659	(0.441)	1.421	(1.033)
Issue: Health Care	−0.050	(0.367)	−0.450	(1.011)
Issue: Taxes	−1.340***	(0.303)	−3.861**	(1.245)
Issue: Economy	0.454	(0.292)	−3.179**	(1.009)
Education × Party ID			−0.347	(0.437)
Health Care × Party ID			0.214	(0.402)
Taxes × Party ID			1.037*	(0.450)
Economy × Party ID			1.641***	(0.412)
Government Approval	0.351***	(0.093)	0.391***	(0.094)
Liberal	0.622*	(0.254)	0.659*	(0.257)
Conservative	−1.024**	(0.319)	−0.663*	(0.313)
Education	0.236*	(0.118)	0.326**	(0.119)
Age	−0.013+	(0.007)	−0.015*	(0.007)
Male	−0.982***	(0.221)	−0.840***	(0.215)
Homeowner	−0.049	(0.285)	−0.085	(0.294)
Constant	−0.748	(0.844)	−1.949**	(0.724)
N	733		733	
Log-Likelihood	−305.119		−303.593	
Pseudo R^2	0.398		0.401	

$+ p < .10,$ $^* p < .05,$ $^{**} p < .01,$ $^{***} p < .001.$

Table B.10. REGRESSION MODELS OF AVERAGE TOP
INCOME TAX RATES IN THE STATES BETWEEN 1987 AND 2012

	State Top Income Tax	
	b	(se)
Awareness of Inequality	0.780*	(0.377)
Public Mood	0.242	(0.191)
State Government Ideology	0.000	(0.036)
Union Membership	−0.115	(0.095)
Initiative Qualification Index	0.123	(0.179)
% White	13.736*	(6.390)
Constant	−71.394*	(32.330)
N	48.000	
Log-Likelihood	−111.229	
R^2	0.191	

$+ p < .10, * p < .05, ** p < .01, *** p < .001.$

Table B.11. EFFECT OF STATE CHARACTERISTICS ON STATE
MINIMUM WAGE LAWS

	Δ State Minimum Wage			
	b	*se*	*b*	*se*
State Minimum Wage$_{t-1}$	−0.165***	(0.017)	−0.164***	(0.017)
Δ Awareness of Inequality	0.006+	(0.003)	0.006+	(0.003)
Awareness of Inequality	0.011***	(0.003)	0.011***	(0.003)
Δ Public Mood	0.017***	(0.003)	0.016***	(0.003)
Public Mood	0.003+	(0.002)	0.003+	(0.002)
Δ Union Membership	0.008	(0.007)	0.008	(0.007)
Union Membership$_{t-1}$	0.000	(0.001)	0.000	(0.001)
Δ Government Ideology	0.002*	(0.001)	0.002*	(0.001)
Government Ideology	0.001**	(0.000)	0.001**	(0.000)
Initiative Qualification Index	0.009**	(0.003)	0.000	(0.005)
Δ Poverty Rate	−0.001	(0.004)	−0.001	(0.004)
Poverty Rate	−0.003	(0.002)	−0.003	(0.002)
Δ % White	−2.923	(1.907)	−2.810	(1.903)
% White	0.203*	(0.086)	0.200*	(0.086)
Has State EITC	0.006	(0.017)	0.005	(0.017)
Federal Minimum Wage Change	−0.038*	(0.018)	−0.038*	(0.018)
Years Since Federal Change	0.025***	(0.004)	0.021***	(0.004)
Initiative × Years Since Fed. Change			0.002*	(0.001)
Constant	−2.095***	(0.297)	−2.061***	(0.297)
N	1152		1152	
Log-Likelihood	462.113		469.165	

+p < .10, *p < .05, **p < .01, ***p < .001.
Note: Each model includes a set of time variables estimating a second- or third-order polynomial to account for any remaining trend in the first-differenced dependent variable (these estimates are not included in the table).

Table B.12. EFFECT OF STATE CHARACTERISTICS ON STATE
EARNED INCOME TAX CREDIT ADOPTION

	State EITC Adoption		
	(1) b / (rob. se)	(2) b / (rob. se)	(3) b / (rob. se)
Δ Awareness of Inequality	0.265**	0.269**	0.269**
	(0.091)	(0.090)	(0.091)
Union Membership	0.119*	0.110*	0.110*
	(0.049)	(0.048)	(0.050)
Public Mood	0.002		−0.002
	(0.060)		(0.059)
Government Ideology		0.020	0.020
		(0.014)	(0.014)
Initiative Qualification Index	−0.172	−0.134	−0.134
	(0.120)	(0.111)	(0.116)
Poverty Rate	−0.229*	−0.277**	−0.277**
	(0.094)	(0.102)	(0.104)
% Income Tax Revenue	0.066**	0.065**	0.065**
	(0.023)	(0.020)	(0.020)
% White	0.955	1.137	1.103
	(4.013)	(3.361)	(3.897)
State Min. Wage Above Fed.	0.318	−0.110	−0.107
	(0.685)	(0.773)	(0.783)
Total State EITC Adoptions	0.559*	0.563*	0.565*
	(0.267)	(0.270)	(0.275)
Regional Diffusion	−1.901	−1.916+	−1.910+
	(1.200)	(1.133)	(1.158)
Constant	−6.357	−7.099+	−6.981
	(6.702)	(4.219)	(6.405)
N	881.000	881.000	881.000
Log-Likelihood	−83.314	−82.215	−82.215

$+ p < .10, * p < .05, ** p < .01, *** p < .001.$

NOTES

CHAPTER 2

1. https://www.census.gov/population/censusdata/table-4.pdf.
2. The initiative may be either immediately binding (a direct initiative) or be first considered by the state legislature (an indirect initiative) before going into effect. With the popular referendum (different from a legislative referendum placed on the ballot for a popular vote by the state legislature), citizens gather signatures to place a disputed law (or a section of the legislation) that has already been enacted on the ballot for voters to reconsider. The recall permits citizens to collect signatures to hold an election to oust an elected official midterm. The recall is rarely used, but recently there has been a resurgence of its use. There was a successful recall of Democratic governor Gray Davis in California in 2003, and a failed attempt to recall Wisconsin governor Scott Walker.
3. For historical data on initiative subject matter see the Initiative and Referendum Institute, http://www.iandrinstitute.org/New%20IRI%20Website%20Info/ Drop%20Down%20Boxes/Historical/Statewide%20Initiatives%201904-2000. pdf.

CHAPTER 3

1. See Xu and Garand (2010) for an exception. Although the authors examine views of inequality at the state-level, data limitations prevent the authors from assessing over time changes in perceptions.
2. As discussed earlier, Bartels (2008) looks at national trends in public perceptions of inequality over time.
3. As another example, Wooldridge (2013) shows that when modeling the effect of gross national product (GNP) on employment, if trending is not accounted for, it appears as though the two measures have a negative and statistically insignificant relationship. When accounting for trending, however, the effect of GNP on employment is positive and statistically significant, as one would expect. Wooldridge demonstrates that trending can be accounted for by either including a trend term in regression analyses (which is our approach throughout this book) or by detrending the variables.
4. All three measures of inequality—the Gini coefficient, the top 10% income share, and top 1% income share—were created by Frank (2009). As with the pioneering work of Piketty and Saez (2003), the author uses Internal Revenue Service tax data to construct the measures, which means they are based on

pretax gross income. The sources of income include wages, salaries, capital income, and entrepreneurial income. The data are available at http://www.shsu.edu/~eco_mwf/inequality.html.

5. State poverty rate data and per capita income were obtained from the US census website (http://www.census.gov/).

6. Estimates of state party identification were developed by Enns and Koch (2013) and are available at http://thedata.harvard.edu/dvn/dv/Enns. State union membership figures were retrieved from the Union Membership and Coverage Database (http://www.unionstats.com/), which is described by Hirsch and MacPherson (2003).

7. The full set of model estimates can be found in appendix table B.1. Additionally, appendix table B.2 presents the results of models replicating those found in table B.1 with the only difference being that the variables in these models have been mean-centered as an alternative way to account for heterogeneity across states and over time. The replication results are substantively similar to those presented in table B.1.

8. The total effect of a variable that has a statistically significant coefficient on the lagged version of the variable (i.e., the long-run coefficient) is calculated by dividing this value by the estimated coefficient on the lagged dependent variable (i.e., the error correction rate). When the short-run coefficient of a variable is statistically different from zero but the long-run coefficient is not, the total effect of the variable is simply the estimated short-term effect. The effects in the plot were calculated by multiplying the total effect of each variable by its standard deviation.

9. In other words, the measure of partisanship provides a theoretical explanation for the downward trending we observe for the inequality awareness measure.

CHAPTER 4

1. See appendix table A.2 for a full list of variables and data sources used in the analyses.

2. We use the preferred DW-Nominate based rather than the ADA-score based measure, though Berry et al. (2013) report that both measures produce similar inferences in most studies that they replicate, which we also observe here.

3. We do this by allowing the intercept in each state to vary when conducting the analysis.

4. To compute the total long-term effect of the lagged level variables, we multiply the coefficient for these variables by the standard deviation, and then divide this value by the value of the lagged dependent variable, which provides information on how quickly the explanatory variable translates into changes in the outcome variable.

5. The union density data set was constructed by Hirsch and Macpherson and can be found at http://www.unionstats.com/.

CHAPTER 5

1. The United States is second to only South Korea as the lowest tax collection countries in the OECD.

2. Using a survey question from the General Social Survey (data available at http://gss.norc.org) similar to the one plotted in figure 5.1, when asked if the taxes of those with high incomes are too low, Democrats were only six percentage points more likely to agree with the question than Republicans in 1987. This partisan

gap grew to 15 percentage points when the same question was asked in 2008. The ideological division is even more impressive, with liberals being only seven points higher than conservatives when asked if the rich pay too little in taxes in 1987, a gap that grew to 19 percentage points in 2008.

3. This point is confirmed when assessing the variation in top income tax rates within states over time and between states. The standard deviation within states (3.09) is nearly double the standard deviation within states (1.67).

4. Proposition 1098 was one of six initiatives on the 2010 ballot, along with one legislatively referred referendum and two legislatively referred constitutional amendments. Details of all ballot measures, as well as information on all of the federal, state, and judicial elections held in 2010, can be found at the Washington Secretary of State website: https://wei.sos.wa.gov/agency/osos/en/press_and_research/previouselections/2010/general/pages/results.aspx.

5. This is the concise description of 1098. The long version of the proposal summary provides more detail: "This measure would establish a tax on 'adjusted gross income' (as determined under the federal internal revenue code) above $200,000 for individuals and $400,000 for married couples or domestic partners filing jointly; reduce the limit on statewide property taxes by 20%; and increase the business and occupation tax credit to $4,800. The tax revenues would replace revenues lost from the reduced levy and increased credit; remaining revenues would be directed to education and health services." These initiative summaries were obtained from the Washington Secretary of State website: http://www.sos.wa.gov/elections/initiatives/people.aspx?y=2010 (retrieved March 3, 2011).

6. These figures were obtained from Washington's Public Disclosure Commission website: http://www.pdc.wa.gov/ (retrieved March 7, 2011).

7. Although our summary of the two campaigns is brief, we believe it is representative of the main arguments made by each side. This was confirmed by also examining the websites of each campaign, http://www.protectwashington.org/yes1098 and http://www.defeat1098.com, as well as viewing the campaign television advertisements aired by each organization (which can be found at http://ballotpedia.org/wiki/index.php/Washington_Income_Tax,_Initiative_1098_%282010%29). Of course, other groups were involved in the debate surrounding Prop. 1098, but nearly all of the major campaigning was done through the Yes on 1098 and Defeat 1098 groups. For example, Washington labor unions actively supported 1098 by contributing to the Yes on 1098 campaign. One of the top donors to Yes on 1098 was the Service Employees International Union (WA). A number of business interests that opposed the initiative also funneled their support through the main 1098 opposition group. Companies such as Microsoft, Amazon, and Bartell Drugs were all top contributors to the Defeat 1098 committee.

8. Although survey respondents have been found to accurately reflect through self-reporting whether they have been exposed to a political advertisement (e.g., see Vavreck 2007), there is no way to verify that the respondents who reported following information related to the ballot proposition actually followed the income tax debates, of course. Though it is clearly valuable to understand how decision-making occurs in actual policy debates as we do here, future research can more closely examine how specific types of information influence opinion with the use of experiments and survey experiments.

9. The question wording is: "There is some talk these days about how the difference in incomes between rich people and poor people in the United States has

continued to grow in the past 20 years. That is, rich people are getting richer, and poor people are getting poorer. Do you think this is a good thing, a bad thing, neither good nor bad, or haven't you thought about it?"

10. The question wording is: "Thinking ahead to the November 2010 elections, what general issues are most important to you as you decide how you will vote?" Responses to this question were coded by poll interviewers according to a predetermined set of issues.

11. While it is difficult to know which ballot measures or office races respondents have in mind when answering the most important issue question, we use the question to measure individuals' general concern for various issue areas. Using this measure we can test whether those who state that the economy (or taxes, education, etc.) is the most important issue for them are more likely to think about economic concerns related to a new state income tax when voting on Proposition 1098.

12. A list of all variables, coding and question wording can be found in appendix table B.6.

13. https://ballotpedia.org/California_Proposition_55,_Extension_of_the_Proposition_30_Income_Tax_Increase_(2016).

14. See appendix table A.2 for a list of the variables and their data sources.

15. The correlation coefficients for inequality awareness, public mood, and government ideology are all statistically significant at the .10 level. Only government ideology is significant at the .05 level.

16. We also conducted a multiple regression analysis that models state top income tax rates as a function of the six variables presented in figure 5.5. It should be noted that since we are focusing on state averages, this model includes only 48 observations (we do not have inequality awareness measures for Alaska and Hawaii). The results, which can be found in appendix table B.10, show that only coefficients for awareness of inequality and the percentage of a state's population that identifies as white are statistically significant from zero.

CHAPTER 6

1. For instance, workers who earn commissions or tips and farmworkers are still exempt from the federal minimum wage.

2. See, for instance: https://americansforprosperity.org/15-minimum-wage-inflict-maximum-pain-workers/.

3. https://ballotpedia.org/South_Dakota_Decreased_Youth_Minimum_Wage_Veto_Referendum,_Referred_Law_20_(2016).

4. The aforementioned minimum wage increase passed in South Dakota in 2014 did not take effect until 2015, which is why figure 6.2 does not indicate that South Dakota has a minimum wage above the federal minimum.

5. We reverse Bowler and Donovan's (2004) original measure so that higher values indicate that initiative qualification is less difficult.

6. A full list of the variables and data sources used in the analysis can be found in appendix table A.2.

7. Since the effect of public concern about income inequality on the adoption of state wage minimums is of central importance to the analysis, the time frame and number of states we can examine is limited to the year and state availability of our measure. We used all existing and available data when developing the measure of public inequality awareness, which led to a measure that covers the

years 1986–2012 and includes all states with the exception of Alaska and Hawaii. See chapter 3 for a more detailed discussion of the measure.

8. State minimum wage law data were obtained from the Department of Labor website (http://www.dol.gov/whd/state/stateMinWageHis.htm).

9. More specifically, we use error correction models to analyze changes in state minimum wage laws. A detailed discussion of our modeling approach can be found in appendix A.

CHAPTER 7

1. The discussion in this section is largely based on Hotz and Scholz (2003) and Ventry (2000).

2. This latter finding is based on analyses discussed below and from the results presented in chapter 6. When examining states with wage minimums above the federal level, we include a variable that indicates whether each state has adopted an EITC and find that this factor does not have a significant effect on minimum wage increases. Below, we also show that states with higher minimum wages are no more or less likely to adopt an EITC.

3. Further details on the power resources theory perspective can be found in chapters 4 and 6.

4. A Pew Research Center (2014) poll found that 73% of adult Americans favored increasing the federal minimum wage from $7.25 to $10.10 an hour.

5. The article counts for each year are based on search results returned from LexisNexis. Any articles published in the *New York Times* (not including blog posts) that included the keywords "minimum wage" or "earned income tax credit" are included.

6. The poll, conducted by the Cooperative Congressional Election Study, interviewed 10,000 American adults. The exact question wording reads: "The earned income tax credit reduces income taxes for low income households (those with at least one child and less than $36,000 or those with no children and less than $14,000). Approximately 1 in 20 Americans qualify for and use this tax credit. Should the government: expand the program; no change; reduce program scale; eliminate the program; or not sure?" More information can be found at http://projects.iq.harvard.edu/cces/home.

7. Since the effect of public concern about income inequality on the adoption of EITCs is of central importance to the analysis, the time frame and number of states we can examine is limited to the year and state availability of our measure. We used all existing and available data when developing the measure of public inequality awareness, which led to a measure that covers the years 1986–2012 and includes all states with the exception of Alaska and Hawaii. See chapter 3 and the appendix for a more detailed discussion of the measure.

8. Data on the state adoption of EITC programs was retrieved from the Hatcher Group's Tax Credits for Working Families website (http://www.taxcreditsforworkingfamilies.org/earned-income-tax-credit/states-with-eitcs/).

9. More specifically, we use event history analysis to model the adoption of state EITCs, which is different from the ECMs we have used for time-series analyses throughout most of the book. The reason for using event history analysis is that the dependent variable is dichotomous (i.e., a state either adopted the policy or it did not). Event history analysis is a commonly used technique in state policy diffusion analyses (e.g., Berry and Berry 1990; Box-Steffensmeier and Jones

2004; Franko 2013) where the researcher is interested in risk. The so-called risk in these instances is the adoption of a particular policy under analysis. Beck, Katz, and Tucker have shown that using adapted logit/probit methods with TSCS data and a binary dependent variable is "identical to grouped duration data" (1998, 1264). The advantage to using typical logit or probit models for these analyses is that the models can be implemented and interpreted in ways that are familiar to the researcher and readers. For these reasons, logistic regression is employed while accounting for duration dependence using a cubic polynomial (Carter and Signorino 2010) and adjusting standard error estimates by state clusters.

10. A full list of the variables and data sources used in the analysis can be found in appendix table A.2.

11. We reverse Bowler and Donovan's (2004) original measure so that higher values indicate that initiative qualification is less difficult.

APPENDIX A

1. In addition to general web searches, the Roper Center's iPOLL Databank (http://www.ropercenter.uconn.edu/data_access/ipoll/ipoll.html) and the Polling the Nations database (http://poll.orspub.com/) were used to find all instances of the "rich getting richer" question being asked.

2. Although all available respondents from all states are included in the individual models, many surveys did not interview residents of Alaska and Hawaii. This means that most years do not have opinion estimates for these states and they are not included in the analysis presented below.

3. The census's Public Use Microdata Samples are used for the poststratification stage, which include the 1990 5% sample of population and housing, the 2000 5% sample of population and housing, and the five-year American Community Survey for years 2005–2011. Linear interpolation is used to estimate each population type for years between these surveys.

4. This is an extension of the initial MRP modeling strategy suggested by Lax and Phillips (2009b). Instead of allowing only a random effect for every state, a random effect is estimated for every state-year. The method extends the logic of partial pooling across states to partial pooling across states and time. It should be noted that simply adding a time component to the multilevel model without interacting the term with the state indicator (or some other geographic identifier) will not produce a dynamic opinion series.

REFERENCES

Abramowitz, Alan I. 1988. "An Improved Model for Predicting Presidential Election Outcomes." *PS: Political Science and Politics* 21(4): 843–47.

Aktas, Oya. 2015. "Intellectual History of the Minimum Wage and Overtime." September 10. Washington, DC: Washington Center for Equitable Growth. http://d3b0lhre2rgreb.cloudfront.net/ms-content/uploads/sites/10/2015/09/09124135/091015-history-min-wage.pdf. Accessed May 4, 2017.

Aldrich, John H. "Did Hamilton, Jefferson, and Madison 'Cause' the US Government Shutdown? The Institutional Path from an Eighteenth Century Republic to a Twenty-first Century Democracy." *Perspectives on Politics* 13(1): 7–23.

Allswang, John. 2000. *The Initiative and Referendum in California, 1898–1998.* Stanford, CA: Stanford University Press.

Amenta, Edwin, and Bruce G. Carruthers. 1988. "The Formative Years of U.S. Social Spending Policies: Theories of the Welfare State and the American States during the Great Depression." *American Sociological Review* 53(5): 661–78.

Amenta, Edwin, Elisabeth S. Clemens, Jefren Olsen, Sunita Parikh, and Theda Skocpol. 1987. "The Political Origins of Unemployment Insurance in Five American States." *Studies in American Political Development* 2: 137–182.

Arceneaux, Kevin. 2002. "Direct Democracy and the Link between Public Opinion and State Abortion Policy." *State Politics and Policy Quarterly* 2: 372–87.

Aristotle. 1984. *The Politics and Constitution of Athens.* New York: Cambridge University Press.

Associated Press. 2014. "City's Gap Between Rich, Poor is 10th Highest." The Daily Record, February 20th. On-line Edition. http://thedailyrecord.com/2014/02/20/citys-gap-between-rich-poor-is-10th-highest/.

Atkins, Toni, and Shirley Weber. 2015. "California Tax Credit Would Help Working Families." *San Diego Union-Tribune*, June 12. http://www.sandiegouniontribune.com/news/2015/jun/12/california-earned-income-tax-credit-families/.

Autor, David H., David Dorn, and Gordon H. Hanson. 2013. "The China Syndrome: Local Labor Market Effects of Import Competition in the United States." *American Economic Review* 103(6): 2121–68.

Bailey, Michael A., and Mark Carl Rom. 2004. "A Wider Race? Interstate Competition across Health and Welfare Programs." *Journal of Politics* 66(2): 326–47.

Baker, Pamela L. 2002. "The Washington National Road Bill and the Struggle to Adopt a Federal System of Internal Improvement." *Journal of the Early Republic* 22(3): 437–64.

Baker Press Office. 2015. "Governor Baker Signs Earned Income Tax Credit Increase for Working Families." http://www.mass.gov/governor/press-office/press-releases/fy2016/governor-signs-eitc-increase-for-working-families.html. Accessed August 14, 2016.

Ballotpedia. 2016. "California 1938 Ballot Propositions." https://ballotpedia.org/California_1938_ballot_propositions.

Barrilleaux, Charles, and Belinda Creel Davis. 2003. "Explaining State Variation in Levels and Change in the Distribution of Income in the United States, 1978–1990." *American Politics Research* 31: 280–300.

Banducci, Susan A. 1998. "Direct Legislation: When Is It Used and When Does It Pass?" In *Citizens as Legislators: Direct Democracy in the United States*, ed. Shaun Bowler, Todd Donovan, and Caroline J. Tolbert, 109–31. Columbus, OH: Ohio State University Press.

Bartels, Larry M. 2005. "Homer Gets a Tax Cut: Inequality and Public Policy in the American Mind." *Perspectives on Politics* 3(1): 15–31.

Bartels, Larry M. 2006. "What's the Matter with What's the Matter with Kansas." *Quarterly Journal of Political Science* 1: 201–26.

Bartels, Larry M. 2008. *Unequal Democracy: The Political Economy of the New Gilded Age*. Princeton, NJ: Princeton University Press.

Bartels, Larry M., and John Zaller. 2001. "Presidential Vote Models: A Recount." *PS: Political Science and Politics* 34(1): 9–20.

Baumgartner, Frank R., and Bryan D. Jones. 1993. *Agendas and Instability in American Politics*. Chicago: University of Chicago Press.

Beck, Nathaniel, and Jonathan N. Katz. 1995. "What to Do (and Not to Do) with Time-Series Cross-Section Data." *American Political Science Review* 89 (3): 634–47.

Beck, Nathaniel, and Jonathan N. Katz. 1996. "Nuisance vs. Substance: Specifying and Estimating Time-Series-Cross-Section Models." *Political Analysis* 6 (1): 1–36.

Beck, Nathaniel, and Jonathan N. Katz. 2011. "Modeling Dynamics in Time-Series–Cross-Section Political Economy Data." *Annual Review of Political Science* 14 (1): 331–52.

Beck, Nathaniel, Jonathan N. Katz, and Richard Tucker. 1998. "Taking Time Seriously: Time-Series-Cross-Section Analysis with a Binary Dependent Variable." *American Journal of Political Science* 42(4): 1260–88.

Benabou, Roland. 2000. "Unequal Societies: Income Distribution and the Social Contract." *American Economic Review* 90(1): 96–129.

Berg, Andrew, Jonathan D. Ostry, and Jeromin Zettelmeyer. 2012. "What makes growth sustained?" *Journal of Development Economics* 98(2): 149–66.

Bernstein, Jared, and Sharon Parrott. 2014. "Proposal to Strengthen Minimum Wage Would Help Low-Wage Workers, With Little Impact on Employment." *Center on Budget and Policy Priorities*. January 7. http://www.cbpp.org/research/proposal-to-strengthen-minimum-wage-would-help-low-wage-workers-with-little-impact-on.

Berry, Frances Stokes, and William D. Berry. 1990. "State Lottery Adoptions as Policy Innovations: An Event History Analysis." *American Political Science Review* 84(2): 395–415.

Berry, William D., Richard C. Fording, Evan J. Ringquist, Russell L. Hanson, and Carl E. Klarner. 2010. "Measuring Citizen and Government Ideology in the U.S. States: A Re-appraisal." *State Politics and Policy Quarterly* 10(2): 117–35.

Berry, William D., Richard C. Fording, Evan J. Ringquist, Russell L. Hanson, and Carl E. Klarner. 2013. "A New Measure of State Government Ideology, and Evidence That Both the New Measure and an Old Measure Are Valid." *State Politics and Policy Quarterly* 13(2): 164–82.

Billis, Madeline. 2016. "Governor Charlie Baker Signs Equal Pay Law." *Boston Magazine*, August 2. http://www.bostonmagazine.com/news/blog/2016/08/02/equal-pay-massachusetts/. Accessed August 10, 2016.

Boehmke, Frederick J., and Richard Witmer. 2004. "Disentangling Diffusion: The Effects of Social Learning and Economic Competition on State Policy Innovation and Expansion." *Political Research Quarterly* 57(1): 39–51.

Bolton, Alexander. 2014. "$10.10 Wage Bill Set to Die." *The Hill*, April 30. http://thehill.com/homenews/senate/204766-1010-wage-bill-set-to-die.

Bonica, Adam, Nolan McCarty, Keith T. Poole, and Howard Rosenthal. 2013. "Why Hasn't Democracy Slowed Rising Inequality?" *Journal of Economic Perspectives* 27(3): 103–24.

Books, John, and Charles Prysby. 1999. "Contextual Effects on Retrospective Economic Evaluations: The Impact of the State and Local Economy." *Political Behavior* 21(1): 1–16.

Bowler, Shaun, and Todd Donovan. 2004. "Measuring the Effect of Direct Democracy on State Policy: Not All Initiatives Are Created Equal." *State Politics and Policy Quarterly* 4 (3): 345–63.

Bowler, Shaun, and Todd Donovan. 1998. *Demanding Choices: Opinion and Voting in Direct Democracy*. Ann Arbor: University of Michigan Press.

Bowler, Shaun, Todd Donovan, and Caroline Tolbert, eds. 1998. *Citizens as Legislators: Direct Democracy in the United States*. Columbus: Ohio State University Press.

Box-Steffensmeier, Janet M., and Bradford S. Jones. 2004. *Event History Modeling: A Guide for Social Scientists*. New York: Cambridge University Press.

Boyd, Eugene. 1997. "American Federalism, 1776–1997, Significant Events." Congressional Research Service Report 95-518:1–18.

Bradley, David, Evelyne Huber, Stephanie Moller, François Nielsen, and John D. Stephens. 2003. "Distribution and Redistribution in Postindustrial Democracies." *World Politics* 55 (02): 193–228.

Brady, Henry, Sidney Verba, and Kay Lehman Schlozman. 1995. "Beyond SES: A Resource Model of Political Participation." *American Political Science Review* 89(2): 271–94.

Branton, Regina P. 2003. "Examining Individual-Level Voting Behavior on State Ballot Propositions." *Political Research Quarterly* 56 (3): 367–77.

Buchanan, Wyatt. 2012. "Big Biz Joins Gov. Jerry Brown in SF for Prop. 30 Push." *SF Gate*. October 25. http://blog.sfgate.com/politics/2012/10/25/gov-brown-sf-businesses-push-for-prop-30/.

Burden, Barry. 2005. "Institutions and Policy Representation in the States." *State Politics and Policy Quarterly* 5: 373–93.

Calfas, Jennifer. 2016. "Trump's Cabinet Picks Have More Wealth Than Third of American Households Combined." *The Hill*, December 15. http://thehill.com/blogs/blog-briefing-room/news/310566-trumps-cabinet-picks-have-more-money-than-third-of-american.

Campbell, Andrea Louise. 2012. "America the Undertaxed." *Foreign Affairs*, September 1. https://www.foreignaffairs.com/articles/united-states/2012-09-01/america-undertaxed.

Campbell, Angus, Philip E. Converse, Warren E. Miller, and Donald E. Stokes. 1960. *The American Voter*. New York: Wiley.

Card, David, and Alan B. Krueger. 1995. *Myth and Measurement: The New Economics of the Minimum Wage*. Princeton, NJ: Princeton University Press.

Carnes, Nicholas. 2012. "Does the Numerical Underrepresentation of the Working Class in Congress Matter?" *Legislative Studies Quarterly* 37(1): 5–34.

Carson, Jamie L., and Benjamin A. Kleinerman. 2002. "A Switch in Time Saves Nine: Institutions, Strategic Actors and FDR's Court Packing Plan." *Public Choice* 113(3–4): 310–24.

Carter, David B., and Curtis S. Signorino. 2010. "Back to the Future: Modeling Time Dependence in Binary Data." *Political Analysis* 18(3): 271–92.

CBS / New York Times. 2015. September Poll. http://www.pollingreport.com/work. htm. Accessed May 22, 2015.

Center on Budget and Policy Priorities. 2015. "Policy Basics: The Earned Income Tax Credit." http://www.cbpp.org/research/policy-basics-the-earned-income-tax-credit. Accessed May 4, 2017.

Central Intelligence Agency. 2012. *The World Factbook*. https://www.cia.gov/library/ publications/the-world-factbook/fields/2172.html. Accessed May 4, 2017.

Chetty, Raj, and Nathaniel Hendren. 2015. "The Impacts of Neighborhoods on Intergenerational Mobility: Childhood Exposure Effects and County-level Estimates." *Working Paper*. http://cms.leoncountyfl.gov/coadmin/agenda/ attach/150609/A0905.pdf.

Chong, Dennis, Jack Citrin, and Patricia Conley. 2001. "When Self-Interest Matters." *Political Psychology* 22(3): 541–70.

Chong, Dennis, and James N. Druckman. 2007a. "A Theory of Framing and Opinion Formation in Competitive Elite Environments." *Journal of Communication* 57(1): 99–118.

Cingano, F. 2014. "Trends in Income Inequality and its Impact on Economic Growth." OECD Social, Employment and Migration Working Papers, No. 163, OECD Publishing.

Chong, Dennis, and James N. Druckman. 2007b. "Framing Public Opinion in Competitive Democracies." *American Political Science Review* 101(4): 637–55.

Cook, Nancy. 2012. "The 51 Percent." *National Journal*, February 9. http://www. nationaljournal.com/magazine/the-51-percent-20120209.

Cronin, Thomas E. 1999. *Direct Democracy: The Politics of Initiative, Referendum, and Recall*. Bloomington Indiana: iUniverse.

Davies, James B., and Ian Wooton. 1992. "Income Inequality and International Migration." *Economic Journal* 102: 789–802.

De Boef, Suzanna, and Luke Keele. 2008. "Taking Time Seriously." *American Journal of Political Science* 52 (1): 184–200.

De Boef, Suzanna, and Paul M. Kellstedt. 2004. "The Political (and Economic) Origins of Consumer Confidence." *American Journal of Political Science* 48(4): 633–49.

Derthick, Martha. 2010. "Compensatory Federalism." In *Greenhouse Governance: Addressing Climate Change in America*, ed. Barry Rabe, 58–72. Washington, DC: Brookings Institution Press.

Desilver, Drew. 2014. "For Most Workers Real Wages Have Barely Budged for Decades." October 9. Pew Research Center. http://www.pewresearch.org/ fact-tank/2014/10/09/for-most-workers-real-wages-have-barely-budged-for-decades/. Accessed May 4, 2017.

Doherty, Daniel, Alan S. Gerber, and Donald P. Green. 2006. "Personal Income and Attitudes toward Redistribution: A Study of Lottery Winners." *Political Psychology* 27(3): 441–58.

Donovan, Todd, Caroline J. Tolbert, and Daniel A. Smith. 2008. "Priming Presidential Votes by Direct Democracy." *Journal of Politics* 70(4): 1217–31.

Downey, Kristin. 2010. *The Woman behind the New Deal: The Life and Legacy of Frances Perkins.* New York: Anchor.

Druckman, James N. 2001. "The Implications of Framing Effects for Citizen Competence." *Political Behavior* 23(3): 225–56.

Druckman, James N. 2004. "Political Preference Formation: Competition, Deliberation, and the (Ir)relevance of Framing Effects." *American Political Science Review* 98(4): 671–86.

Drutman, Lee. 2015. *The Business of America is Lobbying: How Corporations Became Politicized and Politics Became more Corporate.* New York, NY: Oxford University Press.

Dugan, Andrew, and Frank Newport. 2013. "In U.S., Fewer Believe 'Plenty of Opportunity' to Get Ahead." October 25. Gallup. http://www.gallup.com/poll/165584/fewer-believe-plenty-opportunity-ahead.aspx. Accessed May 4, 2017.

Ebeid, Michael, and Jonathan Rodden. 2006. "Economic Geography and Economic Voting: Evidence from the US States." *British Journal of Political Science* 36(3): 527–47.

Edsall, Thomas. 2015. "Why are Asian-Americans Such Loyal Democrats?" *New York Times*, November 4. Opinion.

Eissa, Nada, and Hilary W. Hoynes. 2006. "Behavioral Responses to Taxes: Lessons from the EITC and Labor Supply." In *Tax Policy and the Economy*, vol. 20, ed. James M. Poterba, 73–110. Cambridge, MA: MIT Press.

Enns, Peter K. 2015. "Relative Policy Support and Coincidental Representation." *Perspectives on Politics* 13(4): 1053–64.

Enns, Peter K., Nathan J. Kelly, Jana Morgan, Thomas Volscho, and Christopher Witko. 2014. "Conditional Status Quo Bias and Top Income Shares: How U.S. Political Institutions Benefit the Rich." *Journal of Politics* 76(2): 289–303.

Enns, Peter K., and Julianna Koch. 2013. "Public Opinion in the U.S. States 1956 to 2010." *State Politics & Policy Quarterly* 13(3): 349–72.

Erb, Kelly Phillips. 2016. "Portland Plans to Tax Companies Who Pay CEOs More Than 100 Times Workers." *Forbes* December 19. http://www.forbes.com/sites/kellyphillipserb/2016/12/19/portland-plans-to-tax-companies-who-pay-ceos-100-times-more-than-workers/#5b6dcc035240.

Erikson, Robert S., Michael B. Mackuen, and James A. Stimson. 2002. *The Macro Polity.* New York: Cambridge University Press.

Erikson, Robert S., Gerald C. Wright, and John P. McIver. 1993. *Statehouse Democracy: Public Opinion and Policy in the American States.* New York: Cambridge University Press.

Falk, Gene, and Margot L. Crandall-Hollick. 2014. "The Earned Income Tax Credit (EITC): An Overview." R43805. Washington, DC: Congressional Research Service.

Faricy, Christopher. 2011. "The Politics of Social Policy in America: The Causes and Effects of Indirect versus Direct Social Spending." *Journal of Politics* 73(1): 74–83.

Feldman, Stanley. 1988. "Structure and Consistency in Public Opinion: The Role of Core Beliefs and Values." *American Journal of Political Science* 32(2): 416–40.

Fellowes, Matthew C., and Gretchen Rowe. 2004. "Politics and the New American Welfare States." *American Journal of Political Science* 48(2): 362–73.

Fitz, Nicholas. 2015. "Economic Inequality: It's Far Worse Than You Think." *Scientific American*, March 31st. https://www.scientificamerican.com/article/economic-inequality-it-s-far-worse-than-you-think/.

Flavin, Patrick. 2012. "Income Inequality and Policy Representation in the American States." *American Politics Research* 40(1): 29–59.

Fortin, Nicole M., and Thomas Lemieux. 1997. "Institutional Changes and Rising Wage Inequality: Is There a Linkage?" *Journal of Economic Perspectives* 11(2): 75–96.

Frankfurter, Felix. 1916. "Hours of Labor and Realism in Constitutional Law." *Harvard Law Review* 29(4): 353–73.

Freeman, Richard B., and Joel Rogers. 2007. "The Promise of Progressive Federalism." In *Remaking America: Democracy and Public Policy in an Age of Inequality*, ed. Joe Soss, Jacob S. Hacker, and Suzanne Mettler, 205–27. New York: Russell Sage.

Frank, Mark W. 2009. "Inequality and Growth in the United States: Evidence from a New State-Level Panel of Income Inequality Measures." *Economic Inquiry* 47 (1): 55–68.

Franko, William W. 2013. "Political Inequality and State Policy Adoption: Predatory Lending, Children's Health Care, and Minimum Wage." *Poverty and Public Policy* 5(1): 88–114.

Franko, William W. 2016. "Political Context, Government Redistribution, and the Public's Response to Growing Economic Inequality." *Journal of Politics* 78(4): 957–73.

Franko, William W. 2017. "Understanding Public Perceptions of Growing Economic Inequality." *State Politics & Policy Quarterly* Online First (May): 1–30.

Franko, William W., Nathan J. Kelly, and Christopher Witko. 2016. "Class Bias in Voter Turnout, Representation and Inequality." *Perspectives on Politics* 14(2): 351–68.

Franko, William W., Caroline J. Tolbert, and Christopher Witko. 2013. "Inequality, Self-Interest and Public Support for 'Robin Hood' Tax Policies." *Political Research Quarterly* 66(4): 923–37.

Freund, Elizabeth, and Irwin L. Morris. 2005. "The Lottery and Income Inequality in the States." *Social Science Quarterly* 86: 996–1012.

Gais, Thomas, and R. Kent Weaver. 2002. "State Policy Choices Under Welfare Reform." Policy Brief No. 21. Washington, D.C.: The Brookings Institution. https://www.brookings.edu/research/state-policy-choices-under-welfare-reform/.

Garand, James C. 2010. "Income Inequality, Party Polarization and Roll Call Voting in the US Senate." *Journal of Politics* 72(4): 1109–28.

Garber, Andrew. 2010. "Income-Tax Measure Took Years to Shape." *Seattle Times*, October 23. http://www.seattletimes.com/seattle-news/income-tax-measure-took-years-to-shape/.

Gelman, Andrew, and Gary King. 1993. "Why Are American Presidential Election Campaign Polls So Variable When Votes Are So Predictable?" *British Journal of Political Science* 23(4): 409–51.

Gelman, Andrew, David Park, Boris Shor, Joseph Bafumi, and Jeronimo Cortina. 2008. *Red State, Blue State, Rich State, Poor State: Why Americans Vote the Way They Do*. Princeton, NJ: Princeton University Press.

Gerber, Elisabeth R. 1996. "Legislative Response to the Threat of Popular Initiatives." *American Journal of Political Science* 40(1): 99–128.

Gerber, Elisabeth R. 1999. *The Populist Paradox: Interest Group Influence and the Promise of Direct Legislation*. Princeton, NJ: Princeton University Press.

Gilens, Martin. 1999. *Why Americans Hate Welfare: Race, Media and the Politics of Anti-poverty Policy*. Chicago: University of Chicago Press.

Gilens, Martin. 2009. "Preference Gaps and Inequality in Representation." *PS: Political Science and Politics* 42(2): 335–41.

Gilens, Martin. 2012. *Affluence and Influence: Economic Inequality and Political Power in America*. Princeton, NJ: Princeton University Press.

Gilens, Martin, and Benjamin I. Page. 2014. "Testing Theories of American Politics: Elites, Interest Groups, and Average Citizens." *Perspectives on Politics* 12(3): 564–81.

Gold, Matea. 2014. "In N.C., Conservative Donor Art Pope Sits at Center of Government He Helped Transform." *Washington Post*, July 19. https://www.washingtonpost.com/politics/in-nc-conservative-donor-art-pope-sits-at-heart-of-government-he-helped-transform/2014/07/19/eece18ec-0d22-11e4-b8e5-d0de80767fc2_story.html.

Gold, Matea. 2015. "Ted Cruz, Rand Paul and Marco Rubio Decry Income Inequality, Clash over Foreign Policy." *Washington Post*, January 26. https://www.washingtonpost.com/news/post-politics/wp/2015/01/26/ted-cruz-rand-paul-and-marco-rubio-decry-income-inequality-clash-over-foreign-policy/.

Gonzalez, Francisco E., and Desmond King. 2004. "The State and Democratization: The United States in Comparative Perspective." *British Journal of Political Science* 34: 193–210.

Goodrich, Carter. 1948. "National Planning of Internal Improvements." *Political Science Quarterly* 63(1): 16–44.

Graham, Otis L. 1994. *Losing Time: The Industrial Policy Debate*. New York: Twentieth Century Fund.

Gray, Virginia, and David Lowery. 1990. "The Corporatist Foundations of State Industrial Policy." *Social Science Quarterly* 71(1): 3–24.

Greenhouse, Steven. 2016. "How to Get Low-Wage Workers into the Middle Class." *Atlantic*, August 19. http://www.theatlantic.com/business/archive/2015/08/fifteen-dollars-minimum-wage/401540/.

Greenstone, Michael and Adam Looney. 2012. "The Marriage Gap: The Impact of Economic and Technological Change on Marriage Rates." The Hamilton Project. http://www.hamiltonproject.org/assets/legacy/files/downloads_and_links/020312_jobs_greenstone_looney.pdf.

Grodzins, Morton. 1960. "The Federal System." In *Goals for Americans: The Report of the President's Commission on National Goals*. http://ssihs.wikispaces.com/file/view/The+Federal+System+%285%29.pdf. Accessed May 4, 2017.

Grossman, Jonathan. 1978. "Fair Labor Standards Act of 1938: Maximum Struggle for a Minimum Wage." *Monthly Labor Review* 101(6): 22–30.

Grossman, Kyle. 2015. "The Untold Story of the State Filibuster: The History and Potential of a Neglected Parliamentary Device." *Southern California Law Review* 88: 413–52.

Hacker, Jacob S. 2004. "Privatizing Risk without Privatizing the Welfare State: The Hidden Politics of Social Policy Retrenchment in the United States." *American Political Science Review* 98(2): 243–60.

Hacker, Jacob S., and Paul Pierson. 2005. "Abandoning the Middle: The Bush Tax Cuts and the Limits of Democratic Control." *Perspectives on Politics* 3 (01): 33–53.

Hacker, Jacob S., and Paul Pierson. 2010. *Winner-Take-All Politics: How Washington Made the Rich Richer—and Turned its Back on the Middle Class*. New York: Simon and Schuster.

Hamilton, Alexander. 1791. "Report on Manufactures." *Annals of Congress* 2nd Congress, 1st Session, December 5th 1971, 971-1034.

Hansen, Susan B. 1999. "Life Is Not Fair: Governors Job Performance Ratings and State Economies." *Political Research Quarterly* 52(1): 167–88.

Hasen, Richard L. 2000. "Parties Take the Initiative (And Vice Versa)." *Columbia Law Review* 100 (3): 731–52.

Hatch, Megan E., and Elizabeth Rigby. 2014. "Laboratories of (In) equality: Redistributive Policy and Inequality in the U.S. States." *Policy Studies Journal* 43(2): 163–87.

Hayes, Thomas J. 2013. "Do Citizens Link Attitudes with Preferences? Economic Inequality and Government Spending in the 'New Gilded Age.'" *Social Science Quarterly* 95(2): 468–85.

Hendrick, Rebecca M., and James C. Garand. "Variation in State Economic Growth: Decomposing State, Regional, and National Effects." *The Journal of Politics* 53(4): 1093–110.

Hertel-Fernandez, Alex, Theda Skocpol, and Daniel Lynch. 2016. "Business Associations, Conservative Networks and the Ongoing Republican War over Medicaid Expansion." *Journal of Health Politics, Policy and Law* 41(2): 239–86.

Hibbs, Douglas A. 1977. "Political Parties and Macroeconomic Policy." *American Political Science Review* 71(4): 1467–87.

Hicks, Alexander, Roger Friedland, and Edwin Johnson. 1978. "Class Power and State Policy: The Case of Large Business Corporations, Labor Unions and Governmental Redistribution in the American States." *American Sociological Review* 43(3): 302–15.

Hirano, Shigeo, and James M. Snyder. 2007. "The Decline of Third-Party Voting in the United States." *Journal of Politics* 69(1): 1–16.

Hirsch, Barry T., and David A. MacPherson. 2003. "Union Membership and Coverage Database from the Current Population Survey: Note." *Industrial and Labor Relations Review* 56(2): 349–54.

Hofstader, Richard 1955. *The Age of Reform*. New York: Vintage Press.

Holland, Joshua. 2015. "20 People Now Own as Much Wealth as Half of All Americans." The Nation, December 3rd. On-line Edition. https://www.thenation.com/article/20-people-now-own-as-much-wealth-as-half-of-all-americans/.

Hopkins, Daniel J. 2012. "Whose Economy? Perceptions of National Economic Performance during Unequal Growth." *Public Opinion Quarterly* 76(1): 50–71.

Hotz, V. Joseph, and John Karl Scholz. 2003. "The Earned Income Tax Credit." In *Means-Tested Transfer Programs in the United States*, ed. Robert A. Moffitt, 141–98. Chicago: University of Chicago Press.

Hoynes, Hilary W., and Ankur J. Patel. 2015. "Effective Policy for Reducing Inequality? The Earned Income Tax Credit and the Distribution of Income." July. NBER Working Paper No. 21340. http://www.nber.org/papers/w21340. Accessed May 4, 2017.

Huber, Evelyne, François Nielsen, Jenny Pribble, and John D. Stephens. 2006. "Politics and Inequality in Latin America and the Caribbean." *American Sociological Review* 71(6): 943–63.

Huber, Evelyne, and John D. Stephens. 2001. *Development and Crisis of the Welfare State*. Chicago: University of Chicago Press.

Hungerford, Thomas L. 2010. "The Redistributive Effect of Selected Federal Transfer and Tax Provisions." *Public Finance Review* 38(4): 450–72. doi:10.1177/1091142110373610.

Hungerford, Thomas L., and Rebecca Thiess. 2013. "The Earned Income Tax Credit and the Child Tax Credit: History, Purpose, Goals, and Effectiveness." September 25. Washington, DC: Economic Policy Institute. http://www.epi.org/publication/ib370-earned-income-tax-credit-and-the-child-tax-credit-history-purpose-goals-and-effectiveness/. Accessed May 4, 2017.

Hyclak, Thomas. 1980. "Unions and Income Inequality: Some Cross-State Evidence." *Industrial Relations* 19(2): 212–15.

Inglehart, Ronald. 1997. *Modernization and Postmodernization: Cultural, Economic, and Political Change in 43 Societies*. Princeton, NJ: Princeton University Press.

Jacoby, William G. 2000. "Issue Framing and Public Opinion on Government Spending." *American Journal of Political Science* 44(4): 750–67.

Johnston, Katie. 2015. "Momentum Builds to Raise State Earned Income Tax Credit for Low-Income Workers." *Boston Globe*, March 4. https://www.bostonglobe.com/business/2015/03/04/momentum-builds-raise-state-earned-income-tax-credit-for-low-income-workers/9Ic8MGKXDEIqg21YaE0H7I/story.html.

Jones, Bryan D. 1990. "Public Policies and Economic Growth in the American States." *Journal of Politics* 52(1): 219–33.

Jones, Tim. 2015. "Kansas Schools Close Early as Sam Brownback Tax Cuts Squeeze Revenue." *Bloomberg.com*, May 4. http://www.bloomberg.com/politics/articles/2015-05-04/kansas-schools-close-early-as-brownback-tax-cuts-squeeze-revenue. Accessed August 8, 2016.

Kalet, Hank. 2012. "Senate Hearing on Minimum Wage Follows Last Week's Report on Income Disparity." *NJ Spotlight*. November 19. http://www.njspotlight.com/stories/12/11/19/senate-hearing-on-minimum-wage-follows-last-week-s-report-on-income-disparity/.

Kaminski, John P. 1995. *A Necessary Evil? Slavery and the Debate over the Constitution*. New York: Rowman and Littlefield.

Karp, Jeffrey A. 1998. "The Influence of Elite Endorsements in Initiative Campaigns." In Citizens as Legislators: Direct Democracy in the United States, ed. Shaun Bowler, Todd Donovan, and Caroline J. Tolbert, 149–65. Columbus, OH: Ohio State University Press.

Katz, Bruce, and Jessica Lee. 2011. "Alexander Hamilton's Manufacturing Message." *Brookings*. http://www.brookings.edu/research/articles/2011/12/05-manufacturing-katz-lee. Accessed May 22, 2015.

Katz, Michael B. 1990. *The Undeserving Poor: From the War on Poverty to the War on Welfare*. New York: Pantheon.

Kawachi, Ichiro, Bruce P. Kennedy, Kimberly Lochner, and Deborah Prothrow-Stith. 1997. "Social Capital, Income Inequality, and Mortality." *American Journal of Public Health* 87(9): 1491–98.

Kazin, Michael. 2006. *A Godly Hero: The Life of William Jennings Bryan*. New York, NY: Anchor Books.

Keller, Eric, and Nathan J. Kelly. 2015. "Partisan Politics, Financial Deregulation and the New Gilded Age." *Political Research Quarterly* 68(3): 428–42.

Kelly, Nathan J. 2005. "Political Choice, Public Policy, and Distributional Outcomes." *American Journal of Political Science* 49(4): 865–80.

Kelly, Nathan J. 2009. *The Politics of Income Inequality in the United States*. New York: Cambridge University Press.

Kelly, Nathan J., and Peter K. Enns. 2010. "Inequality and the Dynamics of Public Opinion: The Self-Reinforcing Link between Economic Inequality and Mass Preferences." *American Journal of Political Science* 54(4): 855–70.

Kelly, Nathan J., and Christopher Witko. 2012. "Federalism and American Inequality." *Journal of Politics* 74(2): 414–26.

Kelly, Nathan J., and Christopher Witko. 2014. "Government Ideology and Unemployment in the U.S. States." *State Politics and Policy Quarterly* 14(4): 389–403.

Kenworthy, Lane, and Jonas Pontusson. 2005. "Rising Inequality and the Politics of Redistribution in Affluent Countries." *Perspectives on Politics* 3(3): 449–71.

Kinder, Donald R., and D. Roderick Kiewiet. 1981. "Sociotropic Politics: The American Case." *British Journal of Political Science* 11(2): 129–61.

Kingdon, John W. 1984. *Agendas, Alternatives, and Public Policies*. Boston: Little, Brown.

Kingdon, John W. 1999. *America the Unusual*. New York, NY: Palgrave Macmillan.

Kloppenberg, James T. 1986. *Uncertain Victory: Social Democracy and Progressivism in European and American Thought, 1870–1920*. New York: Oxford University Press.

Kluegel, James R., and Eliot R. Smith. 1986. *Beliefs about Inequality: Americans' Views of What Is and What Ought to Be*. Hawthorne, NY: Aldine de Gruyter.

Kohut, Andrew. 2015. "Are Americans Ready for Obama's 'Middle Class' Populism? *Pew Research Center*, February 19th. http://www.pewresearch.org/fact-tank/2015/02/19/are-americans-ready-for-obamas-middle-class-populism/.

Korpi, Walter. 1978. *The Working Class in Welfare Capitalism*. London: Routledge and Kegan Paul.

Krehbiel, Keith. 1998. *Pivotal Politics: A Theory of U.S. Lawmaking*. Chicago: University of Chicago Press.

Krosnick, Jon A., and Donald R. Kinder. 1990. "Altering the Foundations of Support for the President through Priming." *American Political Science Review* 84(2): 497–512.

La Corte, Rachel. 2010. "Wash. Tax Initiative Divides Big Names in Business." *The San Diego Union-Tribune*. September 22. http://www.sandiegouniontribune.com/sdut-wash-tax-initiative-divides-big-names-in-business-2010sep22-story.html.

Langer, Laura. 2001. "The Consequences of State Economic Development Policies on Income Distribution in the American States, 1976–1994." *American Politics Research* 29: 392–415.

Lau, Richard R., and David P. Redlawsk. 2006. *How Voters Decide: Information Processing during an Election Campaign*. New York: Cambridge University Press.

Lau, Richard R., Richard A. Smith, and Susan T. Fiske. 1991. "Political Beliefs, Policy Interpretations, and Political Persuasion." *Journal of Politics* 53 (3): 644–75.

Lax, Jeffrey R., and Justin H. Phillips. 2009a. "Gay Rights in the States: Public Opinion and Policy Responsiveness." *American Political Science Review* 103 (03): 367–86.

Lax, Jeffrey R., and Justin H. Phillips. 2009b. "How Should We Estimate Public Opinion in The States?" *American Journal of Political Science* 53 (1): 107–21.

Lax, Jeffrey R., and Justin H. Phillips. 2012. "The Democratic Deficit in the States." *American Journal of Political Science* 56 (1): 148–66.

Lee, Don. 2016. "Trump to Preside Over the Richest Cabinet in U.S. History." The Los Angeles Times, December 1st, 2016. On-line edition. http://www.latimes.com/politics/la-na-pol-trump-billionaire-cabinet-picks-20161201-story.html.

Lee, David S. 1999. "Wage Inequality in the United States during the 1980s: Rising Dispersion or Falling Minimum Wage?" *Quarterly Journal of Economics* 14(3): 977–1023.

Lenz, Gabriel. 2009. "Learning and Opinion Change, Not Priming: Reconsidering the Priming Hypothesis." *American Journal of Political Science* 53(4): 821–37.

Leonard, Thomas C. 2015. *Illiberal Reformers: Race, Eugenics and American Economics in the Progressive Era.* Princeton, NJ. Princeton University Press.

Levitin, Michael. 2015. "The Triumph of Occupy Wall Street." *Atlantic*, June 10. http://www.theatlantic.com/politics/archive/2015/06/the-triumph-of-occupy-wall-street/395408/.

Lewis-Beck, Michael S. 1988. "Economics and the American Voter: Past, Present, Future." *Political Behavior* 10(1): 5–21.

Lewis-Beck, Michael S., and Tom W. Rice. 1992. *Forecasting Elections.* Washington, DC: CQ Press.

Lewis-Beck, Michael S., and Mary Stegmaier. 2007. "Economic Models of Voting." In *The Oxford Handbook of Political Behavior*, ed. Russell J. Dalton and Hans-Dieter Klingemann, 518–37. New York: Oxford University Press.

Lindert, Peter H., and Jeffrey G. Williamson. 2012. "American Incomes 1774–1860." NBER Working Paper No. 18396. http://www.nber.org/papers/w18396. Accessed May 4, 2017.

Lipset, Seymour Martin. 1997. *American Exceptionalism: A Double-edged Sword.* New York, NY: WW Norton & Company.

Lowery, Bryan. 2016. "Brownback's Support in Legislature Weakens after Moderates' Big Gains." *Wichita Eagle*, August 3. http://www.kansas.com/news/politics-government/election/article93493722.html.

Lowi, Theodore J. 1984. "Why Is There No Socialism in the United States? A Federal Analysis." *International Political Science Review* 5(4): 369–80.

Lupia, Arthur. 1994. "Shortcuts versus Encyclopedias: Information and Voting Behavior in California Insurance Reform Elections." *American Political Science Review* 88(1): 63–76.

Lupia, Arthur, Adam Seth Levine, Jesse O. Menning, and Gisela Sin. 2007. "Were Bush Tax Cut Supporters 'Simply Ignorant'? A Second Look at Conservatives and Liberals in 'Homer Gets a Tax Cut.'" *Perspectives on Politics* 5(4): 773–84.

Lupia, Arthur, and Mathew D. McCubbins. 1998. *The Democratic Dilemma: Can Citizens Learn What They Need to Know?* New York, NY: Cambridge University Press.

Lupu, Noam, and Jonas Pontusson. 2011. "The Structure of Inequality and the Politics of Redistribution." *American Political Science Review* 105(2): 316–36.

Madison, James. 1789 (1961). *The Federalist Papers.* New York: Penguin.

Magleby, David. 1984. *Direct Legislation: Voting on Ballot Propositions in the United States* Baltimore: Johns Hopkins University Press.

Magleby, David B. 1994. "Direct Legislation in the American States." In *Referendums Around the World: The Growing Use of Direct Democracy*, ed. David Butler and Austin Ranney, 218–257. Washington, D.C.: The AEI Press.

Markus, Gregory B. 1988. "The Impact of Personal and National Economic Conditions on the Presidential Vote: A Pooled Cross-Sectional Analysis." *American Journal of Political Science* 32(1): 137–54.

Matsusaka, John G. 1995. "Fiscal Effects of the Voter Initiative: Evidence from the Last 30 Years." *Journal of Political Economy* 103: 587–623.

Matsusaka, John G. 2004. *For the Many or the Few: The Initiative, Public Policy, and American Democracy.* Chicago: University of Chicago Press.

Matsusaka, John G., and Nolan M. McCarty. 2001. "Political Resource Allocation: Benefits and Costs of Voter Initiatives." *Journal of Law, Economics, and Organization* 17(2): 413–48.

McCall, Leslie. 2013. *The Undeserving Rich: American Beliefs about Inequality, Opportunity, and Redistribution*. Cambridge University Press.

McCall, Leslie, and Lane Kenworthy. 2009. "Americans' Social Policy Preferences in the Era of Rising Inequality." *Perspectives on Politics* 7(3): 459–84.

McCarty, Nolan, Keith T. Poole, and Howard Rosenthal. 2006. *Polarized America: The Dance of Unequal Riches*. Cambridge, MA: MIT Press.

McClosky, Herbert, and John Zaller. 1984. *The American Ethos: Public Attitudes toward Capitalism and Democracy*. Cambridge, MA: Harvard University Press.

McGerr, Michael. 2005. *A Fierce Discontent: The Rise and Fall of the Progressive Movement in America, 1870–1920*. New York: Oxford University Press.

Meier, Kenneth J. 1988. *The Political Economy of Regulation: The Case of Insurance*. Albany, NY: The State University of New York Press.

Meltzer, Allan H., and Scott F. Richard. 1981. "A Rational Theory of the Size of Government." *Journal of Political Economy* 89(5): 914–27.

Miller, Joshua. 2015. "Rosenberg Calls for Fight against Income Inequality." *Boston Globe*, January 7. https://www.bostonglobe.com/metro/2015/01/07/legislature-sworn-stanley-rosenberg-elected-senate-president/STW3sPVGwUIKEEW71MQ80M/story.html.

Mitchell, Greg. 1992. *The Campaign of the Century: Upton Sinclair's Race for Governor of California and the Birth of Media Politics*. New York: Random House.

Moller, Stephanie, Evelyne Huber, John D. Stephens, David Bradley, and François Nielsen. 2003. "Determinants of Relative Poverty in Advanced Capitalist Democracies." *American Sociological Review* 68(1): 22–51.

Morath, Eric. 2014. "Massachusetts Sets Nation's Highest Minimum Wage." *Wall Street Journal*, June 26. http://blogs.wsj.com/economics/2014/06/26/massachusetts-sets-nations-highest-minimum-wage/.

Morris, Martina, and Bruce Western. 1999. "Inequality in Earnings at the Close of the Twentieth Century." *Annual Review of Sociology* 25(1): 623–57.

Mosher, James S. 2007. "U.S. Wage Inequality, Technological Change, and Decline in Union Power." *Politics and Society* 35(2): 225–63.

Mutz, Diana C. 2007. "Effects of 'In-Your-Face' Television Discourse on Perceptions of a Legitimate Opposition." *American Political Science Review* 101(4): 621–35.

Nelson, Thomas E., Rosalee A. Clawson, and Zoe M. Oxley. 1997. "Media Framing of a Civil Liberties Conflict and Its Effect on Tolerance." *American Political Science Review* 91(3): 567–83.

Nelson, Thomas E., and Donald R. Kinder. 1996. "Issue Frames and Group-Centrism in American Public Opinion." *Journal of Politics* 58(4): 1055–78.

Newman, Benjamin J., Yamil Velez, Todd K. Hartman, and Alexa Bankert. 2013. "Are Citizens 'Receiving the Treatment'? Assessing a Key Link in Contextual Theories of Public Opinion and Political Behavior." *Political Psychology* 36(1): 123–31.

Newport, Frank. 2015. "Americans Continue to Say U.S. Wealth Distribution Is Unfair." http://www.gallup.com/poll/182987/americans-continue-say-wealth-distribution-unfair.aspx. Accessed May 22, 2015.

Nicholson, Stephen P. 2005. *Voting the Agenda: Candidates, Elections, and Ballot Propositions*. Princeton, NJ: Princeton University Press.

Niquette, Mark, and Margaret Newkirk. 2015. "Republican Governors Start Learning to Like Tax Hikes." *Bloomberg News*, June 11.

http://www.bloomberg.com/politics/articles/2015-06-11/
norquist-s-no-tax-pledge-chafes-republicans-in-tattered-states.

North, Douglass Cecil. 1981. *Structure and Change in Economic History*. New York, NY: Norton.

Norton, Michael I., and Dan Ariely. 2011. "Building a Better America—One Wealth Quintile at a Time." *Perspectives on Psychological Science* 6(1): 9–12.

O'Brian, John Lord, and Manly Fleischman. 1944. "The War Production Board Administrative Policies and Procedures." *George Washington Law Review* 13(1): 1–246.

Organization for Economic Cooperation and Development (OECD). 2014a. "Focus on Inequality and Growth, December 2014." http://www.oecd.org/social/inequality-and-poverty.htm. Accessed May 4, 2017.

Organization for Economic Cooperation and Development (OECD). 2014b. "Focus on Top Incomes." May, http://www.oecd.org/social/OECD2014-FocusOnTopIncomes.pdf.

Pacheco, Julianna. 2011. "Using National Surveys to Measure Dynamic U.S. State Public Opinion A Guideline for Scholars and an Application." *State Politics & Policy Quarterly* 11 (4): 415–39.

Page, Benjamin I., Larry M. Bartels, and Jason Seawright. 2013. "Democracy and the Policy Preferences of Wealthy Americans." *Perspectives on Politics* 11(1): 51–73.

Page, Benjamin I, and Lawrence R. Jacobs. 2009. *Class War? What Americans Really Think about Economic Inequality*. Chicago: University of Chicago Press.

Page, Benjamin I., and Robert Y. Shapiro. 1992. *The Rational Public: Fifty Years of Trends in Americans' Policy Preferences*. Chicago: University of Chicago Press.

Park, David K., Andrew Gelman, and Joseph Bafumi. 2006. "State-Level Opinions from National Surveys: Poststratification Using Multilevel Logistic Regression." In *Public Opinion in State Politics*, ed. Jeffrey E. Cohen, 209–228. Stanford, CA: Standford University Press.

Parker, Ashley. 2016. "Donald Trump Soaks in the Adulation in Improvised Final Stop." *New York Times*, November 8.

Passell, Peter, and Leonard Ross. 1973. "Daniel Moynihan and President-Elect Nixon: How Charity Didn't Begin at Home." *New York Times*, January 14. https://www.nytimes.com/books/98/10/04/specials/moynihan-income.html.

Perlstein, Rick. 2009. *Nixonland: The Rise of a President and the Fracturing of America*. New York: Scribner.

Peterson, Paul E. 1995. *The Price of Federalism*. New York: Twentieth Century.

Pew Research Center. 2014. "Most See Inequality Growing, but Partisans Differ over Solutions; 54% Favor Taxing the Wealthy to Expand Aid to Poor." January 23.

Piketty, Thomas. 2014. *Capital in the 21st Century*. Trans. Arthur Goldhammer. Cambridge, MA: Harvard University Press.

Piketty, Thomas, and Emmanuael Saez. 2002. "Income Inequality in the United States: 1913–98." *Quarterly Journal of Economics* 68(1): 1–39.

Piketty, Thomas, and Emmanuel Saez. 2007. "How Progressive Is the U.S. Federal Tax System? A Historical and International Perspective." *Journal of Economic Perspectives* 21 (1): 3–24.

Pines, Christopher L. 1993. *Ideology and False Consciousness: Marx and His Historical Progenitors*. Albany: State University of New York Press.

Piven, Frances Fox, and Richard A. Cloward. 1979. *Poor People's Movements: Why They Succeed, How They Fail*. New York: Vintage Books.

Piven, Frances Fox, and Richard A. Cloward. 1982. *The New Class War: Reagan's Attack on the Welfare State and Its Consequences*. New York: Pantheon.

Plotnick, Robert D., and Richard F. Winters. 1985. "A Politico-Economic Theory of Income Redistribution." *American Political Science Review* 79(2): 458–73.

Polanyi, Karl. 1944. *The Great Transformation*. Boston: Beacon Press.

Poole, Keith T., and Howard Rosenthal. 1998. "The Dynamics of Interest Group Evaluations of Congress." *Public Choice* 97 (3): 323–61.

Prillaman, Soledad Artiz, and Kenneth J. Meier. 2014. "Taxes, Incentives, and Economic Growth: Assessing the Impact of Pro-business Taxes on U.S. State Economies." *Journal of Politics* 76(2): 364–79.

Quadagno, Jill. 1994. *The Color of Welfare: How Racism Undermined the War on Poverty*. New York: Oxford University Press.

Radcliff, Benjamin, and Martin Saiz. 1998. "Labor Organization and Public Policy in the American States." *Journal of Politics* 60(1): 113–25.

Rae, Nicol C. 1998. *Conservative reformers: The Republican Freshmen and the Lessons of the 104th Congress*. Armonky, NY: ME Sharpe.

Reeves, Andrew, and James G. Gimpel. 2012. "Ecologies of Unease: Geographic Context and National Economic Evaluations." *Political Behavior* 34(3): 507–34.

Rehm, Phillip, Jacob S. Hacker, and Mark Schlesinger. 2012. "Insecure Alliances: Risk, Inequality and Support for the Welfare State." *American Political Science Review* 106(2): 386–406.

Reuters. 2015. "Hershey: US Income Inequality Is Transforming the Chocolate Business." *Huffington Post*, October 28. http://www.huffingtonpost.com/entry/hershey-income-inequality_56317721e4b0c66bae5afcd2.

Rigby, Elizabeth, and Melanie J. Springer. 2010. "Does Electoral Reform Increase (or Decrease) Political Equality?" *Political Research Quarterly* 64(2): 420–34.

Robison, Peter. 2010. "Gates's Dad Says Rich 'Aren't Paying Enough' in Taxes." *Bloomberg Businessweek*. http://www.businessweek.com/news/2010-05-20/gates-s-dad-says-rich-aren-t-paying-enough-in-taxes-update1-.html. Accessed March 3, 2010.

Saez, Emmanuel. 2015. "Striking it Richer: The Evolution of Top Incomes in the United States." January 25. http://eml.berkeley.edu/~saez/saez-UStopincomes-2013.pdf. Accessed May 4, 2017.

Saez, Emmanuel, and Gabriel Zucman. 2014. "Wealth Inequality in the United States since 1913: Evidence from Capitalized Income Tax Data." NBER Working Paper No. 20625. http://www.nber.org/papers/w20625. Accessed May 4, 2017.

Schattschneider, E. E. 1960. *The Semi-sovereign People: A Realist's View of Democracy in America*. New York: Holt, Rinehart and Winston.

Schlesinger, Arthur M. 2003. *The Coming of the New Deal, 1933–35*. New York: Mariner Books.

Schmitt, John. 2009. "Inequality as Policy: The United States since 1979." October. Washington, DC: Center for Economic and Policy Research. http://www.cepr.net/index.php/publications/reports/inequality-policy. Accessed May 4, 2017.

Schmitt, John. 2013. "Why Does the Minimum Wage Have No Discernible Effect on Employment?" February. Washington, DC: Center for Economic and Policy Research. http://www.cepr.net/publications/reports/why-does-the-minimum-wage-have-no-discernible-effect-on-employment. Accessed May 4, 2017.

Schneider, Saundra K., and William G. Jacoby. 1996. "Influences on Bureaucratic Policy Initiatives in the American States." *Journal of Public Administration Research and Theory* 6(4): 495–522.

Schneider, Saundra K., and William G. Jacoby. 2005. "Elite Discourse and American Public Opinion: The Case of Welfare Spending." *Political Research Quarterly* 58(3): 367–79.

Schnurman, Mitchell. 2014. "Texas Is a Leader in Income Inequality, Too." *Dallas News*, January 4. http://www.dallasnews.com/business/columnists/mitchell-schnurman/20140104-texas-is-a-leader-in-income-inequality-too.ece.

Schrag, Peter. 1998. *Paradise Lost: California's Experience, America's Future.* New York: New Press.

Schwartz, Nelson. 2014. "The Middle Class Is Steadily Eroding: Just Ask the Business World." *New York Times*, February 2. http://www.nytimes.com/2014/02/03/business/the-middle-class-is-steadily-eroding-just-ask-the-business-world.html?_r=0.

Sears, David O., Richard R. Lau, Tom R. Tyler, and Harris M. Allen Jr. 1980. "Self-Interest vs. Symbolic Politics in Policy Attitudes and Presidential Voting." *American Political Science Review* 74(3): 670–84.

Shapiro, Ian. 2002. "Why the Poor Don't Soak the Rich." *Daedalus* 131(1): 118–28.

Shipan, Charles R., and Craig Volden. 2008. "The Mechanisms of Policy Diffusion." *American Journal of Political Science* 52(4): 840–57.

Siders, David. 2016. "Jerry Brown Signs $15 Minimum Wage in California." *Sacramento Bee*, April 4. http://www.sacbee.com/news/politics-government/capitol-alert/article69842317.html.

Singleton, Jeff. 2000. *The American Dole: Unemployment Relief and the Welfare State in the Great Depression.* Santa Barbara, CA: Praeger.

Slonimczyk, Fabián, and Peter Skott. 2012. "Employment and Distribution Effects of the Minimum Wage." *Journal of Economic Behavior and Organization* 84(1): 245–64.

Smeeding, Timothy M. 2005. "Public Policy, Economic Inequality, and Poverty: The United States in Comparative Perspective." *Social Science Quarterly* 86(s1): 955–83.

Smith, Daniel A., and Caroline J. Tolbert. 2001. "The Initiative to Party: Partisanship and Ballot Initiatives in California." *Party Politics* 7(6): 739–57.

Smith, Daniel A., and Caroline J. Tolbert. 2004. *Educated by Initiative: The Effects of Direct Democracy on Citizens and Political Organizations in the American States.* Ann Arbor: University of Michigan Press.

Smith, Daniel A., and Caroline J. Tolbert. 2010. "Direct Democracy, Public Opinion, and Candidate Choice." *Public Opinion Quarterly* 74(1): 85–108.

Smith, Richard Norton. 2014. *On His Own Terms: A Life of Nelson Rockefeller.* New York: Random House.

Snyder, Brad. 1995. "GOP Is Cutting Tax Credit for Poor Begun by Nixon, Expanded by Reagan. Republicans Hope to Save $42 Billion by 2002 from Earned Income Tax Credit." *Baltimore Sun*, October 27. http://articles.baltimoresun.com/1995-10-27/news/1995300027_1_earned-income-tax-raise-taxes-credit-for-poor.

Soley-Cerro, Ashley. 2012. "Prop. 30 Tax Increase for Education Funding Passes." *The Sundial*. November 7. http://sundial.csun.edu/2012/11/prop-30-too-close-to-call/.

Solt, Frederick. 2008. "Economic Inequality and Democratic Political Engagement." *American Journal of Political Science* 52(1): 48–60.

Solt, Frederick. 2009. "Standardizing the World Income Inequality Database." *Social Science Quarterly* 90(2): 231–42.

Solt, Frederick, Philip Habel, and J. Tobin Grant. 2011. "Economic Inequality, Relative Power, and Religiosity." *Social Science Quarterly* 92(2): 447–65.

Soss, Joe, Sanford F. Schram, Thomas P. Vartanian, and Erin O'Brien. 2001. "Setting the Terms of Relief: Explaining State Policy Choices in the Devolution Revolution." *American Journal of Political Science* 45(2): 378–95.

Steinmo, Sven. 1995. "Why Is Government So Small in America?" *Governance* 8(3): 303–34.

Stepan, Alfred, and Juan J. Linz. 2011. "Comparative Perspectives on Inequality and the Quality of Democracy in the United States." *Perspectives on Politics* 9(4): 841–56.

Stiglitz, Joseph E. 2012. *The Price of Inequality: How Today's Divided Society Endangers our Future*. New York, NY: WW Norton & Company.

Stimson, James A. 1999. *Public Opinion in America: Moods, Cycles, and Swings*. Boulder, CO: Westview Press.

Stimson, James A., Michael B. Mackuen, and Robert S. Erikson. 1995. "Dynamic Representation." *American Political Science Review* 89(3): 543–65.

Storing, Herbert J. 1981. *What the Anti-Federalists Were For: The Political Thought of the Opponents of the Constitution*. Chicago: University of Chicago Press.

Tankersley, James. 2016. "Middle Class Incomes Had Their Fastest Growth on Record Last Year." *Washington Post*, September 13.

Tax Foundation. 2015. "U.S. Federal Individual Income Tax Rates History, 1862–1913." October 17. http://taxfoundation.org/article/us-federal-individual-income-tax-rates-history-1913-2013-nominal-and-inflation-adjusted-brackets. Accessed May 4, 2017.

Tax Policy Center. 2015. "Historical Capital Gains and Taxes." http://www.taxpolicycenter.org/taxfacts/displayafact.cfm?Docid=161. Accessed May 4, 2017.

Teske, Paul. 2004. *Regulation in the States*. Washington, D.C.: Brookings Institution.

Theen, Andrew. 2016. "6 Things to Know about Oregon's New Minimum Wage Law." *Oregonian*, June 26. http://www.oregonlive.com/education/index.ssf/2016/06/5_things_to_know_about_oregons.html

Thomson-DeVeaux, Amelia. 2011. "Most Americans Support Raising the Minimum Wage, Except for Tea Partiers and Fox News Viewers." *PRRI*. November 15. https://www.prri.org/spotlight/most-americans-support-raising-the-minimum-wage-except-for-tea-partiers-and-fox-news-viewers/.

Tocqueville, Alexis de. 1945. *Democracy in America*. New York: Vintage.

Tolbert, Caroline J. 2003. "Direct Democracy and Institutional Realignment in the American States." *Political Science Quarterly* 118 (3): 467–89.

Tolbert, Caroline, Daniel C. Bowen, and Todd Donovan. 2009. "Initiative Campaigns: Direct Democracy and Voter Mobilization." *American Politics Research* 37(1): 155–92.

Tope, Daniel, and David Jacobs. 2009. "The Politics of Union Decline: The Contingent Determinants of Union Recognition Elections and Victories." *American Sociological Review* 74(5): 842–64.

Tritch, Teresa. 2014. "F.D.R. Makes the Case for the Minimum Wage." *New York Times*, March 7. http://takingnote.blogs.nytimes.com/2014/03/07/f-d-r-makes-the-case-for-the-minimum-wage/.

US Department of Labor. 2015. "History of Federal Minimum Wage Rates under the Fair Labor Standards Act, 1938–2009." http://www.dol.gov/whd/minwage/chart.htm. Accessed May 19, 2015.

Vavreck, Lynn. 2007. "The Exaggerated Effects of Advertising on Turnout: The Dangers of Self-Reports." *Quarterly Journal of Political Science* 2(4): 325–43.

Ventry, Dennis J. 2000. "The Collision of Tax and Welfare Politics: The Political History of the Earned Income Tax Credit, 1969–99." *National Tax Journal* 53(4): 983–1026.

Verba, Sidney. 1987. *Elites and the Idea of Equality: A Comparison of Japan, Sweden, and the United States*. Cambridge, MA: Harvard University Press.

Volscho, Thomas W. 2005. "Minimum Wages and Income Inequality in the American States, 1960–2000." *Research in Social Stratification and Mobility* 23: 343–68.

Volscho, Thomas W., and Nathan J. Kelly. 2012. "The Rise of the Super-rich: Power Resources, Taxes, Financial Markets, and the Dynamics of the Top 1 Percent, 1949 to 2008." *American Sociological Review* 77(5): 679–99.

Wang, Te-Yu, William J. Dixon, Edward N. Muller, and Mitchell A. Seligson. 1993. "Inequality and Political Violence Revisited." *American Political Science Review* 87(4): 979–93.

Waltman, Jerold L. 2000. *The Politics of the Minimum Wage*. Urbana: University of Illinois Press.

Weisbecker, Lee. 2013. "McRory Signs Bill Eliminating Tax Credit." *Triangle Business Journal*, March 13. http://www.bizjournals.com/triangle/news/2013/03/13/mccrory-signs-bill-eliminating-tax.html. Accessed August 14, 2016.

Western, Bruce, and Jake Rosenfeld. 2011. "Unions, Norms, and the Rise in U.S. Wage Inequality." *American Sociological Review* 76(4): 513–37.

Whitaker, Eric A., Mitchel N. Herian, Christopher W. Larimer, and Michael Lang. 2012. "The Determinants of Policy Introduction and Bill Adoption: Examining Minimum Wage Increases in the American States, 1997–2006." *Policy Studies Journal* 40(4): 626–49.

Wildavsky, Aaron. 1985. "Federalism Means Inequality." *Society* 22(2): 42–49.

Wilkinson, Richard, and Kate Pickett. 2011. *The Spirit Level: Why Greater Equality Makes Societies Stronger*. New York, NY: Bloomsbury Publishing.

Williams, Eric. 1994. *Capitalism and Slavery*. Chapel Hill: University of North Carolina Press.

Williams, Eric, and Nicholas Johnson. 2013. "ALEC Tax and Budget Proposals Would Slash Public Services and Jeopardize Economic Growth." Center on Budget and Policy Priorities. http://www.cbpp.org/research/alec-tax-and-budget-proposals-would-slash-public-services-and-jeopardize-economic-growth. Accessed August 14, 2016.

Williams, Roberton C. 2011. "Why Do People Pay No Federal Income Tax." Tax Policy Center. http://www.taxpolicycenter.org/taxvox/why-do-people-pay-no-federal-income-tax. Accessed August 14, 2016.

Winters, Jeffrey A., and Benjamin I. Page. 2009. "Oligarchy in the United States?" *Perspectives on Politics* 7(4): 731–51.

Wilson, Sven E., and Daniel M. Butler. 2007. "A Lot More to Do: The Sensitivity of Time-Series Cross-Section Analyses to Simple Alternative Specifications." *Political Analysis* 15 (2): 101–23.

Witko, Christopher. 2003. "Cold War Belligerence and U.S. Public Opinion toward Defense Spending." *American Politics Research* 31(4): 379–403.

Witko, Christopher. 2013. "When Does Money Buy Votes? Campaign Contributions and Policymaking." In *New Directions in Interest Group Politics*, ed. Matt Grossman, 165–84. New York: Routledge.

Witko, Christopher. 2016. "The Politics of Financialization in the United States, 1949–2005." *British Journal of Political Science* 46(2): 349–70.

Witko, Christopher, and Sally Friedman. 2008. "Business Backgrounds and Congressional Decision-Making." *Congress and the Presidency* 35(1): 71–86.

Witko, Christopher, and Adam J. Newmark. 2005. "Business Mobilization and Public Policy in the US States." *Social Science Quarterly* 86(2): 356–67.

Witko, Christopher, and Adam J. Newmark. 2010. "The Strange Disappearance of Investment in Human and Physical Capital in the U.S. States." *Journal of Public Administration Research and Theory* 20(1): 205–32.

Woodward, Curt. 2010. "Washington Wealthy Clash over Income Tax on Rich." *Seattle Times*, October 1. http://seattletimes.nwsource.com/html/localnews/2013047820_apuswashingtonincometax1stldwritethru.html.

Wooldridge, Jeffrey M. 2013. *Introductory Econometrics: A Modern Approach.* 5th ed. Mason, OH: Cengage Learning.

Xu, Ping, and James C. Garand. 2010. "Economic Context and Americans' Perceptions of Income Inequality." *Social Science Quarterly* 91(5): 1220–41.

Xu, Ping, James C. Garand, and Ling Zhu. 2016. "Imported Inequality? Immigration and Income Inequality in the American States." *State Politics & Policy Quarterly* 16(2): 147–71.

Zaller, John R. 1992. *The Nature and Origins of Mass Opinion.* New York: Cambridge University Press.

Zelizer, Julian. 2015. *The Fierce Urgency of Now: Lyndon Johnson, Congress, and the Battle for the Great Society.* New York: Penguin.

INDEX

Fair Labor Standards Act (FLSA), 26, 129
farmers, 23, 25. *See also* agriculture
FDR, 18, 27. *See also* Roosevelt, Franklin
federalism, 40–2
    federal inaction, 20–36, 46–8
    inequality, and, 36–40
filibuster, 35, 43, 76
financial sector,
    2008 crisis, 9, 18, 32, 50, 77, 120, 174
    deregulation of, 9–10, 31, 39
firms, 7–9, 25–6, 120
foreign trade, 8–9, 21, 23, 34, 40, 80,
        165, 171, 174
France, 2, 6, 22

Gates, Sr., Bill, 108–9
Germany, 2, 6
Gilded Age, 2, 44, 165, 168
Gini coefficient, 2, 51–7, 63, 67–9, 74,
        90–4, 166
GI Bill, 28–9
globalization, 6, 8
Goldwater, Barry, 30
Gridlock, 15, 33, 41, 75–6
Great Depression, 2, 5, 7, 9, 11, 18, 27–9,
        32, 36, 40, 44–5, 102, 127–8, 172–3
Great Society, 6, 22, 27–33, 41, 77, 171

ham and eggs initiative, 45
Hamilton, Alexander, 23
Hanna, Mark, 25
Hoover, Herbert, 27
Hopkins, Harry, 28
House of Representatives, 31–2, 165
household income, 1, 52
    inequality in, 54–5

ideology
    government, 13, 43, 81, 84–7, 121,
        137, 141, 153
    public, 21, 51, 64, 112, 166
    See also conservatism; liberalism
individualism, 58, 64
inequality
    attitudes toward, 99, 102–3
    awareness of, 51, 58, 61–77, 84–9,
        93–4, 96, 121–2, 126, 136, 141,
        146, 152, 157, 159–61, 166–7, 169
    federal government and (*see*
        federalism)

historical state, 51–7 (*see also* Gini
    coefficient; top income shares)
state variation in, 51–7, 105–7, 111–12,
    121–3, 169 (*see also* Gini coefficient;
    top income shares)
income distribution, 7–8, 10, 41, 47, 49,
    52–3, 56, 58–9, 72, 74, 77–83, 86,
    90–5, 113, 125–6
income share, 2–3, 53, 66–71, 90–4, 166
industrialization, 24–6, 42, 44–5, 127,
    171. *See also* deindustrialization;
    manufacturing
inflation, 7, 31, 62, 79, 81, 101, 126
    minimum wage and, 129–35, 146, 149
initiative, 12–14, 19, 49
    campaigns, 44, 103, 107–14,
        116–17, 120
    citizen voting on, 102–4, 107, 114
    history of, 26, 43–6
    majoritarian policy tool, 43–6, 94–5,
        98–102, 153–4
    minimum wage and, 15, 137–8
    taxes and, 119–22
interest groups, 10, 38, 43–4, 91. *See also*
        business groups; organized interests

Jackson, Andrew, 23
Johnson, Lyndon Baines, 147. *See also* LBJ

Kansas, 48

labor regulation, 82, 128
laissez faire, 20–2, 26, 174
LBJ, 30, 148, 170. *See also* Johnson,
        Lyndon Baines
liberalism
    government, 15, 43, 73–7, 81–5,
        88–96, 126, 146, 157, 167, 170
    public, 86–7, 137, 175
libertarianism, 20
limited government, 20–2, 26

Madison, James, 12, 42
    Madisonian institutions, 34–5
manufacturing, 8, 23, 36, 42, 91, 128.
        See also deindustrialization;
        industrialization
market-conditioning, 10, 14, 37, 49,
        79–80, 125
Medicaid, 32, 77–9, 148, 165